What

M000311569

"Gary Hoover is the best kind of scholar. He understands business history intimately as a serial entrepreneur himself. Add a lively exposition to the mix and you have a must-read collection of fascinating stories."
- **Todd E. Petzel**, Chief Economist and Co-Chief Investment Officer, Offit Capital

"Gary is one of the great students of business and entrepreneurship. Enjoy this fun bedtime read!"
- **Ryan Mannion**, Co-founder of BookThinkers

"Gary Hoover brings an analytical perspective in viewing industries - their birth, growth, transformation, and the lessons learned from their decline and reformation - without useless buzzwords."
- **Thomas M. Bodenberg**

"Today theories of strategy, finance, and even economics itself, are in flux. Businesspeople can find more solid guidance in the study of business history. Gary Hoover is an entrepreneur, educator, bookworm, and business historian. His essays are a delight."
- **Fred Phillips**, Editor-in-Chief Emeritus, *Technological Forecasting & Social Change*

"I love reading Gary Hoover's research on the history of American Businesses. This book will be taken off the shelf time and time again for referencing, learning, appreciating, and entertaining."
- **Aaron Considine**

"Gary Hoover is one of the most insightful business thinkers I know. He is also a gifted writer. His ability to understand the critical success factors of a business and communicate them in a straight-forward but entertaining manner, is a skill that animates the stories in this book."
- **Kevin Williams**, Senior Lecturer, McCombs School of Business, The University of Texas at Austin

★ ★ ★

BEDTIME BUSINESS STORIES

*Short Sagas of Business
Creation, Success, and Failure*

GARY HOOVER

AMERICAN BUSINESS HISTORY CENTER

Copyright © 2021 by American Business History Center.
Published by American Business History Center
Flatonia, Texas

AmericanBusinessHistory.org

First Edition: December 2021
Paperback ISBN 978-0-9991149-5-7
ebook ISBN 978-0-9991149-7-1

Library of Congress Cataloging-in-Publication Data
Names: Hoover, Gary E. 1951-, author.
Title: Bedtime Business Stories: Short Sagas of Business Creation,
Success, and Failure/ Gary Hoover.
Description: First edition. | Flatonia, TX: American Business History
Center [2021]
Library of Congress Control Number: 2021951093

Cover design: Alexander Atkins Design, Inc.
www.alexatkinsdesign.com

If you would like permission to use material from the book (other than
for review purposes), please contact
gary@americanbusinesshistory.org. Thank you.

Interested in bulk copies? Email gary@americanbusinesshistory.org

The author is available for speaking events. Please contact him at
gary@americanbusinesshistory.org.

Table of Contents

Industry Battles

Some Most Interesting Characters

Lessons

About This Book

If you dream of being an entrepreneur, if you love history, or if you lead a business, this book is for you.

Bedtime Business Stories includes 34 seldomly-told stories of how business leaders and their companies have succeeded (and failed) throughout American history. These stories were originally published in the American Business History Center's free weekly email newsletter and posted on Americanbusinesshistory.org.

Most of our readers are also booklovers, so we have produced this book, hopefully the first of many we will publish in the future.

Each of our original stories, on the website, were full of color pictures illustrating the stories. Rather than printing the color pictures in this book and increasing its price, we have opted to produce a separate PDF with all the pictures in it, which is downloadable for free at Americanbusinesshistory.org/BedtimeStories.

Our lifelong study of business success and failure has led us to the conclusion that the critical elements of business are timeless and unchanging. Tactics, techniques. and technologies continuously change, from advertising on streetcars to advertising on Facebook, from communicating by telegraph to using smartphones. Yet the principles of serving others through innovation, product development, marketing, and competition remain the same.

Those leaders who fail to learn the lessons of history, who fail to be inspired by the pioneers of the past, do so at their peril.

Understanding how our present world evolved from the personalities and events of the past is also the gateway to grasping the future. As Steve Jobs said, "You can't connect the dots looking forward; you can only connect them looking backwards."

Any business history story can be seen through three lenses, much like watching a movie shot from three camera angles. These different perspectives thus have a great deal of overlap.

The Arc of a Company

One way to understand business history is to study the "arc" of a company – how it was born, how it rose to success. The first eighteen chapters of this book tell such stories, in roughly chronological order. We start with our take on the three greatest companies in American history. Next are the histories of nine companies which still prosper today, covering industries ranging from elevators to paint, from soft drinks to retail stores.

We also tell the sagas of companies that no longer exist. These stories have the added benefit of teaching how companies go into decline, how they fail, or how they get acquired. Eight more chapters touch on such former companies, ranging from tractors to musical instruments, from food making to movie making.

These first eighteen chapters are written through the lens of a complete understanding of each company's story.

Industry Histories and Competition

Next, six chapters look at business through the lens of industry histories, studying the various competitors in any industry and how they started, fought each other, rose, and fell. Industries covered include aspirin, gas stations, watches, and bicycles. Every business has competition; seeing how an industry evolves and who "wins" (and how and why) is worthy of our study.

The Human Story

The third lens we apply is through the life stories of interesting business leaders. As Ralph Waldo Emerson said, "All history is biography." None of these companies or industries could exist without people, often pioneers taking great risks and dreaming big dreams. While every story we write contains biographical information, the next nine chapters look at the "arc" of individual lives, often involving multiple companies and industries in the life of one person. The people covered range from the man who invented modern sales techniques to the men who created the famous Woodstock music festival.

There is no better way to understand business and entrepreneurship, success and failure, than to study these lives: how these individuals thought, how they dealt with obstacles, and how they continued to learn and grow over time.

The book closes with some of our overall conclusions that flow from our multitude of stories: "Six Simple Steps to Building a Great Lasting Company."

We hope you enjoy these stories. We trust that they will inspire you, no matter your goals and dreams. We plan to produce more books in the future as we continue to report the saga of American Business.

We encourage you to visit the American Business History website at Americanbusinesshistory.org and subscribe to our free weekly newsletter, both of which contain over one hundred more such stories and other charts and information on business history.

I thank Alex Atkins for the cover design for this book, and Dave Stanwick, who compiled and published the book.

Gary Hoover
Flatonia, Texas
November 2021

About the American Business History Center

The rich mine of business history yields rewards for business leaders, scholars, teachers, students, and anyone who loves history or biography. The great stories of triumph and defeat, of men and women, remain unknown to most everyone, even stories about companies whose products we use every day and often love.

In 2019, four of us founded the American Business History Center, a 501(c)3 nonprofit organization, to promote interest in business history.

Failing to learn from our own history costs our society a great deal of time, energy, and money. We also fail to recycle the thinking patterns and innovations of the past, ideas often forgotten but still relevant if adapted to today's world.

Our first goal was to create an online nexus of information, stories, links, book recommendations, videos, and charts about business history and business leaders. Our stories, published in our free weekly newsletter and posted at Americanbusinesshistory.org, tend to focus on the less well-known stories, in every industry, every era, and every part of America.

In our first year and a half of operation, our newsletter subscription list and website pageviews grew very slowly as we created and assembled more content. Then, in 2021, as we drew more attention on the Internet and in appearances on the History Channel, our "traffic" began to accelerate.

In the first ten months of 2021, our website traffic has been over four-and-a-half times the "eyeballs" we attracted in the same period of 2020. For the full year 2021, we project that over 100,000 users will access the website. The newsletter will also have been read about 100,000 times during 2021.

In 2021, we began an annual high school essay contest, asking students to write up the story of a local business, with $7,500 in prizes. The best essay submissions are on our website.

Our efforts are still in the early stages but growing rapidly. We have a long list of future ideas to further engage the public with the great stories of American Business. With the publication of this book, we take yet another big step toward our long-term goals.

Gary Hoover
Executive Director and
Board Member

Dave Stanwick
Chairman of the Board
and Publisher

Bill Leake
Board Member

Larry Siegel
Board Member

American Business History Center
113 W. South Main Street
Flatonia, Texas 78941

About the Author

Gary Hoover was raised in a General Motors factory town, Anderson, Indiana. His teachers and friends could not answer his questions about GM, its history, leaders, and founders. Gary's inability to learn more about the giant company led him to discover *Fortune*, the great American business magazine, starting a subscription at the age of twelve. In the succeeding fifty-eight years, Gary has studied economics, worked on Wall Street, founded multiple companies, and taught and spoken about business success and failure worldwide.

After earning a degree in economics at the University of Chicago, studying under four future Nobel Prize winners including Milton Friedman, Gary analyzed the stocks of retail companies for Citibank in New York. He then learned retailing by spending seven years working for Federated Department Stores (now called Macy's) and May Department Stores in tasks ranging from buyer to financial analyst to shopping center planning and marketing.

Gary and his friends had started three small businesses in college and went on to found the first chain of book superstores, Bookstop, in Austin, Texas, in 1982. Barnes & Noble bought that company for $41.5 million in 1989. He and his friends then founded the business information company that became Hoovers.com, which was listed on the NASDAQ stock exchange in 1999 and bought by Dun & Bradstreet for $119 million in 2003. Gary then founded the first chain of travel superstores, TravelFest, but this business failed when airlines drastically cut the commissions paid to travel agencies. He has thus participated in both success and failure, including every aspect of founding and building businesses.

Gary served as the first Entrepreneur-in-Residence at the McCombs School of Business of the University of Texas at Austin in the 2009-10 academic year, working with hundreds of entrepreneurial dreamers. He has also made thousands of speeches to entrepreneurs and corporate managers in over thirty countries and across North America.

Gary's lifelong love of business and business history led him to join three friends in creating the American Business History Center in 2019. He has appeared on numerous podcasts and several programs on the History Channel.

Gary Hoover lives in Flatonia, Texas, in his 60,000-book personal library, including almost every issue of *Fortune* magazine back to the first issue, published in 1930. He can be reached at gary@americanbusinesshistory.org.

Other books by Gary Hoover:

The Art of Enterprise (as PDF only, available at Hooversworld.com)

The Lifetime Learner's Guide to Reading and Learning (available on Amazon)

Chapter 1
The Three Greatest American Companies of All Time

For the last 52 years, I have been obsessed with understanding what makes a company great. What leads to success; what leads away. This led me to ruminate on which might be the greatest US companies so far.

I grew up in a General Motors factory town (Anderson, Indiana) in the 1950s and 1960s. GM at the time was the largest and most profitable company on earth. At the peak, they employed 877,000 people worldwide. It was considered a premier place to work. It was a great technological inventor and an innovator in business methods without peer.

When my teachers taught about leadership, competition, and strategy, I discovered political and military leaders. But what about the people who started, built, and ran this enterprise? At the age of 12 I discovered the *Fortune* 500 list of largest companies, began my lifelong subscription to that magazine, and fell in love with lists and rankings.

Though I am also interested in the greatest companies globally, such a list would likely be these same three. The 20th century was not only the American Century, it was also in many ways the era of the giant corporation, dominated by American corporations along with a few European giants like Shell and Unilever. The biggest difference between this list today and this list in 100 years will be the great rise of companies based in Asia and the Southern Hemisphere.

What makes a company great? That can be very subjective and hard to pin down. It includes size, but it is not determined by size alone. I believe a great company changes society: through innovation, impact on business practices at other companies, and pure reach – the number of people it affects. I have thought long and hard about the three companies that top my list. They are:

1. Pennsylvania Railroad from about 1870 to 1920
2. General Motors from about 1925 to 1975
3. IBM from about 1930 to 1980

Note that Apple, Google, Microsoft and many other more recent companies are not on my list. I think it is still too early to tell how those companies will pan out. A company can appear great and permanent one day and be gone, transformed, or acquired not long after. The digital age is just beginning to build up steam; we have a lot of history ahead of us.

Here is why I chose these three firms, whose rich histories I only skim:

Pennsylvania Railroad from about 1870 to 1920

The railroads were our first huge industry. They opened up the nation to trade and communication. Alongside them came the telegraph and Western Union, the first giant company consolidated from smaller ones. The big railroads were leaders in technology, employment, and as investments.

The railroads were the first giant, geographically-spread enterprises. Districts, regions, supervisory structures, middle management, forms, pay scales, and ultimately use of computers (punch card machines) were pioneered by the railroads.

The greatest railroad of all, the largest in revenue and most innovative, called "The Standard Railroad of the World," was the Philadelphia-based Pennsylvania Railroad. Competing to open the west with Vanderbilt's New York Central System, the Pennsylvania was not family-run, but hired professional managers. Executives like J. Edgar Thomson and Thomas Scott trained youngsters like Andrew Carnegie and Thomas Edison.

By the 1870s, the Pennsylvania was the largest business enterprise in the world. Around 1900, the Pennsylvania's securities on the stock market exceeded 10% of the value of all such securities. That would roughly equal the combined importance of Apple, Microsoft, ExxonMobil, and Berkshire Hathaway today. The company paid dividends starting in the 1850s for over 100 years in a row, a remarkable record.

Peaking at a 1920 employment of 279,787, the "Pennsy" did everything from serve food to build its own locomotives at its giant Altoona shops. Just west of Altoona is the great engineering feat of the Horseshoe Curve. East near

Harrisburg was the enormous railyard at Enola, which sorted over 20,000 freight cars in one day at the peak of World War II, and was later replaced by Conway Yard west of Pittsburgh.

But perhaps the railroad's greatest accomplishment was under the Presidency of Alexander Cassatt, brother of the painter Mary Cassatt. The Pennsylvania, unlike the New York Central, did not reach Manhattan Island. People and freight arriving from the West were taken by ferry from the rail's end in New Jersey to piers in Manhattan.

Cassatt conceived and executed (but did not live to see the completion of) a set of tunnels under the Hudson, extending across Manhattan and then under the East River to railyards in Queens. Between, in Manhattan, the railroad built an enormous beautiful terminal, Pennsylvania Station. Across the street, they built the largest hotel in Manhattan, the Pennsylvania Hotel. This great railroad station was demolished in the 1960s, perhaps the greatest loss ever to historic American architecture. But the hotel lives on, quite profitably last I looked. The area has in recent years come back to vibrancy, with massive new construction planned.

Taken in its entirety, this construction cost over $100 million when completed in 1910. 100,000 people came to see it on opening night. This was reportedly the most expensive project ever built by private enterprise and private capital at that time. It would cost many billions today. At its peak in 1945, 100 million passengers passed through Penn Station.

The Pennsylvania had imagination and cared about design. They hired one of the founders of the industrial design profession and one of its greatest practitioners, Raymond Loewy, to design their locomotives. Their advertising, calendars, and car interiors reflected high design standards.

This is the only company in my list that no longer exists.

What brought down this amazing enterprise?

The Pennsylvania and other eastern railroads ran into severe financial difficulties in the mid-20th century. As always, there were multiple causes: truck competition, over-regulation, poor leadership to name a few. Facilities and service decayed. In the 1960s they merged with their arch-rival New York Central to form the Penn Central, which lasted less than three years before collapsing into the then-biggest corporate bankruptcy in history. I was working as a summer teller in the bank in my hometown on the day it happened, and we were told not to cash Penn Central paychecks; luckily none came in. Today the old Pennsylvania routes and track are still hard at work, mainly as Norfolk Southern but in some places as CSX or other railroads. Both of these rail giants are healthy, profitable companies today, and the railroads are efficient and busy. The key Amtrak line between New York and Washington is another remnant of the late, great Pennsylvania Railroad.

General Motors from about 1925 to 1975

By 1920, Billy Durant had assembled a hodgepodge of smaller automakers into General Motors, including former industry leaders Buick and Oldsmobile. But even taken together, they were like a flea to Henry Ford, who was making over $100 million a year in profit in some years – a company wholly owned by him, his wife, and his son. In 1921, GM sold 12% of the automobiles sold in the US. In 1954, GM outsold all others combined, with a 52% market share, in what was by far the world's largest and most competitive auto market. For 77 years, from 1931 to 2007, GM was the largest automaker in the world. No company has since equaled its size relative to US GNP.

In those roughly 35 years, an amazing team of leaders under the ultimate guidance of Alfred P. Sloan created the first great modern corporation. Sloan had sold his Hyatt Roller Bearings company to Durant, who wanted to control his key automobile parts suppliers. The DuPont chemical company invested in GM. Pierre S. DuPont and the board gave Sloan the task of thinking through the best organization for the disorganized group of companies. Durant stepped aside and Sloan became chief. The result was the most famous organization chart in business, the birth of the decentralized company. Operations were controlled locally or by brand, whereas finance, accounting, capital allocation, staff functions, and general corporate-wide policies were overseen centrally.

In technology, GM had Charles Kettering, one of the top patent holders in US history and the inventor of the commercially successful electric starter, which eliminated the need to crank the car. The company's research centers created innovation after innovation in the auto industry, as well as significant efforts in aerospace and other fields. The diesel locomotive pioneered and commercialized by GM drove the stake through the heart of the steam locomotive, in one of the biggest productivity gains ever for world industry.

In design, eccentric chief of design Harley Earl gave us most of the great American cars of this classic era. From fins to long low slung babies, "concept cars" to stunning Futurama exhibits at the great World's Fairs, his visions were seen by millions.

At the peak, GM employed 877,000 people worldwide.

GM's collapse provides enough examples to fill another newsletter. There are many challenges that are widely discussed, such as labor unions, management mistakes, bureaucracy, Asian competition, and perhaps most importantly: cultural isolation (an ingrown corporate culture).

But I would also note that, after the 1937 sit-down strikes and ensuing labor-management relations, no one who ever worked on a car assembly line or hand-built a car led the company, and very few ever crossed through the huge wall that labor and management built between themselves. (Compare, for example, the restaurant business, in which most CEOs and founders began as cooks or waitstaff.)

By 2009, at age 101, the company was bankrupt and effectively a ward of the state.

Today a new, restructured General Motors is still among the largest employers and still one of the largest global automakers. Chevy and Cadillac have some hot products going, including an awesome-looking new Corvette. I will personally continue to root for them, but refrain from making any forecasts after their tortured history.

IBM from about 1930 to 1980

It is hard for technology companies to make this list, because it is especially hard for them to endure. The business and its requirements change so fast compared with, say toothpaste or beer, that few technology companies can retain leadership and maintain innovation for decade after decade (3M being the great exception).

The IBM I list here is the predecessor of, but not the same as, the IBM of today, which represents a remarkable turnaround. Today's IBM, like the first one, employs over 400,000 workers and is again a prosperous innovator. The IBM of old was the world's largest computer hardware company and the world's largest computer software company. In 1993, between those "two companies," IBM had an $8 billion loss, the then-biggest in US history, approaching death.

The first arc of this history, the rise of the first IBM, is one of the great beauties of corporate history.

Thomas J. Watson, Sr., was the head of sales at John H. Patterson's dominant National Cash Register Company in Dayton. Patterson was the great American salesman and sales innovator, developing pitches and attitudes that worked. (R. H. Grant whose sales methods drove Chevy past Ford in the 1920s also came from "the Cash.") Watson was hired by Charles Flint, George Fairchild (semiconductor pioneer Sherman Fairchild's father), and other major stockholders of the Computing-Tabulating-Recording Company to run the small combination of punched card, time clock, and other office equipment makers. Watson soon adopted the name of their Canadian subsidiary, International Business Machines.

The punched card machine had been developed by Herman Hollerith, whose old company was now part of IBM. He leased his machines rather than sold them. During the depression, IBM was far more profitable than its older competitors: while new machine sales collapsed, IBM's monthly lease payments kept coming in.

In the early 1950s, Remington Rand (and its predecessors) had pioneered the Univac machine and was poised to dominate the rapidly emerging market for mainframe computers. But Watson's IBM, by focusing on what customers were looking for and making technology serve them, overtook the pioneer and went on to 30+ years of global dominance. Competitors from NCR to GE, RCA to Honeywell were dwarfed.

In those same 1950s, Watson handed the reins to his son, perceived playboy Thomas Watson, Jr., who then took the company to much greater heights.

Watson the younger knew how to take bold moves, betting

the company on the totally new IBM System 360, which was premiered to a group of the press at a secret warehouse on launch day – precursor of Steve Jobs!

The company was one of the first big American companies to develop a complete corporate identity and design program, which touched everything from the office buildings and notepads to the computers themselves. IBM hired top designers including Eliot Noyes and Paul Rand.

The company also became a huge employer, highly regarded as a great place to work. It was one of the top "corporate citizens" in supporting education and other important and popular causes.

By the mid-1980s, IBM peaked at over 400,000 employees. By 1993, they were posting enormous losses, threatening the company's survival. Luckily for the people of IBM and their stockholders, Louis Gerstner came along and re-energized this great company. The reborn IBM continues to be a leader in patents, ideas, revenues, and profits.

Conclusions

I am sure we could go on at length debating this list, adding more thoughts on these companies, and seeking to discover what made them great in their best days. Not unlike remembering Rome or Constantinople in their most glorious days.

Do not take what I say to claim any of these companies was or is perfect. Any human enterprise has weaknesses and makes mistakes. Alfred Sloan said that you would be a hero if you were right 51% of the time. Any organization of size is going to have a few crooked employees and some unhappy ones. And most, if not all, technologies have in one way or another a dark side. None of this detracts from the achievements of these great companies.

What did they have in common?

Each was highly regarded among business people worldwide at its peak. Each was an ambitious company, without modest goals. They were highly creative. Each created enormous numbers of jobs. But they also created things that worked, that served a purpose, that were often beautiful, and whose vestiges, descendants, and visual impact remain with us today. Many of our parents and grandparents spent their lifetimes working and socializing at such companies. Taking employees together with customers and suppliers, millions of people's lives were affected by their actions and innovations.

Each of these companies in its best days followed a consistent vision crafted by outstanding leaders. They understood what mattered, what the purpose and priorities of the company were. These companies were all about will and imagination, not the management fad or financing method of the day.

To learn more

There is an enormous amount written, in print and online, about each of these companies, their products, and their industries. If you can only get one book on each company, here are my choices:

Pennsylvania Railroad

A serious history: *The Pennsylvania Railroad Vol. 1 Building an Empire* by Albert Churella.

A more informal illustrated book: *Pennsylvania Railroad*

(Railroad Color History) by Mike Schafer

For more about the building of Penn Station and tunnels: *Conquering Gotham: Building Penn Station and Its Tunnels* by Jill Jonnes

General Motors – *My Years with General Motors* by Alfred P. Sloan.

IBM – *IBM: The Rise and Fall and Reinvention of a Global Icon* by James Cortada.

This article first appeared on January 16, 2015 on Hooversworld.com.

The Diverse World of Business

Chapter 2
Billiards, Bowling, and Boating: 175 Years of Brunswick

A current buzzword is "pivoting," which means changing your company's strategy and direction, often into entirely new businesses. Pivots are frequent in young companies trying to find the best markets and a footing for future opportunities. Here we look at a very old company which has survived wave after wave of mergers and remained independent, but over its life has made an amazing array of products, including widely known consumer products. Despite 175 years of ups and downs, Brunswick Corporation soldiers on toward its third century.

John Moses Brunswick was born to a Jewish family in the German-speaking part of Switzerland in 1819. Seeking new opportunities, John took the forty-day Atlantic crossing to the United States just before he turned fifteen. Landing in New York in 1834, he found work as an errand boy for a German butcher. John Brunswick observed the massive number of carriages of all types, shapes, and sizes jamming Gotham's streets. But the intensity was too much. Brunswick soon moved to the quieter Philadelphia, where he got on as an apprentice to a carriage-maker.

For four years, Brunswick learned carriage building in Philadelphia for before moving to Harrisburg as a journeyman to a German woodworker named Greiner. Brunswick soon married Greiner's daughter Louisa and could have inherited Greiner's business, but wanted to start out on his own. The booming city of Cincinnati, Queen of inland America and home to a large German community, drew John and Louisa, who settled there in 1840.

In Cincinnati, John worked for a series of carriage makers as a journeyman. When one employer closed up, he took a job as a steward on an Ohio River steamboat. Brunswick showed a head for trading, buying low and selling high along the river. He soon had a nest egg big enough to start his own firm. The twenty-five-year-old woodworker opened The John M. Brunswick Company to make carriages in 1845. The company soon expanded into making chairs, tables, and cabinets. Brunswick said, "If it is wood, we can make it. And we can make it better than anyone else." Shortly after founding the new company, someone showed young Brunswick a beautiful, heavy, expensive English billiards table. Despite historical connections with gambling and "the low life," three-cushion and pocket billiards began to catch on in America. John knew he could build equally beautiful billiard tables, saving the expense of importing them from Europe.

The competition in billiard tables was intense. Brunswick battled Julius Balke's Great Western Billiard Manufactory of Cincinnati and the leading eastern company, Phelan & Collender of New York. In 1873, John's son-in-law Moses Bensinger played a key role in Brunswick's merger with Balke. The combined company produced 700 tables a year with a value of $400,000. In 1879 Phelan & Collender was acquired. The company was renamed Brunswick-Balke-Collender in 1884, a name used until 1960, when the company became Brunswick Corporation, the title used today.

Thus, by the late 1880s, Brunswick-Balke-Collender dominated the American billiards industry and was the largest billiards manufacturer in the world. The company's leaders were innovators in billiards rules, billiards organizations, and billiards equipment, producing better cues and rubber cushions (bumpers). Brunswick's products won award after award at international expositions. Between 1881 and 1883, the company built a new Chicago complex at Huron and Sedgwick streets. Designed by famous architect Louis Sullivan, the facility included a factory, warehouse, and lumber-drying plant.

John Brunswick died in 1886; Moses Bensinger (who had moved to Chicago) became President in 1890. The company's great strength was in beautiful, quality woodworking: Bensinger expanded the company into building elaborate wooden bar backs. A new factory was built in Dubuque, Iowa to produce the bars. As was always the case, Brunswick made hundreds of specialty and accessory products such as billiard table lamps, coolers, and lunch counters to serve the same markets.

Moses Bensinger noted a rising sport in America: bowling. Descended from ancient games, bowling began to appear in

America as taverns added a few lanes. Brunswick began making lanes, pins, and wooden bowling balls. The sport was not well-organized, using different rules, lane lengths, and ball sizes. In the 1890s, Bensinger led an effort to standardize bowling, resulting in the formation of the American Bowling Congress (ABC) in 1895. The first ABC tournament using standard rules took place in Chicago in 1901. Brunswick produced all the equipment for the match, as they did for the next 40 years.

Moses Bensinger's son Benjamin, who had joined the company in 1885, took over as President at the age of thirty-six upon his father's death in 1904. In his efforts to keep up with rising sales, Benjamin opened a 100,000 square foot factory in Muskegon, Michigan on the Lake Michigan shore. The big new facility was near Brunswick's 1,000 acres of timberland and an easy crossing of Lake Michigan from the Chicago factories (on Brunswick's ships). By the 1940s, this plant, Brunswick's largest, would grow to one million square feet.

Ever searching for ways to improve its products, the company introduced the revolutionary Mineralite rubber bowling ball in 1906. (Because of their continual research into the properties of wood, rubber, and other materials, the Brunswick of 100 years ago might today be called a "materials science company.")

Brunswick-Balke-Collender moved its headquarters from Cincinnati to Chicago in 1908. The company had sales offices and showrooms in twenty-seven US cities, Honolulu, London, Paris, Buenos Aires, and Mexico City. It was the world's largest buyer of hardwoods and operated the largest lumber drying kilns on earth. Maple went into 400,000 cues a year, dark woods into billiards tables weighing up to 2,700 pounds. No company had a finer reputation for woodworking and product quality. Brunswick was becoming a household name. Yet there was a cloud on the horizon.

In 1846, Maine passed the first state temperance law. Gradually, prohibitionists swept the nation. The 1906 formation of the Anti-Saloon League accelerated and intensified the movement, as bars were attacked and busted up. Demand for new bars began to shrink. Benjamin Bensinger saw the writing on the wall and feared for the future of the bar furnishing business, which made up one-fourth of company's four million dollars in sales. He began cutting back on the production of the beautiful, expensive bars, ending production in 1912, seven years before the passage of national Prohibition. Benjamin began a search for new products to replace the lost sales.

Beginning a long history of expansion into related niche products, Benjamin found several opportunities. First was another use for rubber, with which the company had expertise in both billiards and bowling. In 1912, Brunswick introduced the first rubber toilet seat, the Whale-Bone-Ite. The company was soon selling 120,000 toilet seats a year. An early adopter was Chicago's Pullman Company, operator of the nation's railroad sleeping cars.

For a brief period, Brunswick jumped on the piano boom, using its woodworking skills to make piano cases that were sold to the major piano makers. Getting in and out of different businesses became a Brunswick tradition throughout the 20th century.

Headlines were made when American billiards star Willie Hoppe shockingly beat "the world's best," Maurice Vignaux, in Paris in 1906. Hoppe then toured the US doing trick shots, drawing enormous crowds. The popularity of billiards took a leap upward: by the 1920s, there were more than 42,000 American pool rooms, 4,000 in New York City alone. Detroit's Recreation pool hall had an amazing 142 tables. San Francisco's Graney had a 400-seat spectator gallery. Brunswick supplied the boom, organized tournaments, and published the rules. Brunswick-Balke-Collender WAS billiards.

Another industry that soared in the 1910s and 1920s was the automobile business. Benjamin used the company's expertise in rubber to enter the tire business in 1912. By 1921, the Muskegon factory was turning out 2,000 tires a day. Yet competition intensified as two hundred tire companies were founded. In 1922, Brunswick sold their tire business to BF Goodrich, which continued to make Brunswick tires.

In the midst of that era, Brunswick made wooden airplane wings and other defense materials during World War I.

Benjamin Bensinger's next expansion was into phonograph cabinets, responding to another booming consumer trend. Brunswick-Balke-Collender soon had a million dollars in orders for these exquisite pieces of wooden furniture, largely from the Edison Phonograph company. It was not long before the company began making complete phonographs. In 1916, Brunswick introduced a model that sold for $150 (about $3700 today) but was the equal of competitors' models priced at $250. In 1915, there had only been eighteen phonograph makers; four years later, in 1919, two hundred manufacturers produced over two million phonographs. That year, Brunswick made $700,000 in profits from cabinets and complete phonographs, of which the company built 750 a day.

Brunswick-Balke-Collender went public in 1924, allowing outsiders to own stock in the company for the first time.

The company added radio manufacturing when the radio boom hit in the early 1920s. In 1925, Brunswick joined with General Electric to produce the first all-electric phonograph (as opposed to hand-cranked), the Panatrope, for $350 and up.

The company's success with phonographs led Benjamin to enter the record business. The first Brunswick record was produced in 1922. Soon Duke Ellington, Cab Calloway, and many other recording artists, including classical performers, were making records for Brunswick.

Few companies have jumped on (and off) and profited from as many different "hot" industries as has Brunswick.

By 1928, Brunswick-Balke-Collender was a large company for the time, recording sales of $29 million. The next year, the stock market collapsed, and with it, the economy. Discretionary and recreational spending went into a tailspin. Benjamin Bensinger realized dramatic measures would be required if the company, $9 million in debt, were to survive. In 1930, he sold the Brunswick Panatrope & Radio Corporation, including the record division, to Warner Brothers for $10 million. While some might say that he sold a business with big potential, most believe the move saved the company. Brunswick Records, after several owners, continue to be sold today.

Benjamin Bensinger's oldest son Robert assumed the Presidency in 1930, an inauspicious time to take the helm of any company. "Bob" Bensinger was thirty-two years old and had eleven years' experience at the company. He was assisted by younger brother Ted. Father Benjamin died five years later.

In that brief period, the company hit the rocks. 1928's record sales of $29 million dried up. In 1932, the sales figure was $3.9 million, a drop of almost 90%. Few companies were hit that hard even in the Great Depression, but most of Brunswick's revenue was from recreational spending. The continuation of prohibition (until 1933) did not help.

After years of profits, in the early 1930s Brunswick recorded losses of a million dollars a year. It is impressive that the Bensingers even bothered carrying on.

Yet carry on they did. Bob Bensinger quickly searched for new opportunities. With the end of Prohibition in 1933, Brunswick began producing coolers and table top refrigerators, led by "the Blue Flash." Soda fountains were added in 1935. Gradually the bowling and billiards businesses began to come back. Bob Bensinger also recruited new talent and managers to revive the company. But it took World War II to really restart things.

Brunswick cranked up rapidly to meet the nation's wartime needs. Included in the long list of items manufactured by the company were parachute bomb flares, assault boats, aircraft fuselages, landing skids for gliders, mortar shells, aircraft instrument panels, and rubber fuel cells. Adding to its arsenal of materials knowledge, Brunswick developed Brunsalloy, a lightweight but extremely strong metal alloy used as a substitute for aluminum in airplanes. Brunswick was back in business, registering $20 million in sales in 1942. At the same time, the rise of the USO to entertain service personnel led to better recreational facilities on military bases. Thirteen thousand billiard tables and three thousand bowling lanes were installed on bases worldwide by the end of World War II.

After the war, Americans returned to "normal" and the economy boomed. This should have been a great time for Brunswick. The company had also entered the school furniture business, seeing the coming boom in education and school construction. (Most Americans have experienced the award-winning Brunswick school chair.). Sales rose to $30 million in 1948. But another problem soon arose.

The American Machine and Foundry Company, commonly called AMF, was the leader in tobacco machinery which rolled cigars and cigarettes. Like Brunswick, AMF was always on the lookout for new markets. Brunswick had been toying with the idea of an automated pinsetter for years, but in the 1930s turned away two inventors who thought they could make one. Those inventors took their idea to AMF, which decided to pursue the project. In 1946, AMF began to introduce their automatic pinsetters. At first, they did not work, but by 1952 AMF was successfully producing its machines, branded "AMF Pinspotters." Alley owners and bowlers loved them. Brunswick was literally "behind the eight ball." And, in 1950, Bob's brother Ted was named President of the company, with Bob remaining as Chairman of the Board. The two brothers faced a challenge perhaps as great as the Depression had been.

Under Ted's leadership, the company needed to develop an automatic pinsetter, but did not have the $10 million required for research and development. Ted cut a deal with the Murray Corporation of America, which made automobile bodies for Ford but had just lost that contract. Murray had cash and was looking for new opportunities to apply its metal engineering skills. Brunswick and Murray formed a 50-50 partnership, the Pinsetter Corporation. Using Murray's cash, the first pinsetters were manufactured for the partnership by the Otis Elevator Company, which also understood machinery. Sensing a major opportunity, Murray tried to buy Brunswick out of the partnership. But Ted Bensinger was able to arrange a $55 million line-of-credit with financier CIT Financial Corporation. When the Murray executives showed up at a meeting, planning on buying out Brunswick's interest in Pinsetter, Ted instead handed them an $18 million check for Murray's share of Pinsetter. Brunswick now had total control of the new product line, finally ready to ship in the spring of 1956.

By that time, AMF had already sold 9,000 of its Pinspotters. Nevertheless, Brunswick's long history in bowling paid off. Revenues took off. Brunswick soon had $30 million in pinsetter orders to fill. By the end of 1956, 2,000 of Brunswick's $8,000 Pinsetters were installed, followed by 7,000 more in 1957. Boosted by the "pinsetter wars" between Brunswick and AMF, bowling took off in the 1950s. Thousands of lanes were opened across America, often financed by Brunswick and AMF. Bowling alley owners included Mickey Mantle, Stan Musial, and Yogi Berra. AMF and Brunswick eventually operated their own large chains of bowling alleys (today consolidated into Bowlero Corporation). Between 1946 and 1960, the number of women bowlers rose from 82,000 to six million; youth bowlers from 8,000 to 185,000. Bowling was supported by over one hundred specialty magazines and newspapers. Brunswick continued to play a key role in promoting the sport.

With additional support from billiards and school furniture, Brunswick boomed. From 1958 to 1961, the company expanded from 5,500 employees to over 16,000. In 1954, Brunswick-Balke-Collender earned profits of $700,000 on sales of $33 million. Seven years later, in 1961, profits were $45 million on sales of $422 million. The company had grown from being a niche industry supplier to become a Fortune 500 company. The company was loaded with cash, with more flowing in every day. The Bensingers were, finally, on top of the world. The family held about 10% of Brunswick stock, which rose dramatically.

Ted, rising to CEO in 1954, had a vision for the company. With the post-war growth in consumer spending, recreation looked like the place to be. Ted said he wanted the company to become "the General Motors of Sports." With their newfound corporate war chest, in 1958 Brunswick bought sporting goods maker MacGregor, which made balls for all sports, golf clubs and bags, shoes for baseball and football, tennis balls and rackets, and many other items.

Brunswick continued making acquisitions over the next few years, including Red Head outdoor clothing and equipment and Union Hardware, the largest maker of roller skates. A glimpse of the future took place when Brunswick bought the Owens Yacht and Larson boat companies (later sold). A more successful purchase was Zebco, the leading maker of closed-face spinning reels for fishing. (The company was originally named the Zero Hour Bomb Company, making time bombs for oil wells.) Zebco sales almost quadrupled from 1954 to 1957 alone.

Brunswick added new factories for its sporting goods empire and sold over 5,000 products in America and around the world. The company began a joint venture in Japan, Nippon Brunswick, to serve another exploding market for bowling. The billiards business boomed briefly as a result of the 1961 Paul Newman and Jackie Gleason movie, *The Hustler*. Perhaps the big strategic concept, "General Motors of Sports," would work out.

At the same time, the Bensingers seem to have caught the "conglomerate bug" that swept through Wall Street and American industry in the 1960s. "Diversification" and "synergy" were the buzzwords of the era. Maybe sports alone was not enough.

In 1959, Brunswick bought the AS Aloe Company, a medical supply house in St. Louis. By buying four more medical equipment companies, the company became a major competitor in hypodermic needles, catheters, and other categories. Brunswick consolidated these businesses into a unit named Sherwood Medical Industries, the nation's second largest manufacturer and distributor of medical supplies. The company produced 4.5 million needles a week, four times the nearest competitor. Brunswick was now well-positioned in three industries with promising futures: recreation, education (school furniture), and healthcare. An extensive 1959 article in *Fortune* magazine entitled "Brunswick's Automatic Money- Maker" included Ted's remark that the company would become "The Mr. Big in recreation, education, and health."

Brunswick also expanded upon its expertise in materials and defense products. They spent $10 million developing Brunsmet, a metal fiber product with many uses from jet engine seals to anti-static carpet. A later acquisition made parts for the Viking Mars Lander. Brunswick became a major producer of aircraft radomes and camouflage materials for the military. A vast array of unusual and niche products made up a meaningful portion of the company's revenues. In view of the company's diversity, the name was finally shortened from Brunswick-Balke-Collender to simply the Brunswick Corporation in 1960.

Amidst this diversification and acquisition spree, Ted Bensinger made a purchase that would change the company long-term. In the summer of 1961, Brunswick bought the Mercury Marine Company from company founder Carl Kiekhaefer for $34 million in Brunswick stock. Kiekhaefer was a pioneer in the outboard boat motor industry, later producing inboard engines and stern drives as well. Mercury's top-end engines competed with the Johnson and Evinrude lines of the industry's dominant company, Outboard Marine Corporation (OMC). Under Brunswick, Mercury added the lower-priced Mariner line, produced in Japan by a joint venture with Yamaha.

Then, more quickly than it had risen, the bowling boom came to an end. A 1961 study commissioned by Brunswick indicated a US potential of 300,000 lanes (vs. 125,000 at the time). But that future was not to be. In 1962, demand for new bowling lanes came to a virtual halt. The thousands of bowling alleys that had been financed by Brunswick and

AMF could not make their payments. Brunswick found itself almost $400 million debt. The stock dropped from $75 in 1961 to $13 the next year. The Bensingers were once again "up against the wall." For the first time in the company's 118-year history, the family chose an outsider, Jack Hanigan, to take over as President of the company in 1963.

Hanigan and his successors continually restructured and streamlined the company. Businesses continued to be bought and sold. Organized into the four realms of recreation, marine power (Mercury), technical products, and medical products, Brunswick's sales reached $450 million in 1969, the highest since 1961. Under Brooks Abernathy, Hanigan's protégé, sales reached one billion dollars for the first time in 1977, generated by 25,000 employees. Still apparently bitten by the conglomerate bug, Brunswick entered fields as far removed as doors and fare collection boxes for mass transit.

In 1981, Brunswick's profits set a record at $66 million on sales of $1.1 billion. Half the sales and two-thirds of the profits came from the health and technical divisions, including strong international results. Wall Street looked at the company and believed it might be worth more if broken into pieces. The fast-growing medical supply business was the gem. Diversified company Whittaker Corporation made an offer to buy Brunswick in 1982. To save Brunswick from the raider, the company sold Sherwood Medical to American Home Products (later Wyeth, then Pfizer) for $425 million. Brunswick maintained its independence at the cost of losing a promising division.

For the next twenty years, Brunswick continued to try new things, ranging from bicycles (Roadmaster, bought from AMF) to re-entering the boat and yacht business. They bought into the camping business, including Igloo coolers. The acquisition spree continued in July 1997 as Brunswick paid $310 million for Life Fitness, maker of stationary bicycles, treadmills, stairclimbers, rowers, cross trainers, and strength training equipment for fitness centers worldwide. Finally, by the start of the 21st century, Brunswick began to narrow its focus. The Technical division was spun out as the company slimmed down to boats, marine engines, and fitness equipment. Today this interesting, very old company generates annual sales of three billion dollars in marine engines and about one billion dollars in the boat business (including Sea Ray, Bayliner, Meridian, Boston Whaler, Crestliner, Lowe, and Princecraft). The company is the world's largest maker of pleasure boats and certainly one of the top makers of marine engines. In recent years, virtually all of the company's profits have derived from marine engines. Bowling, billiards, and the other components of Brunswick's history have been sold off to an array of buyers. (Many products are still sold under the Brunswick brand name.)

It is worth noting that former arch-rival AMF also diversified into more recreational products, including billiards and Harley-Davidson motorcycles (from 1969 to 1981). That did not work, either; today AMF no longer exists. The same fate ultimately befell Brunswick's other key rival, Outboard Marine, a billion-dollar-company in the 1990s, though new owner Bombardier Recreational Products continued to produce Evinrude outboard engines until 2020.

Most great companies focus on one business and central skill. UPS, Deere, Caterpillar, Paccar, and Home Depot come to mind. Diversification (LACK OF FOCUS) as a business strategy grew in the conglomerate era of the 1960s. Many of the companies that existed before the 1960s went the conglomerate route, then later "deconglomerated" (Colgate-Palmolive among the most successful). Other companies "pivot" once or twice, at most. Few companies make it to 100 years of age as an independent company.

Brunswick is the exception to all these "rules." The company has shown a strong will to live, a survival instinct that has kept it an independent company for 175 years.

Blowing with the wind, including conglomeration, Brunswick has usually been a leader in each of its many fields. From jazz records to camouflage, the company has a history of quality. In its 175 years, Brunswick has successively been the dominant factor in the billiards industry, the bar industry, the bowling industry, the hypodermic needle industry, and now the boat and engine industries.

Our study of great companies implies that they should usually stick to one industry. Perhaps even rename their company after their most important operation, as did Dayton-Hudson and Melville Corporation (becoming Target and CVS, respectively). Mercury Marine might be a good moniker for Brunswick as it stands today.

At the same time, the long history of this most interesting company forces us to wonder, "What industry will they try next, then lead, in the coming fifty years?"

Originally published on AmericanBusinessHistory.org on October 16, 2020.

Chapter 3

Two Billion Passengers a Day: The Otis Story

On this 4th of July, it is appropriate to honor the long history of one of America's great companies. Elisha Otis perfected the first commercially successful elevators, both for freight and passengers, before the Civil War. The organization he founded, the Otis Elevator Company, has labored on for almost 170 years, through wars, depressions, competition, managements good and bad, and changes of ownership. Yet, after all that time, Otis circles the world and continues to lead the "vertical transportation industry." The modern city as we know it would be impossible without the elevators, escalators, and moving walkways developed by the company.

Today carrying two billion passengers a day over hundreds

of millions of vertical miles in over 200 nations, Otis is one of those relatively rare cases where the "first mover" in an industry went on to lead – and dominate – that industry for over a century. (Note that none of the companies we nominated as the three greatest companies in American history invented their industry in the same way that Otis did.) Here is a brief look at the Otis story.

Beginnings

Elisha Otis, born in Vermont in 1811, was a natural tinkerer and inventor who loved machinery. Otis moved around the nation to different jobs while he worked on inventions in bread-baking, woodturning, and railroad brakes. His attention ultimately turned to "hoists." Dating back to the construction of the pyramids, mankind had developed ingenious combinations of pulleys and ropes to lift heavy things up in the air. Shafts for hoists were even built into medieval castles. (St. Peter's in Rome had a shaft in place in 1626, but no elevator was built in the shaft until 1900!) Accidents and injuries were commonplace when the ropes or other components broke. By the early 1850s, Elisha Otis had developed a braking system that stopped a hoist (also called a "lift") from falling to the ground.

In 1853 the first American World's Fair was held in New York City, including the beautiful Crystal Palace, where Bryant Park is today (next to the New York Public Library). The fair opened late and was not a success the first year, so the organizers brought in P.T. Barnum to manage it in the second, 1854 season. Barnum paid Elisha Otis $100 to erect and demonstrate his invention. Otis rode the lift up into the air, then shocked the crowd by cutting the rope which held the lift. His braking system kicked in, holding the lift in place.

Elisha Otis began his company, which had several names

before becoming the Otis Elevator Company, selling hoists primarily to factories for lifting freight. His two sons Charles and Norton came into the business with him. In 1857 they installed the world's first passenger elevator in Manhattan's five-story Haughwout Building, powered by a steam engine in the basement. It moved up and down at about eight inches per second. Haughwout was a dealer in china, glass, and silverware; his customers included Mary Todd Lincoln. The building still stands today at the corner of Broadway and Broome in the SoHo district.

Nevertheless, most of the public was not ready to trust the new contraption to carry people. Inventors around the nation tinkered with different types of lifts, many of which failed. Newspapers were full of stories of the dangers of elevators. Otis and his sons labored away selling lifts to factories. In 1858, the company almost went bankrupt, but Elisha kept it going with the support of his creditors.

In 1861, Elisha Otis died of diphtheria at the age of forty-nine and his sons took over the business. Norton traveled the country promoting their products while Charles ran the factory, always obsessed with product quality and treating his workers well, paying them more than competing factories. Over time, the company developed a large works in Yonkers, New York, with easy access to railroads and shipping. The entire elevator machinery was made in Yonkers, then broken into individual parts and shipped to the customer, where a local installer would actually build the final device in the customer's shaft. (This process of shipping parts for local assembly would continue for decades, reinforced by the later rise of the elevator constructors' union.)

Over time, Otis earned the reputation as having the best and safest hoists and elevators available. Every year brought improvements in safety devices and the heavy machinery and counterweights required to lift heavier loads and lift them higher, as buildings rose in height. Otis switched from steam-driven elevators to hydraulic systems. The company crowed that it had never had a fatality, whether working with freight or passenger elevators. Otis's catalogs implied that buying any other brand amounted to "criminal recklessness and wholesale manslaughter." The company began shipping its elevators all over the world. Otis built new factories and acquired dozens of smaller elevator companies and local installers.

By the end of the Civil War, people began to accept the idea of elevators for passenger use. The earliest passenger elevator "cages" were sumptuous affairs, built into hotels and fine stores. Saratoga, New York's Congress Hotel had such an elevator installed by 1870. The passenger car had an overhead dome with skylights, gaslit chandeliers, sofas on three sides, carvings and moldings of French walnut and ebony, and "appropriate touches of gilding." Operators, often wearing uniforms and gloves, were present in each elevator.

Rising Up

The 1870s and 1880s witnessed more tall buildings. The elevator joined the development of steel frame construction (in place of stone and brick) to permit the rise of the skyscraper. The increasing value of land in New York City drove developers to build higher and higher. The devastating Chicago fire of 1871 provided another opportunity for new construction in that booming city. Prior to the perfection of the safe elevator, about five stories were the most stairs that any tenant would climb. The highest floors earned the lowest rents. With the elevator, the top floors became even more valuable than lower floors due to better sunlight, ventilation, and views. By the 1880s, some buildings reached the unprecedented height of over two hundred feet, with ten and more stories.

taining ten times the weight which can ever be brought to bear upon it. In the works of the Messrs. Otis Brothers & Co., not only is all the machinery of their apparatus made, but also the cars used in the elevators. In the construction of these the same consum-

MANUFACTORY OF HOISTING MACHINERY, YONKERS, N. Y.

mate care is taken, and strength, with a luxury of tasteful decoration, is a characteristic of their passenger elevators. An examination of this modern convenience in use at the St. Nicholas Hotel, at Arnold, Constable & Co's, N. York; at Congress Hall, Saratoga; the Galt House, Louisville; the Maxwell House, Nashville; the St. Charles Hotel, New Orleans; and the Occidental Hotel, San Francisco, and as specimens, among the other numerous ones they have built, will show conclusively the merit of their work, and exhibit the reasons for the reputation they have gained.

The works of Messrs. Otis Brothers & Co., at Yonkers, N. Y., —

Excerpt from "Great Industries of the United States" 1872

Charles and Norton Otis had partnered with another elevator maker, William Hale, and in 1882 they sold the business to Hale for $350,000 (about $9 million in 2021 dollars) and retired. But for some reason the brothers could not stay away from the elevator business, and in 1887 returned to the company, investing some of their money, with Charles running the factory. In just three years, Charles made further improvements in Otis's elevators, before his 1890 resignation. Norton continued with the company until 1905.

By 1884, Otis had installed 1,250 passenger elevators in New York City alone. By 1886, over one hundred of those elevators were more than one hundred feet tall. An even more complex challenge was Paris' Eiffel Tower, opened in 1889 for another World's Fair. The French sponsors were opposed to using American technology, but no French company could figure out how to run an elevator up the curved legs of the tower. Otis figured it out and won the contract for the elevators in the sloping legs. The Otis elevators were smoother, faster, and quieter than those installed in other parts of the tower by French elevator manufacturers.

In the late 1880s and early 1890s, Otis began to apply a newly emerging technology to its elevators: electricity. 1892 witnessed the addition of the first push buttons to call elevators. Soon New York had over 5,000 apartment elevators in use, with Otis leading the field. Partnerships with local elevator companies from Canada to Australia were formed, and over time more of these companies were acquired by Otis. (Between 1887 and 1900, Otis acquired thirteen other elevator makers.)

In 1898, the brothers' associate William Baldwin became President of Otis. The Otis Elevator Company was incorporated that year with a capitalization of $11 million. Otis also went public that year, one of the earliest companies (outside of railroads) to do so. Baldwin ran the company until 1930.

At the same time, Otis acquired the rights to a new invention, "moving stairs." The first machine was installed in the New York subway station at Sixth Avenue and 23rd Street in 1899, followed by Bloomingdale's New York department store in 1901, then by large orders from competitors Gimbel's and Macy's (for their new Herald Square store in 1902). Soon renamed "Escalators," Otis owned the trademark on that term until 1950.

In 1904, Otis built 175 elevators for the London Underground, at a total cost of $2 million, the largest job the company had ever undertaken.

In 1902, Otis had introduced its "gearless traction (electric) elevators." These allowed the elevators to reach even greater height and were installed in a new wave of taller buildings. New York witnessed the opening of the 46-story, 612-foot Singer Building in 1908, the 700-foot Metropolitan Life Building in 1910, and the 780-foot Woolworth Building in 1912, each the tallest building in the world at the time. All used Otis elevators and were considered modern wonders of the world (both the buildings and their majestic elevators).

Big and Global

By 1906, with demand booming, Otis operated seven factories across the United States, one in Canada, and generated annual revenues of $15.7 million. In the following decade, major new factories were added in Buffalo and Harrison, New York to supplement the main plant in Yonkers. The number of employees rose to 5,000. In 1909, the company boasted that its elevators were in use in the Forbidden City in Beijing and the Mikado Palace in Japan. Others using the company's products in their palaces were the Emperor of Austria-Hungary and the Czar of Russia (in the Kremlin).

From 1911 to 1944, Otis's advanced electrical engineering efforts were led by a Swede, David Lindquist. His efforts led to continuous improvements – lighter materials, faster and quieter elevators, automated control and timing systems, and lower costs. Lindquist paid especial attention to the people using elevators – how fast they entered, how fast they left, and what their travel patterns were. A high point was reached in 1931's Empire State Building, with 58 passenger elevators serving 102 floors (and using 119 miles of rope).

The roaring twenties were good to Otis. Between 1922 and 1929, the number of Otis employees rose from 8,000 to 19,500. From 1926 to 1929, the stock rose from a price of $70 a share to $450. But those times did not last, as the Great Depression hit. Otis's stock price collapsed as did the business, forcing the layoff of half the employees and the slashing of dividends. In 1933 and 1934 the company recorded losses, the first in the corporation's history (since 1898). The 1930s were also a period of labor unrest, and Otis reached agreements with major unions, including the elevator constructors/installers, perpetuating the practice of building elevators onsite from parts shipped from the Otis plants.

The 1920s and 1930s also saw the development of an idea that helped the company. Against the better judgment of management, one Otis employee began promoting the idea that the company should maintain its products after installation, a job previously done by thousands of independent repairmen. By the late 1930s, Otis had over 10,000 maintenance contracts, which provided a steady flow of cash even when demand for new elevators rose and fell. A Modernization department soon followed, going back to old customers and modernizing their machines. (Today, service and modernization provide the bulk of Otis's profits.)

Otis survived the Depression and was ready for the demands of wartime America. Like other companies, Otis made war materiel: guns, machine tools, radar, and of course hoists and elevators for ships (including aircraft carriers). Germans bombed Otis's London plant, killing eleven people, and seized the company's Berlin factory.

Struggling in the 1950s and 1960s

The post-war expansion of the US economy served Otis well, with 1951 revenues reaching $120 million. The late 1950s saw the full development of automatic, push-button elevators which understood daily traffic patterns, signaling the end of the line for America's 90,000 elevator operators. Yet the 1950s and 1960s brought a new challenge to the company.

The challenge was the rise of the south and west, with new cities more horizontal than vertical. Unlike New York and Chicago, Phoenix, Los Angeles, Dallas, and Atlanta were more spread out, with fewer skyscrapers. The number of new skyscrapers built in the older cities declined. Like its long-time competitor, Westinghouse Electric, Otis focused on big, tall, high status jobs. Small hydraulic elevators only serving two to five floors were not of much interest to Otis, though those were the most common building heights for offices, hotels, stores, and apartments in the sunbelt. Smaller companies, led by Dover Elevator, seized the opportunity in small elevators and Otis lost share. Otis was slow to react, only gradually entering the small elevator industry segment. By 1975, Otis's share of the American new elevator and escalator market had fallen from 45% to 31%.

The 1960s was also the era of the conglomerate craze, the idea that a company could acquire totally unrelated businesses to alleviate fluctuations in your core business and achieve "synergies" (2+2=5) across these diverse businesses. Before the concept was largely proven ill-advised by the 1980s, most major companies went "diversification" crazy. Otis, under CEO Leroy Petersen (in charge from 1944 to 1966), was one of them, deciding that Otis should be a "short distance transportation company." Under his leadership (or lack thereof), Otis bought a forklift truck maker, ventured into electric vehicles including buses, and purchased electronics companies. Going even further afield, Petersen even tried the bowling pinsetter business, then in a short-lived boom, against industry giants Brunswick and AMF. None of this worked, the new ventures lost money, and Otis gradually became a weakened company despite its continuing leadership in elevator technology.

The Big Changes

Meanwhile, in Hartford, Connecticut, the United Aircraft Company had problems of its own. United's Pratt & Whitney division made over 90% of the engines for jet airliners, but General Electric was gaining market share on them and would eventually become #1 in jet engines. The other parts of United, including Sikorsky, were too dependent on defense department spending, which had fallen as the Vietnam War ended but were always unpredictable. United's new CEO, Harry Gray, hired from early conglomerate Litton Industries, was committed to diversification. Looking around for companies with solid futures but inexpensive stock, his advisors pointed him to Otis, whose stock was selling in the high $20s. In 1975, Gray offered over $40 in cash to buy Otis, a total of under $300 million. While Otis at first fought the deal, they finally caved when no other buyers could be found. United Aircraft, renamed United Technologies by Gray, made back that much money off Otis within a few years, and went on to buy air conditioning pioneer and giant Carrier in 1979.

While United Technologies swallowed Otis, two key executives from Otis rose to power in the combined company. One was Hubert Faure, a Frenchman who built Otis's International business to be bigger than its American side, partially by building small elevators to serve the "less tall" European market. The other was one of Faure's hires,

George David, who became President of the Otis division in 1986 and president of United Technologies in 1992. David ran United Technologies until 2007, building a stronger company and winning many kudos as a top CEO from industry groups and trade publications.

For forty-five years, Otis served as an important revenue and profit contributor to United Technologies. Over time, as more companies moved away from diversification and toward focusing on their "core competencies," it became clear that perhaps the parts of United Technologies were worth more than the whole. United decided to spin off its two key non-defense businesses. In March 2020, United's shareholders each received one share of a new company, Carrier Global, and one half-share of another "new" company, Otis Worldwide, for each share they owned in United. The remaining aerospace business merged with Raytheon and is now called Raytheon Technologies.

Since the split-up, as of July 2021, Raytheon Technologies' stock has risen about 40%, Otis has almost doubled, and Carrier has almost tripled.

In 2020, under CEO Judy Marks, Otis Worldwide generated profits of $900 million, 83% from services, on revenues of almost $13 billion. 85% of its 69,000 employees are located outside the United States. The company's two million installations carry two billion passengers every day, perhaps making Otis the world's biggest transportation company. Otis elevators and escalators are found in eight of the ten tallest buildings in the world, including the record-setting 2700-foot Burj Khalifa in Dubai. Among other large recent jobs were 670 elevators and escalators built for the Hyderabad, India, metro system.

When one steps into an elevator in a modern skyscraper, we usually do not realize the immense complexity of the overall machine. Dozens of elevators in one building are controlled by central systems which determine which car to send to which floor when and where to have them waiting before they are called. Otis now has Internet technologies that allow the systems to be controlled and monitored remotely. To test their new ideas, Otis has built massive test towers around the world, with one in China 886 feet tall. Otis's elevators and escalators can be found everywhere, even on the outside of tall buildings and in cruise ships.

While the global "vertical transportation" industry remains highly competitive, Otis still tops the field, leading key competitors Schindler of Switzerland (which bought Westinghouse's elevator division), Mitsubishi of Japan, KONE from Finland, and ThyssenKrupp from Germany (which bought Dover). And thus, this very old company, started by one tinkerer with an idea, has lived on through times good and bad, through changes in its environment, but still leads its industry. And that industry is one which is required for the existence of the world as we know it and use it every day.

Originally published on AmericanBusinessHistory.org on July 4, 2021.

Chapter 4
Success Lost & Found: Sherwin-Williams

While most big companies disappear over time, some figure out how to survive and prosper decade after decade, even century after century. But is the journey from founding to long-term durability a straight path? Today one of America's most successful companies, one that does not make many headlines, is Sherwin-Williams, the world's largest paint company, based in Cleveland, Ohio for 151 years. Here is a quick look at the ups and downs of a true survivor.

The Start

In 1866, twenty-four-year-old Henry Sherwin invested his $2,000 life savings in a prosperous local paint wholesaler. Four years later (1870), he convinced two friends, Williams and Osborn, to each put up $15,000 to become equal one-third partners with him in taking over the wholesale business and adding a retail store. The new organization, Sherwin, Williams & Co, generated $422,391 in revenue in its first year. Relative to other businesses of the era, that was a large figure, the equivalent of almost $9 million in 2021 dollars.

Henry Sherwin was the driving force behind the company. According to company records, he was obsessed with neatness and organization, even checking for dust behind machinery and under desks. Any sign of clutter could get you fired. But he was also intent on making the business large, an attribute not common among the thousands of paint dealers around the nation.

In a time when paints were hand-mixed from raw pigments and fillers and other ingredients, Sherwin and his associates focused their energies on making the best paints and charging a full price for them. And they were committed to growth. In 1871, the one-year-old company began making its own paints. For its factory, the company acquired a former cooperage (for barrel making) from John Rockefeller's main company, Standard Oil of Ohio, on the Cuyahoga River in the heart of Cleveland. In its first year, Sherwin, Williams' paint factory made 450 pounds of paint using 83 different formulas.

The Rise

By 1874, the firm employed twenty people. 1875 witnessed the company's first ready-mixed paint, a major step forward, and in 1880, it opened a branch in Chicago. The firm was incorporated as Sherwin-Williams in 1884. In the ensuing years, Sherwin-Williams continued its geographical expansion, making use of the emerging railroad system. It also hired chemists and led the industry in new innovations. Finding new markets, the firm produced paints for horse-drawn coaches, railroad cars, and farm implements. It even made its own paint cans. All of this growth was financed from profits, avoiding debt. Henry Sherwin continued as the key person, first as President and then Chairman of the Board, until his death in 1916. (Sherwin was also responsible for the first use of the "Covers the Earth" logo, one of the most recognized in the world.)

By World War I, Sherwin-Williams had become the world's largest paint manufacturer. By then, the company was about the same size as Standard Oil of Ohio, the Brunswick Company, or the powerful National Cash Register Company of Dayton, Ohio. While the company opened a few retail stores in this era, the emphasis was on paint manufacturing, with the products being sold through a large dealer network. In 1917, Sherwin-Williams acquired Chicago's Martin-Senour Paint Company, a brand still in use today. The company also expanded overseas. Between 1900 and 1919, Sherwin-Williams' revenues grew from $2.3 million to $34.2 million, generated by 600 different products. The first sale of stock to the public took place in 1920.

The man who drove this growth was Walter Cottingham, President from 1909 until 1922, who came into the company when they acquired his Canadian paint company, one of many acquisitions. Cottingham was a master salesman, preaching the importance of enthusiasm to the company's growing sales force. Like John Patterson, the head of National Cash Register and often considered the creator of modern sales methods, Cottingham developed incentive systems, slogans, company songs, and handbooks covering every aspect of sales. Sherwin-Williams ran national advertising campaigns, including billboards, magazines, and later radio. Due to the quality of the products, the company's paints often sold for substantially more than those made by competitors.

From a distance, the paint business might seem simple. But "coatings," as the industry calls itself, are highly complex. Each paint, varnish, lacquer, finish, and stain must be customized for its intended use. Coatings that stick to metal are different from those that stick to wood. Those used on the interiors of houses are very different from those that work on automobile exteriors. Sherwin-Williams developed extensive research laboratories to figure out the best formula for every application. Developing paints for aircraft exteriors was especially challenging, given that those surfaces expand and contract as they experience temperature extremes. Sherwin-Williams rose to meet all these challenges, becoming an important source of automotive and airplane paints.

The chemistry of paints also changed dramatically in the early twentieth century. In World War I, supplies of critical dyestuffs and other ingredients from the big German chemical industry were cut off. All of American industry scrambled to come up with synthetic substitutes, which also lowered the cost of paint ingredients. New plastics resulted in the creation of latex-based and other paints. Sherwin-Williams was at the forefront of all these developments.

The Great Depression hit the company hard like it did other firms. Yet by 1939, when company revenues reached $95.8 million, business had bounced back.

From 1940 through 1960, Sherwin-Williams was led by Arthur Steudel, who introduced fat books which showed customers how rooms might look in different color schemes, along with paint chips to take home. The company operated a large printing plant, which in 1959 produced 500,000 "Color Harmony Guides" and 12 million copies of the company's *Home Decorator* magazine.

In 1941, Sherwin-Williams introduced Kem-Tone Paint, which required only one coat and dried within an hour. The new product was a huge success, quickly outselling all the other products the company made. By 1945, 37 million gallons had been sold and by 1955, 100 million gallons. Another new product was the paint "Roller-Koater," one of the first paint rollers and another big winner for the company.

World War II brought new demand for paints for the military, and Sherwin-Williams even operated a bomb factory on behalf of the government, due to its reputation as outstanding manufacturers. 2,700 company men and women served in the armed forces.

After the War, the great housing boom of the 1950s drove demand up, resulting in one of the best eras in the company's history. New factories and new product innovations continued apace. By 1964, when Sherwin-Williams stock was listed on the New York Stock Exchange, the company had 1,850 branch offices and 33,000 dealers. Revenues that year were $313.5 million and profits $17 million, making Sherwin-Williams one of the two hundred largest American industrial companies, larger than Gillette, Merck, Xerox, or Pepsi-Cola.

The Fall

That same post-war boom also brought innovations in retailing and other forces which were not favorable to the company. By the early 1960s, the discount store phenomenon began to arise: Kmart, Target, and Walmart all opened their first stores in 1962. Sherwin-Williams had historically been able to set the prices retailers sold its products at, but changes in the law allowed retailers to sell at any price. Discount stores sometimes sold the company's products at half-off in order to drive traffic, crushing the profit margins for Sherwin-Williams dealers and its own branches.

At the same time, after years of falling ingredient prices, inflation increased, raising the cost of making paint. Labor costs also rose. The rise of aluminum siding for houses posed another challenge to the traditional paint market. Sherwin-Williams' revenues stagnated and profits started to decline.

Struggling to regain its footing, new management tried a variety of strategies. Investment in new plants to replace outdated facilities accelerated. A large new research center was built. Much larger stores called "Decorating World" carrying many more products for do-it-yourselfers were tested but proved too complex to operate, outside the company's "wheelhouse." More acquisitions were made, some of them well beyond the company's expertise. The company even dropped the renowned "covers the earth" logo, spending $15 million on "rebranding" and introducing the new logo.

To finance all these activities, Sherwin-Williams went deeply into debt for the first time in its history. The acquisitions and new ideas resulted in the company's first billion-dollar sales year in 1977. But that same year also resulted in the first loss, $8 million that year, compared with annual profits of $15-20 million in the 1960s. For the first time, no dividends were paid to stockholders. Long-term debt totaled $197 million. According to its own financial executives, Sherwin-Williams was on the verge of bankruptcy.

The Rebirth

Likely in a state of panic, in January 1979, the hundred-year-old company's Board of Directors brought in a new leader, John Breen. Breen was the first chief in company history to come from outside the company (and outside the paint industry), having served as an executive at Cleveland's Gould battery and defense company. Breen brought with him other key executives, especially in finance and strategic planning. Breen and his new team brought higher productivity standards to the company. Authority was decentralized and re-organized into profit centers, the heads of which were expected to deliver results. Every aspect of the business was reviewed, with many parts sold off. Many long-time executives quit or were fired. The transition was not easy.

The new leadership was not perfect. In 1981, Sherwin-Williams bought leading Cleveland drug store chain Gray Drug for $55 million, thinking the drug stores' year-round business would balance the company's dependence on the warm weather painting business. (Acquisitions in radically different fields, which peaked in the "conglomerate" fad of the 1960s and 1970s, were in part motivated by intensified antitrust action by the federal government, which often prohibited a company from buying companies in the same industry.) Gray Drug was later sold to Rite Aid.

But, over time, the most profitable parts of Sherwin-Williams were enhanced and expanded, and the weak parts sold off. The classic old logo was revived. Profits began to rise. Debt was paid down and dividends restarted.

The Sherwin-Williams brand of paint was no longer sold at competing stores; it became exclusively available in the company's own retail stores (which are owned, not franchised). For the first time in company history, its retail stores became meaningfully profitable, and as many as 100 new stores a year were opened. The stores followed successful chain retail principles, looking alike, becoming instantly recognizable across the nation. At the same time, to support independent paint dealers and the new home improvement chains (Home Depot, Lowe's, Menard's), Sherwin-Williams developed separate brands including Martin-Senour and Dutch Boy (an old brand it acquired).

In the following decades, Sherwin-Williams really "got its act together." The company returned to its roots as a premium paint manufacturer, complemented by its ever-expanding chain of stores. As it became more profitable and on a solid financial footing, Sherwin-Williams made the right kind of acquisitions, which fit its strategy to be the best (as well as biggest) paint company in the world. These efforts culminated in the 2017 acquisition of large coatings company Valspar for $9.3 billion. Sherwin-Williams continues to introduce new products and innovations in all segments of the coatings and finishings markets, serving do-it-yourselfers, contractors, and the industrial coatings markets. Every segment of the company is profitable.

Sherwin-Williams Stock Chart 1980 to 2012

In the year ended December 31, 2020, Sherwin-Williams' 61,000 employees generated revenues of $18.4 billion in 120 countries and through 4,900 company-owned stores. Net profits exceeded $2 billion for the first time in company history, compared with $1.5 billion the prior year and $1.1 billion two years earlier, a phenomenal result for a company over 100 years old. As of late April 2021, the company is valued (market capitalization) at about $72 billion, among the 250 most valuable public companies in the world.

Sherwin-Williams Stock Chart 2012 to 2021

Painting the Big Picture

Long-term corporate survival is not easy. In fact, it is rare. Adapting to changing technologies, markets, and competitors can challenge even the best of companies and the smartest leaders. Only those companies which can repeatedly learn and adapt – sometimes even return to their roots – remain in business as independent enterprises decade after decade. Sherwin-Williams is a great example of this, making life better for its customers, suppliers, employees, and stockholders. Cleveland, America, and the world are fortunate to have a company as excellent as Sherwin-Williams. Only time will tell if future managements can live up to such a high standard.

Originally published on AmericanBusinessHistory.org on April 29, 2021.

Chapter 5
The Corporate Giant Whose History Almost Nobody Knows

Who would have guessed that a medium-sized retailer which never put its name on a store would evolve to become the 7th largest company in America, a place where millions of Americans shop every day?

My first job after studying economics at the University of Chicago was as an analyst of retail stocks for New York's Citibank, then one of the largest institutional investors in the United States. I was lucky to learn the business from my boss, veteran retail analyst Charles A. "Pete" Wetzel.

When I arrived at Citibank in 1973, one of Pete Wetzel's favorite retail stocks was a company then called Melville Shoe. One of his retail heroes was Francis C. "Frank" Rooney, the Chief Executive Officer (CEO) of Melville. Soon Pete turned over responsibility for covering Melville to me.

Melville, founded by Frank Melville in 1892, rose to eminence as the operator of the highly profitable Thom McAn shoe store chain, one of the two industry giants alongside Kinney Shoes (owned by the F. W. Woolworth dime store company, which later evolved into Foot Locker).

Melville's real goldmine and "growth engine" came when, in the 1960s, they took over the shoe departments in the Kmart discount store chain, which was growing dramatically at the time. These leased departments were operated as a separate subsidiary, Meldisco, in which Kmart held a minority interest (under 25%).

While I covered the company, Kmart went to Melville and demanded a half-interest in the highly profitable Meldisco. Melville had no choice but to comply, giving away millions of dollars in profits to their "partner." Life was not always easy for the smaller company.

Frank Rooney had 8 kids, and they later reported that every Saturday morning he would pile a couple of them in his car and go out driving around to his shoe stores, probing managers and customers on "what worked" and what didn't.

At the same time, Frank Rooney was very adventurous. He knew there were risks in the shoe store business, and that there were risks with Kmart. Despite the exceptional profitability and growth of Thom McAn and Meldisco, he began diversifying and experimenting with various retail concepts. Melville bought Marshall's and turned it into the largest off-price apparel retailer. They bought Chess King in young men's apparel. They operated Foxmoor Casuals for young women, Linens and Things for the home, and eventually Kay-Bee Toys. The name "Melville" was never seen on a store.

Few retail companies have ever been as aggressive at "trying things" to see what works. It was as if the company was doing R&D – research and development – like an aerospace or pharmaceutical company might do.

Years after my exposure to Frank Rooney and Melville, Jim Collins wrote the business bestseller *Built to Last*. In it he picked a great company and a "comparison" company in each of several industries. The "comparison" companies supposedly ranged from good (not great) to sick. In the shoe retailing business, he picked Nordstrom, which had begun as a shoe retailer and morphed into one of the hottest retailers in the country, for his great company. The comparison (weaker) company was lowly and "boring" Melville Shoe. The thesis was that the "greats," as understood through Collin's findings and theories, were vastly superior to the comparison firms. And had far brighter futures.

But in the midst of this history, in 1969, Frank Rooney's Melville picked up a tiny six-year old Rhode Island drug store chain called Consumers Value Stores. We at Citibank worried that this was a misfire, but with his diverse portfolio of stores, we did not lose sleep over our investment in Melville's future. Nevertheless, how could the apparel- and shoe-centered Melville compete in this new field against established drug store chains like Walgreen's, Jack Eckerd, Rite Aid, Revco, People's, Long's, Thrifty, and many others?

Melville Shoe was later renamed Melville Corporation to reflect its diversity. When Frank Rooney stepped down in

1987, after 23 years in the driver's seat (and 34 years with the company), the value of Melville's shares had risen 60-fold (19.5% per year compounded). Annual sales had risen from $180 million to $7 billion. The company had grown year-in, year-out, quarter-in, quarter-out, always among the most profitable retailers in America.

When Frank Rooney retired, two things happened:

First, Stanley Goldstein, son of one of the founders of Consumers Value Stores (now renamed CVS), took over the helm of Melville. He went on to shed the shoe businesses, Marshall's, and the other non-drug store businesses. The company evolved into CVS Health.

Second, despite his age, three years after he retired, Frank Rooney took over his father-in-law's small shoe company, H.H. Brown. Within a year H.H. Brown caught the attention of Warren Buffett, whose Berkshire Hathaway bought the company but kept the aging Frank Rooney as CEO. Rooney and Buffett became friends, and Rooney became a key advisor on Buffett's many retail investments.

Buffett wrote his shareholders, "Much of my enthusiasm for this purchase came from Frank's willingness to continue as CEO. Like most of our managers, he had no financial need to work but does so because he loves the game and likes to excel. Managers of this stripe cannot be "hired" in the normal sense of the word. What we must do is provide a concert hall in which business artists of this class will wish to perform."

By 2017, CVS Health had gone on to become the 7th largest company in the United States, with annual revenues of $184 billion and profits of over $6 billion. This places the company just ahead of Amazon, AT&T, and longtime number one General Motors on Fortune magazine's list of the 500 largest American companies.

Over the years, Melville/CVS stock has far out-performed that of Jim Collins' favored Nordstrom.

Frank Rooney died in 2015 at age 93, undoubtedly still visiting his beloved stores up until the end. That love of stores, but above all else a rare willingness to try new ideas, created the roots for the CVS behemoth of today.

(For another story of a retailer that experimented with new concepts and then re-invented itself, see Chapter 10: Can Companies Re-invent Themselves? The Target Story.)

Originally Published on Hooversworld.com on May 22, 2018

Chapter 6
Same Town, Same Family: The Smucker Saga

In 1752, Amish/Mennonite farmer Christian Schmucker migrated from Switzerland to Pennsylvania. In 2016, his son's son's son's son's son's son's son's son's son, forty-six-year-old Mark Smucker, became Chief Executive of the J. M. Smucker Company of Orrville, Ohio. That makes him a ninth-generation American. This is the story of this great family and its iconic company.

By 1817, the Schmuckers had changed their name to Smoker, which did not last because these Pennsylvania Dutch people opposed the use of tobacco, changed it again to Smucker, and settled in Ohio. The area around their town of Orrville had plenty of apple trees, some reportedly planted by Johnny Appleseed. Christian's grandson's grandson, Jerome Monroe ("JM") Smucker, operated a cider mill in 1897. He charged one cent a gallon to press apples into cider for the local farmers. Out of this operation, JM developed a method for making better-tasting apple butter, which the family began to sell in neighboring counties. JM's sons Willard and Welker went to work in the family business by the time they were fifteen.

In 1921, JM incorporated the private company, wholly-owned by him and his children. Annual sales were $147,000. Soon after, they began making jams and jellies, added a siding of the Pennsylvania Railroad for more efficient shipping, and started selling their products in surrounding states.

The company was tiny compared to the big canning companies or the jelly-making Welch's company. But they kept plugging away, and under Willard Smucker's leadership, improved their products, created a custom-shaped glass jar, and opened a plant in Washington state to be near the best and least expensive apples. By 1939, sales reached $1,000,000 per year.

By the early 1960s, the J. M. Smucker Company under Willard's son Paul had gone public, broken the $10 million sales barrier, and made a few acquisitions. It took until the 1970s to become number two in jams and jellies, behind Welch's. By 1980, Smucker's was number one, and Paul's son Tim was climbing into the driver's seat. Tim represented the 8th generation American Smucker, and the 4th generation to run the company.

Under Tim, the company saw dramatic change. In 1989, sales reached $367 million. Several smaller acquisitions added to the continuing natural growth of the company. The big shift in the company's product mix began with the 2002 acquisition of Jif Peanut Butter from fellow Ohio company Procter and Gamble. The Cincinnati-based giant had started to re-evaluate its product "portfolio," entering fast-growing fields and leaving others where it felt the future was less promising. Smucker's also bought Crisco from P&G. Though P&G might not have been excited by the future of these brands, they were natural additions to the Smucker line and the Smucker grocery store distribution system.

The next year, Smucker's bought Pillsbury flour, though they later sold off that business. While these acquisitions propelled Smucker's into a larger company, they were small potatoes (or apples?) compared to the acquisition, announced in late 2008, of Folgers Coffee, another Procter & Gamble castoff. The $2 billion purchase doubled Smucker's size and resulted in P&G's shareholders owning over half of the Smucker company's stock, through an unusual, tax-saving transaction called a "Reverse Morris Trust."

Folgers had begun as a San Francisco coffee roaster in 1850. By the time Procter and Gamble bought the company in 1963, it had passed up California rival Hills Bros. Coffee in the west and Midwest but was not strong in the big east coast market. The national market was dominated by General Foods' Maxwell House coffee for at least the previous fifty years. With P&G's marketing, sales, and distribution brilliance, Folger's entered new markets and passed up Maxwell House by 1980. (These things don't happen overnight!).

Yet almost thirty years after winning the grocery store ground coffee crown, P&G was less excited about Folgers' future and their friends in Orrville decided to give it a try.

The coffee industry has always been extremely competitive. Maxwell House, named after a Nashville hotel, had been purchased in the late 1920s by the emerging General Foods Company, under the leadership of Marjorie Merriweather Post and her husband E.F. Hutton. Ms. Post had inherited the old Postum Company when her father committed suicide. She became famous for her interior designs and her homes, including Mar-A-Lago in Florida.

The Folger family had an even more tragic fame: young heiress Abigail Folger was killed with Sharon Tate and others by Charles Manson's evil crew.

From the 1960s onward, the leading coffee brands raged an intense war, producing many memorable television commercials. By the time of Smucker's 2008 acquisition of Folgers, Starbucks and craft coffees had come along, and old-fashioned canned ground coffee on supermarket shelves had lost its momentum.

Smucker's entered another new field, this one booming, when the company bought Big Heart Pet Brands in 2015. This acquisition added Meow Mix, Milk Bone, 9Lives, Kibbles 'n Bits, and Gravy Train to the company's list of products. Three years later, they bought the Nutrish line of pet foods.

All this history brings us to today. In the fiscal year ending April 30, 2019, the last year for which full results have been reported, the J. M. Smucker Company racked up sales of almost $8 billion. $2.9 billion of the total was generated by pet foods, followed by $2.1 billion worth of coffee, where Folgers has more than double the U.S. market share of Maxwell House (now owned by Kraft Heinz). The famous jams and jellies are almost insignificant, except to the heart, soul, and reputation of the Smucker company.

In *Fortune* magazine's most recent list of the 500 largest American companies, based on 2018 results, Smucker's was the 12th largest of 14 food makers listed, but 4th in profits and highest in profit as a percent of sales. Bigger companies Hershey, Conagra, and Campbell Soup made less money. The company – and the family – have come a long way from apple butter!

As students of the global corporate scene for the last fifty years, we cannot help but look at how the stockholders have fared. With the 2008 acquisition of Folger's, P&G's stockholders received over half the stock in Smucker's, though the Smucker family retained hundreds of million dollars' worth of company stock and remained in the management driver's seat. Over the next several years, P&G hit a rougher spot and their stock under-performed the market, while Smucker stock did well and beat the market. But over the last few years, Smucker's sales and profits have not grown significantly, while P&G has gotten back on track. Smucker stock has dropped in price while P&G stock has done well. Taking both periods of time together, since January of 2009 when the Folger's acquisition closed, stocks in the two companies have performed almost exactly the same, rising about 132%. (The S&P 500 index of stocks, reflecting the overall stock market, has tripled in the same period.)

As we look back at this illustrious history of two great American companies – Procter & Gamble this year celebrating 183 years in business and Smucker's reaching 123 – we can only conclude that both companies have seen many storms before, have stayed true to their roots and "core values," and are likely to persist for many decades to come.

Mark Smucker, who turns fifty this year and the fifth generation to head the "family business," still based in Orrville, now faces competitive challenges, just like his predecessors. In the key pet food category, the two giants are the Swiss company Nestle, the world's largest food and beverage company, and the extremely private pet food and candy empire of the Mars family. In coffee, Maxwell House battles on and upstarts like Starbucks grow stronger. But with a name like Smucker's, "it has to be good." Those of us at the American Business History Center are rooting for another hundred years of Smucker success.

Originally published on AmericanBusinessHistory.org on January 17, 2020.

Chapter 7
The Little Soft Drink That Could: The Pepsi Story

Happy Valentine's Day! Here is a sweet story of candy and soda pop, and of incredible persistence which overcame failure and controversy.

In 1893, young Caleb Bradham bought the drugstore at the corner of Middle and Pollock Streets in New Bern, North Carolina. Jumping on the soda fountain craze sweeping the country, by 1898 he had invented his own drink, which he named "Pepsi-Cola." Bradham promoted the drink, expanding to fifteen bottlers in the Carolinas, Virginia, and West Virginia by 1906. By 1910, he had lined up 280 bottlers.

After World War I, the price of sugar, a key ingredient, quadrupled from a nickel a pound to over twenty cents. Bradham bought heavily in anticipation of even higher prices. But when sugar then dropped to two or three cents, the business failed, filing for bankruptcy in 1923. By this time, Coca-Cola had already emerged as the dominant brand, being sold around the United States and numerous foreign countries. The future could not have looked worse for tiny Pepsi.

Nevertheless, New York investment broker Roy Megargel saw a future in the product. As Pepsi was losing money on sugar, he tried to raise money to save the company, but the market was not interested and his efforts failed. When Pepsi declared bankruptcy in the spring of 1923, a group of creditors took control of the company's trademark, patents, and other assets for just $30,000. That summer, Roy Megargel created a new Pepsi-Cola company and bought the creditors out for $35,000.

With full control of Pepsi, Megargel worked to keep the company alive, personally loaning it money and moving the offices and plant to Richmond, Virginia. Despite his valiant efforts, Megargel was unable to keep the company solvent when the Great Depression hit. In June 1931, Megargel's renamed National Pepsi-Cola Corporation was declared bankrupt. Again.

At this juncture, another man entered the game. Charles Guth owned Mavis Candies, a Long Island company which made chocolate candies and chocolate soft drinks. In 1929, he sold his candy company to Loft, Inc., for about $600,000 in Loft stock. Loft operated over one hundred candy stores, largely in the New York area, under the names Loft, Mirror, and Happiness. Most had soda fountains.

As the depression arrived, Loft's stock and profits collapsed and Guth grew impatient with the old management. After a bitter proxy fight, Guth prevailed and took control of Loft. A man of strong opinions and will, Guth was not happy with Loft's relationship with key supplier Coca-Cola. Loft used 31,000 gallons of Coca-Cola syrup a year – the magic ingredient which, when mixed with carbonated water, yielded the famous drink. Guth thought that, at that volume of business, Loft deserved a jobber's or wholesaler's discounted price on the syrup. But the Coca-Cola Company would not budge; to the company, Loft was a retailer, not a wholesaler. Guth asked his managers to find an alternative to Coke.

Roy Megargel telephoned Charles Guth, the two men met in New York, and in the summer of 1931, a new Delaware corporation was formed, the Pepsi-Cola Company. Half owned by Guth personally and half by Megargel and friends, the new company bought the good will, trademark, and business of the bankrupt old Pepsi for $10,500. Guth exercised total management control, and soon bought out Megargel's shares. Charles Guth now owned 91% of Pepsi.

Guth was not pleased with the taste of Pepsi and had his chemist at Loft change the formula until it was to Guth's liking.

Loft's quickly replaced Coke with Pepsi in its big candy and soda fountain chain. But no one in the New York market had ever heard of Pepsi, and Loft's use of cola syrup dropped from 31,000 gallons a year to 21,000. Guth was nevertheless not dissuaded, continuing to believe that Pepsi had a future.

Soft drinks were mainly consumed at soda fountains, but bottled drinks were also becoming more popular. The standard size was 6 ounces, priced at 5 cents. In 1932, Guth experimented with a 12-ounce bottle for 10 cents, replete with a fancy foil wrapper at the top of the bottle. Seeking better awareness and demand for Pepsi, Guth thought about dropping the standard bottle nickel price to 3 cents but resisted. In another experiment in late 1933, he dropped the price of the large 12-ounce bottle to the same nickel that others charged for 6 ounces. That one decision changed everything: Pepsi-Cola sales skyrocketed.

Charles Guth knew that for Pepsi to survive, especially with the lower profit margin generated by the nickel 12-ounce bottle, he had to grow – today it would be called "scaling." He built bottling plants around the country and signed up hundreds of bottlers. In Long Island City, facing Manhattan across the East River, he built one of the largest soft drink plants in the world, replete with docks for unloading sugar from ships.

By 1936, Pepsi-Cola, owned 91% by Guth, was making two million dollars a year in profit. But there was a hitch.

While Guth owned Pepsi, he had continued as the head of Loft's, where he was a major shareholder but not in absolute control. Guth put all his attention into Pepsi. He made sure Loft's loaned money to Pepsi to finance Pepsi's growth. Loft employees and facilities were used to make Pepsi successful.

In the meanwhile, Loft's core candy store business slid from making a profit to losses approaching a million dollars a year. In a cost-saving move, Guth laid off some Loft's employees and cut the pay of many others. The employees went on strike, trapping Guth in his office at Loft's headquarters. He had to be escorted out by the police. Not a good situation!

The Loft's Board of Directors accepted Guth's resignation, and he was replaced with a new President at Loft's. At first everything seemed smooth, at least for Guth, who was now free to focus on his booming Pepsi business.

But the new head of Loft's, James Carkner, found his situation dire. The company was losing money and out of cash. Carkner scrambled to raise money, but no investors were interested. Then it was brought to his attention that maybe Loft's should claim ownership of Pepsi, since Pepsi had been built with Loft's people, money, and facilities. Pepsi was worth perhaps $30 million, as its profits climbed to $3 million, then $4 million. Carkner, with great effort, found a law firm willing to take on the Loft's case against Guth and Pepsi on a contingency basis, since Loft's had no funds with which to pay a guaranteed retainer fee. He also found a financial firm willing to take a risk on the outcome of the suit, providing cash to Loft's to keep the doors open while the lawsuit proceeded.

What followed was an intense proxy fight between Guth and Carkner and his backers over voting control of Loft's. Angry letters to shareholders flew back and forth, with each side accusing the other of lying. Guth lost that battle, and Loft's ended up being controlled by the financial firm which had bailed it out, led by one Walter Mack, Jr.

Still, Guth battled on, trying to maintain control of Pepsi. More lawsuits and appeals to higher courts, more lawyers' fees. (The lawyers who took the Loft suit on a contingency basis ended up with about $5 million worth of stock, equivalent to $90 million today.) When the dust finally settled, Guth received some compensation and the rights to bottle Pepsi in some cities, perhaps worth a few million dollars. But 80% of the Pepsi-Cola company was now owned by the candy store chain Loft's, whose stock soared in value. In 1941, Loft's renamed itself the Pepsi-Cola Company, under the leadership of Walter Mack.

Pepsi continued to build on Bradham's brand and Guth's foundation. Walter Mack was succeeded by former Coca-Cola executive Albert Steele, whose wife, actress Joan Crawford, became a public face for Pepsi. The company innovated with newly designed bottles and catchy advertising slogans and became THE competitor to Coca-Cola. Pepsi began a long tradition of having great CEOs, though it was still far behind Coca-Cola by every measure.

In 1965, Pepsi's highly regarded CEO Don Kendall, who led the company until 1986, put together a merger with Frito-Lay of Dallas, Texas. Frito-Lay itself was the result of the 1961 merger between Herman Lay's Atlanta company, the nation's largest potato chip maker, and the San Antonio Doolin family's Frito Company. Frito-Lay owners received about 30% of the stock in the combined company, renamed PepsiCo. Revenues jumped from $250 million in 1964 to $500 million in 1965, including Frito-Lay.

Most studies indicate that perhaps 70-80% of all mergers do not produce the great results anticipated. In retrospect, the Pepsi merger with Frito-Lay must be considered one of the most successful business combinations in history.

While gaining some success on supermarket shelves, Pepsi struggled to compete with Coke in the restaurant market. To assure a good customer for Pepsi products, in 1977 PepsiCo bought Taco Bell, followed by Pizza Hut the next year and Kentucky Fried Chicken in 1986. Under PepsiCo management, this group became one of the largest restaurant organizations in the world. In 1997, PepsiCo spun off the restaurant business to shareholders as the Tricon Global Restaurants. That business continues very successfully today as Yum Brands, based in Louisville, Kentucky. (In 2016, Yum Brands spun off the big Yum China operation, including about 6,000 KFC locations in that country.)

Over time, PepsiCo acquired other businesses, including Tropicana, Gatorade, and Quaker Oats. They also introduced new products, such as Aquafina water. In 2006, Indra Nooyi, born in India, became Pepsi's CEO. She compiled one of the best records of any female CEO of a *Fortune* 500 company, leading the company until 2018.

In 2018, the last full year for which data is available, PepsiCo posted revenues of $64.7 billion and net profits of $12.5 billion, making it America's 48th largest and 18th most profitable public company, and the largest food and beverage company based in the United States (Switzerland's Nestle is larger). PepsiCo's return on assets of 16% was exceptional, ranking 34th of the 500 companies in *Fortune*'s list. The still-great (and cola-dominant) Coca-Cola Company posted profits of $6.4 billion on revenues of $31.9 billion and a return on assets of under 8%, half the profitability of PepsiCo.

How did this performance gap evolve? Attribute it to Donald Kendall and Herman Lay. According to PepsiCo's financial statements, in 2018 the company made just 20% of its operating profits from "Beverages North America" but 43% of profits from Frito-Lay North America. 54% of total company sales were from food, 46% from beverages. Salty snacks seem to go well with non-alcoholic beverages! And persistence pays off, even if it takes several attempts and leaders to make it work.

Originally published on AmericanBusinessHistory.org on February 14, 2020.

Chapter 8
Jeep: The Little Brand That Could

Earlier this week, Fiat Chrysler Automobiles ("FCA"), technically a Dutch Company, proposed a marriage with the seriously-French automaker Renault. Initial investor reaction to the marriage was strong. If the deal is approved by shareholders and regulators, it would create the world's third-largest automaker, behind Volkswagen and Toyota, but ahead of General Motors and Ford. One of the most valuable children in the family would be the Jeep line. Few great brands have had so many owners and such a tortuous history.

The Jeep story began in June of 1940. American military leaders foresaw the coming of war, and needed a light, all-terrain reconnaissance vehicle. In less than a month, they created specifications and sent them to 135 potential manufacturers, requesting bids. The only hitch was that plans were required in less than a month, by July 22, to be followed by a "finished" prototype within 49 days. Due to the impossible deadline, only two companies responded, American Bantam and Willys-Overland.

Willys-Overland, built by the ambitious car salesman John North Willys, had in 1915 been America's second-largest carmaker after Ford. In the 1920s, it remained among the five or six largest producers. But the 1930s witnessed the rise of General Motors and Chrysler in the midst of the Great Depression. Willys-Overland crashed, was reorganized, and barely survived. Still, they had large factories in Toledo.

American Bantam was a tiny company based in Butler, Pennsylvania. Only ten days before the tight deadline, they convinced automotive engineer Karl Probst to design the vehicle for them. He started on a Wednesday and had plans drawn by Friday.

When the military opened the two bids, Willys-Overland's was incomplete. They begged for more time. American Bantam won the initial design contract, and delivered the first prototype on time.

Realizing that they'd need many more of these little vehicles than American Bantam could build, the government also gave Willys-Overland and Ford Motor the rights to produce the Bantam-designed vehicle with Willys motors.

While it is generally thought that the name "Jeep" came from GP for "general purpose" vehicle, there were other possible sources. Before the war, the Minneapolis-Moline agricultural implement company had called some of their tractors Jeeps, and Popeye cartoons had a character named "Eugene the Jeep."

In any case, Jeeps in various models became critical to the

war effort. Between November of 1941 and September of 1945, American Bantam built 2,675 Jeeps, Ford built 282,356, and Willys-Overland 362,896, for a total of 647,927. Only a dreamer would think America would ever again need Jeeps in such enormous quantities.

After the war, only Willys-Overland stayed in the business, providing Jeeps in various forms to the government, businesses, and a few consumers. In the late 1940s, production was around 100,000 per year and the company was finally profitable, even without the demands of war.

In the interim, the great Oakland-based industrialist Henry J. Kaiser, who had helped build Hoover Dam and provided ships, steel, and aluminum to the war effort, decided to enter the auto industry. In partnership with experienced auto executive Joseph Frazer, he created Kaiser-Frazer to build cars. Unsuccessful in competing with General Motors, Ford, and Chrysler, Kaiser-Frazer bought Willys-Overland for $60 million in 1953. Kaiser's automotive interests were soon renamed Kaiser Jeep.

Jeep added new models, including the famous Wagoneer, and modified the traditional CJ line. Nevertheless, by the late 1960s, annual U.S. Jeep sales dropped below 40,000. Henry Kaiser's son Edgar finally tired of the auto business.

On the other hand, American Motors' (AMC) CEO Roy Chapin, Jr., was seeking new opportunities. Formed in 1954 from the failing independent automakers Hudson and Nash, AMC had briefly prospered in the 1960s under CEO George Romney with its bestselling Rambler line of compact cars. (Romney went on the become Governor of Michigan and a Presidential hopeful like his son, Mitt.)

Chapin, whose father had run Hudson, had tried to convince his boss Romney to buy Kaiser Jeep, to no avail. But Chapin thought the brand had an upside, so after he became head of AMC, he re-opened talks with Edgar Kaiser. In early 1970, AMC bought Kaiser Jeep for $82.5 million in cash and stock. Kaiser's company ended up owning 20% of AMC, making it the largest shareholder.

In 1970, AMC made 45,000 Jeeps and 276,000 other cars. With AMC's retail expertise and dealer network, Jeep sales boomed. Only eight years later, in 1978, the company made 153,000 Jeeps and 214,000 other cars.

In 1979 and 1980, French automaker Renault bought 46% of AMC, gaining effective control. But the partnership did not work, and AMC's sales of cars other than Jeeps declined. In 1986, after another eight years, the company produced 243,000 Jeeps and only 49,000 other cars.

Meanwhile, former Ford executive and creator of the Mustang Lee Iacocca was "turning around" the ever-cyclical Chrysler Corporation. Iacocca believed that, despite troubles and losses, AMC had potential, but only because it owned the Jeep brand. He thought the demand for "recreational vehicles" would grow in coming years. The original "sport utility vehicle" (SUV), the Jeep, had a strong tradition and reputation. In 1987, Chrysler paid about $1.5 billion to buy AMC from Renault and the other stockholders.

The roller-coaster ride of Chrysler could fill several books. From its stunning start in the 1920s under the brilliant former GM executive Walter P. Chrysler through post-war struggles, the Iacocca "turnaround," two government bailouts, and failed ownership by both Germany's Daimler-Benz and U.S. private equity firm Cerberus, the company has been through the wringer. Nevertheless, between 1990 and 2000, Jeep sales rose from 196,000 to 495,000.

In 2009, Chrysler went bankrupt, wiping out its shareholders. The company appeared hopeless, despite the continuing success of its Jeeps and its Ram trucks, spun off from the Dodge division.

Italy's largest automaker, Fiat, controlled by the wealthy Agnelli family, had a similarly troubled history and seemed the unlikeliest of saviors for Chrysler. But Fiat's CEO, Sergio Marchionne, merged the companies, creating Fiat Chrysler Automobiles (FCA). Marchionne seemed to understand the U.S. auto buyer more than many Americans, boosting the Chrysler brands, particularly Jeep, Ram, and Dodge. He pulled off the miraculous and the combined company prospered.

In 2018, FCA sold 2.2 million cars and light trucks in America, ranking 4th, after GM, Toyota, and Ford, but well ahead of Nissan and Honda. Of those 2.2 million, 973,000 were Jeeps, up 17.5% from 2017, ranking as the 6th best-selling and the fastest-growing of the top fifteen brands. Ram sold 587,000, up 7.3%, the second-largest increase among the top fifteen.

Marchionne's success in America and abroad led to the proposed FCA-Renault merger now proposed. Marchionne had advocated such an alliance but died in 2018. His successors and the Agnelli family moved ahead, in 2021 creating a new company named Stellantis.

Despite some bad owners, numerous near-bankruptcies, and continuously changing ownership, the venerable Jeep has not only survived, but prospered. Without the vision of men like Henry Kaiser, Roy Chapin, Jr., Lee Iacocca, and Sergio Marchionne, the Jeep might have died and been long-forgotten, alongside many other formerly famous American brand names.

Originally published on AmericanBusinessHistory.org on June 3, 2019.

Chapter 9

The Non-Profit Where the World Sleeps: Best Western

The lodging industry is one of the oldest industries on earth, and one of the most important.

No one can do business, trade, spread ideas, practice diplomacy, explore the world, or migrate without temporary lodgings. From the lowliest hostel to the finest resort, from giant chains to locally owned independents, lodging touches the lives of most people in the developed world. But even in the poorest countries, people stay with relatives or find cheap lodgings. Travelers are everywhere, for every reason.

Today, one of the largest lodging organizations in terms of number of locations and total number of rooms is Best Western, based in Phoenix. Few of Best Western's millions of annual guests know the unusual story behind this great, highly successful non-profit enterprise. Here is the story.

The Rise of Highway Travel

As Americans began to own cars in the first twenty years of the twentieth century, they also began to travel along routes inaccessible by the railroads. Highways began to be paved; filling stations were built. Alongside our expanding highway system, roadside inns began to appear. The inexpensive hotels near city railroad stations became less important, as did urban boardinghouses, the original cheap stay.

The first roadside lodgings were often clusters of small cottages, called Tourist Camps or Tourist Courts. Over time, these inns evolved first into Motor Courts and were eventually known as motels. The large hotel chains like Statler and Hilton ignored the new opportunity, but independent "mom and pop" motels had sprung up across America by the 1930s. Their quality and cleanliness varied dramatically.

Various associations had been created to promote travel – the Lincoln Highway Association was started in 1913 by Packard Motor Company President Henry Joy, Indianapolis motor speedway founder Carl Fisher, and others to promote their coast-to-coast route. Two years later, Fisher also helped start the Dixie Highway Association, promoting a route from Chicago and Detroit to Miami. These associations published guides to their routes, advertising gas stations, hotels, and restaurants along the way.

While business had boomed in the 1920s, the Great Depression brought new challenges to the embryonic motel industry. In an effort to promote business, in 1933 the United Motor Courts Association was founded by a group of west coast "moteliers." This group was a non-profit which published directories of its members, available at each inn. The idea was to "refer" customers to other members. By 1937, United had almost three hundred member locations, stretching along the west coast and across the sunbelt, with concentrations in California, Texas, and Florida. Other similar "referral" groups were founded, but none were as big as United.

After World War II, pent-up demand for new automobiles and for the chance to see America resulted in a boom in highway travel, further facilitated by the Eisenhower Interstate System that followed in the 1950s and 1960s. The family vacation and the road trip became iconic American experiences.

At the 1947 convention of United Motor Courts, board member M.K. Guertin, who owned the Beach Motel in Long Beach, California, expressed dissatisfaction with United. The organization was slow or reluctant to kick out motels which did not meet their standards or failed to maintain their properties. Others shared Guertin's concerns, and by late 1947 had broken off to form Best Western, with an initial membership of sixty-six motels stretching to Chicago but concentrated in the far west. In 1939, a similar break-away from United had occurred in the eastern United States, with the creation of Quality Courts due to the same desire to uphold more rigorous quality standards. By 1949, the people at Quality Courts had invited Guertin to meet, and the two organizations agreed to promote each other, with Best Western members west of the Mississippi and Quality Courts members to the east of the river. Both Best Western and Quality Courts distributed hundreds of thousands of travel guides along America's highways.

M.K. Guertin, born in Liberty, Texas in 1891, had migrated with his daughter to California in the 1920s, where he helped promote a relative's motel and learned the advertising business. In 1933, he had bought his own motel, the Beach, and then joined United. When he and a few close friends founded Best Western in the late 1940s, he immediately hit the road, inspecting 507 motels up and down the west coast, driving 4,956 miles in twenty-nine days. He accepted no payment for his time or travel expenses – Best Western had become a labor of love.

As Guertin signed up new members, he required each to become an informal inspector on Best Western's behalf. If he heard of a prospective member, he'd send an existing member to the property to see if it met his high standards. If he heard that a member was not keeping their property up, he'd call another member and tell them to check on it. Unlike United, Best Western under Guertin did not hesitate to kick out a poor performer – Best Western has forced out as many as 15% of its members each year. By 1951, Best Western had grown to 197 members.

At the beginnings of this, there were few if any real motel chains. Alamo Courts, based in Texas, tried to build a chain, but did not get very far. In 1952, Kemmons Wilson of Memphis opened his first Holiday Inn, which was to change (and dominate) the motel industry for years. In 1963, the United States had about 60,000 motels, up from 10,000 thirty years earlier. By that year, Holiday Inn had expanded to 415 locations, but Best Western had 699, by far the largest of any lodging organization.

Also, in 1963, Quality Courts was restructured as a for-profit franchising organization, which continues today as industry giant Choice Hotels. As a result, Best Western discontinued the co-marketing program with Quality, and began to enter the eastern United States. For a couple of years, these eastern members were called Best Eastern, but were soon rebranded as Best Western.

The growth of the industry, coupled with intensified

competition, kept Best Western on its toes. In the mid-fifties, they banned coin-operated "Magic Fingers" from beds in the belief that they cheapened the overnight experience. Best Western led the way with the first national reservations system, placing a teletype machine in each motel. The "parent" non-profit organization gradually added services for its members: group buying of furniture, linens, and soap; accounting and consulting services; and motel planning and building advice. Best Western provided travel guides, signs, and advertising materials to its members.

Throughout this period, M.K. Guertin apparently ran Best Western with an iron hand. Even his friends called him a dictator. His single-minded drive, ambition, and high standards created the basis for the Best Western we know today. In 1966, the seventy-five-year-old Guertin lost control of Best Western in an internal board of directors' fight. He unwillingly retired and died four years later.

Nevertheless, Best Western retained its standards and its desire to grow. Headquarters moved from Guertin's motel in Long Beach to new facilities in Phoenix. In 1967, the company began its first national advertising campaign (in *Life* magazine), to keep up with all the new chains including Holiday Inn, Ramada Inns, and others. In 1969, Holiday Inn's 1,071 locations finally caught up with Best Western, at 1,068 inns. Television advertising appeared in 1972, on the *Merv Griffin Show* and *Let's Make a Deal*. Best Western began to expand outside the United States, adding Australia in 1975, Mexico in 1976, and Great Britain and Ireland in 1978, renaming itself Best Western International that year. The company was by then printing over six million of its travel guides each year, each copy replete with tiny color photographs of each member inn.

Over time, the "referral chains" in America went into decline – all but Best Western. Quality Courts converted to a for-profit company, as did others. United Motor Courts, the original leader, declined due to low standards and was gone by the mid-fifties. Yet the concept remains popular abroad, especially in Europe, where organizations like the French Relais & Chateaux (over 500 members) and Logis de France (2,400 members) operate on the same principle as Best Western.

In 2018, Best Western's management and board recommended that the company convert to a for-profit, franchised organization, as Quality Courts had done fifty-five years earlier. They believed this would allow the company access to more capital and be better able to invest in technology and marketing. But the members voted down the proposal, and as of today, Best Western continues as the non-profit group of independent inns as envisioned by Guertin.

Today the "parent" Best Western has annual revenues of about $400 million, representing over 3,500 hotels and inns in more than 100 countries and territories. All together, their 300,000 rooms generate in excess of $5 billion per year in revenue. Best Western's guest loyalty program is considered one of the best in the industry.

The company has added "Premier" and "Signature" collections for its most luxurious members, as well as the innovative Glo, Vib, Aiden, and Sadie brands. Best Western has also entered the economy segments of the industry with SureStay and SureStay Plus. Most of the original member inns are now called Best Western, Best Western Plus, or Best Western Premier. Each member inn has its own personality and history. Through thick and thin, through industry change, Best Western remains one of the largest lodging organizations in the world, owned by its members.

Originally published on AmericanBusinessHistory.org on May 8, 2020.

Chapter 10
Can Companies Reinvent Themselves? The Target Story

Much has been written about the idea of "reinventing" your company. However, in my 50+ years of studying big business, I have rarely seen it happen — successfully. Here, from the treasure trove that is business history, one of the few cases of a great company which against all odds actually did "reinvent" itself.

Wind the clock back to 1962. The US was covered from coast-to-coast, in cities big and small, with family-owned department stores. These stores were the dominant retailers of general merchandise (not food) everywhere. They not only sold most of the clothing and home furnishings but were also the primary buyers of newspaper display advertising and centers for the community and events (think Thanksgiving Day parades).

Over the early part of the century, many had joined or sold out to holding companies, including May Department Stores (formed in 1911), Associated Dry Goods (1916), Mercantile Stores (1916), and R.H. Macy and Allied Stores (acquisitions starting in the 1920s). The biggest of all, Federated Department Stores, was formed in 1929 by three independent stores: Lazarus of Columbus, Filene's of Boston, and Abraham & Straus of Brooklyn (Manhattan's Bloomingdale's joined a year later).

But most of these stores remained independent, including the leading stores of Chicago, Philadelphia, Cleveland, Indianapolis, Washington, Atlanta, San Francisco, Detroit, and Minneapolis. The largest store that remained privately owned by the founding family was J. L. Hudson in Detroit. Another one of the best-run family-owned stores was Dayton's in Minneapolis, where this story begins.

George Draper Dayton was a straight-shooting Presbyterian who arrived in Minneapolis seeking real estate investments. In order to help out a church, he bought their former location and lured an existing "dry goods" store to the site. In 1902 he bought out the store, aptly named Goodfellow's, and renamed it Dayton's. Over time, Dayton's became the dominant store in Minneapolis, even against competitors owned by the far larger Allied Stores and Associated Dry Goods. But unlike most other independents, neither he nor his descendants went public, availing the company of the equity markets. A laggard, sleepy company? Hardly.

In 1950, his 5 grandsons took control of the company, each owning 20%. By 1959, Dayton's single downtown store generated revenue of $70 million each year, disproportionate to Minneapolis' size and equivalent to $600 million in 2021 dollars. The grandsons debated whether to live off the fat of the land, keeping the extremely profitable store along its historic track, or whether to become more ambitious. They realized most wealthy families ended up fighting each other, and figured if they grew the business, they'd more likely maintain harmony among the extensive Dayton families.

One of the grandsons' early moves was to build the first major enclosed shopping mall in the US, Southdale, in 1956, which they developed and owned. They took the unprecedented step of inviting into the mall their long-time downtown Minneapolis competitor, Donaldson's, owned by the big Allied Stores group. (Two years earlier, in 1954, fellow department store operator Hudson's in Detroit had built a pioneer open-air shopping center Northland in suburban Detroit but had not invited any other department stores from downtown Detroit. Hudson's Northland soon became the highest revenue branch department store in America.)

At the same time, on the great retail stage long dominated by these huge, high revenue stores, the 1950s and 1960s saw the rise of a scary phenomenon — the discount department store. Thundering out of the northeast after World War II, but copied everywhere, these new stores rented old warehouses or built new but plain one-story buildings and filled them with cheap fixtures loaded with whatever national brands (or factory overstocks) they could get their hands on. They ran dense black and white newspaper ads, in sharp contrast to the department store fashion ads with plenty of white space. The discounters proclaimed, "Price Busters!" and "How can we sell so cheap?" Leading early discount store names included Korvette's, Arlan's, White Front, Two Guys, Topps, Gibson's, Zayre, and many others.

Most of the old department stores were unsure of how to react. The new business required a whole new mindset and plenty of capital. The ugly, often dirty new stores repulsed the old merchants. Even if they could copy the discounters with new stores, wouldn't they cannibalize their existing, highly profitable businesses? Nevertheless, a few had the courage to give it a try, among the earliest was L. S. Ayres of Indianapolis with its Ayr-Way discount stores in 1961.

The great dime store chains were quick to enter the fray. The business of F. W. Woolworth, W. T. Grant, S. S. Kresge, and others was already in serious decline, yet they had national systems for inventory, distribution, advertising, and management in place. After a year of study, Kresge executive Harry Cunningham launched Kmart in 1962, which went on to lead the discount store industry for the next thirty years. Also in 1962, franchised "Ben Franklin" dime store operator Sam Walton opened his first Walmart in Rogers, Arkansas.

In that same historic year 1962, the Dayton brothers decided that there was an opportunity to open an "upscale" discount store with a more fashionable approach to the business, opening three Target stores in the Minneapolis area, and one in Duluth. While they knew these new stores might hurt their Dayton's business, they also knew that if it worked, they could take the concept anywhere in the US, and not be limited to their Minnesota markets.

The idea of an upscale discounter seemed logical, and several other department store companies followed Ayres and Dayton's leads. Rich's of Atlanta opened Rich-way, Federated Department Stores opened Gold Circle and other concepts, Strawbridge & Clothier of Philadelphia opened Clover Stores, and May Department Stores created Venture Stores (designed by the brains behind Target, the highly creative John F. Geisse). Other players bought or opened discount chains. Each of these companies had the same fashion merchandising know-how as Dayton's that might have paid off in the discount world. But none of them had the conviction and commitment that the Dayton brothers did. By 1968, Target was the largest of the department-store-owned discount store operations. The following table lists America's largest discount store chains in 1968.

Rank	Company	Store Names	1968 # of Stores	1968 Revenue ($MM)	1964 Revenue ($MM)
1	SS Kresge	K Mart, Jupiter	356	$ 1,310	$ 325
2	Gibson	Gibson's	434	$ 1,021	$ 190
3	Spartans Industries	EJ Korvette	45	$ 687	$ 529
4	Interstate Stores	White Front, Topps	86	$ 581	$ 323
5	Vornado	Two Guys, Unimart	53	$ 530	$ 316
6	Zayre	Zayre, Shopper's City	131	$ 525	$ 176
7	Arlan's	Arlan's, Play World	91	$ 335	$ 170
8	Parkview-Gem	Gem, Dixie Mart, Corondolet	39	$ 329	$ 250
9	FW Woolworth	Woolco	65	$ 312	$ 58
10	Spartan Dept. Stores	Atlantic Thrift	96	$ 285	$ 278
11	Food Fair	JM Fields	65	$ 272	$ 162
12	Alexander's	Alexander's	8	$ 259	$ 153
13	McCrory	S Klein	13	$ 233	$ 185
14	Cook Coffee	Uncle Bill's, Ontario, Clarks	77	$ 230	$ 60
15	Baza'r	Baza'r, Cal, Gov-Mart, Save-Co	19	$ 210	$ 40
16	Grand Union	Grand Way	32	$ 207	$ 137
17	Diana Stores	Millers, Great Eastern, Gulf Mart	38	$ 200	$ 118
18	King's	King's, Miracle Mart	78	$ 193	$ 103
19	Dayton's	Target	11	$ 175	$ 39
20	Stop & Shop	Bradlee's	52	$ 165	$ 73

Dayton's didn't just pursue its discount store strategy. In 1967, the company finally went public, and in 1969 acquired the larger Hudson's stores in Detroit, renaming the company Dayton-Hudson. With this move, the company became the 14th largest retailer in the US.

Besides expanding its core department store business, Dayton-Hudson became an ambitious tester of new retail ideas, very rare in the retail industry. Much like the R&D departments of big industrial companies, Dayton-Hudson acquired or experimented with concepts in hard goods and electronics discounting, jewelry stores, bookstores, and many other categories. Their 1966 concept B. Dalton went on to become America's largest bookseller in the 1970s and 1980s. Over two decades, the parent company reportedly tried as many as 18 different ideas. The company also expanded in other ways, buying California soft-goods discounter Mervyn's in 1978 and Chicago's great Marshall Field department store for $1 billion in 1990.

(For another retailer that also experimented with new concepts, resulting in that company becoming one of the world's largest corporations, even bigger than Target, see Chapter 5: The Corporate Giant Whose History Almost Nobody Knows.)

The path to the "right idea" was a rocky road.

Making the upscale discount stores work was anything but easy. If you invested in nicer stores, you might not be able to deliver the low prices required to compete with the Kmarts of the world. If your stores felt too nice, your customers might assume your prices were un-competitively high, whether they were or not.

In 1973, I arrived at Citibank in New York as a junior securities analyst covering the retail industry, my first job after college. My veteran analyst boss, Pete Wetzel, gave me an assignment to get my feet wet: write up a recommendation that our investment management department sell all our Dayton-Hudson stock. This was purely a training exercise, as the bank had already sold off the stock. Why? Because Target, consuming much capital and with the hopes of Wall Street riding on it, had had a terrible year. Dayton-Hudson had not delivered on promised profit levels, and the stock collapsed. We got out. I told Pete, after looking into the company, that I thought it still might be a good long-term investment. He said, "You are probably right, but it will take a few years for the Street to forgive them; the stock will be dead for a while."

The other department store companies which had opened discount stores struggled with the concept. Few of them met financial expectations. Their hearts were not in the business, and neither were their wills. Over time, they all gave up, many of them selling off their experiments to

Target, which continued to press ahead come hell or high water.

Throughout this history, Dayton-Hudson became well known for its values and unique approach to business. Always considered a well-run, highly ethical company and employer, the company focused on developing and supporting great people from top to bottom. They led the way in "transparency" with investors, revealing more detailed data than the Securities and Exchange Commission and stock market regulators required. The company aggressively developed advanced information and measurement systems. Dayton-Hudson has always been among the most generous of big companies, donating 5% of pre-tax income to charities in its markets. No New York Stock Exchange company has been more generous. And the Dayton family as individuals have been extremely active politically and in nature and environmental causes.

In 2000, no longer under direct management of the Dayton family, but continuing these strong traditions, Dayton-Hudson was renamed Target Corporation after its primary business. In 2004, the company effectively sold off its own parentage, selling the large department store operations to the May Department Stores Company. This had to have been one of the hardest decisions in the company's history. These steps completed the transition from being one of the top department store operators in America to being the only valid, direct competitor to Wal-mart, given the long and continuing decline of Kmart.

By 2005, most of the big US department stores, including the former May Company, Allied Stores, Dayton's, Hudson's, and Marshall Field, had been consolidated into Macy's.

In 2019, Target Corporation registered revenues of $77.1 billion, over three times the sales of Macy's at $24.6 billion. Target made a net profit of $3.3 billion vs. Macy's $564 million. Target even made a higher profit as a percent of sales (4.3%) than either Wal-mart (2.8%) or Macy's (2.3%). Return on Assets (ROA), a good measure of a retailer's profitability, was 7.7% at Target compared to 6.3% at Walmart and 2.7% at Macy's.

Due to Covid, 2020 comparisons were distorted, because Macy's was forced to close many of their stores while Walmart and Target stayed open, considered essential stores because they sold groceries. As shown in the table below, in 2020, Target posted far higher sales and profit growth than Walmart. Macy's lost money.

	2020	2019
FINANCIAL RESULTS (in millions)		
Sales	$ 92,400	$ 77,130
Other revenue	1,161	982
Total revenue	93,561	78,112
Cost of sales	66,177	54,864
Selling, general and administrative expenses (SG&A)	18,615	16,233
Depreciation and amortization (exclusive of depreciation included in cost of sales)	2,230	2,357
Operating income	6,539	4,658
Net interest expense [b]	977	477
Net other (income) / expense	16	(9)
Earnings from continuing operations before income taxes	5,546	4,190
Provision for income taxes [c]	1,178	921
Net earnings from continuing operations	4,368	3,269
Discontinued operations, net of tax	—	12
Net earnings	$ 4,368	$ 3,281

Target Financials

In the big picture, this is one of the most important and successful "reinventions" in US business history. But the trek from regional department store to discount industry leader was not easy. What can we learn from this story?

First, **nothing is more important than corporate will.**
How committed to the future is your company? Do you
clearly see the future? Are you willing to take the risks and
lumps that come with change? Would you be willing to
cannibalize or even sell off your core business as this
company did?

Second, your **institutional principles and values matter**.
If Dayton-Hudson had not had a strong emphasis on ethics,
philanthropy, people, and information, would it have been
able to pull this off, in the face of the fiercest competitor in
global retailing, Walmart?

Third, **are you experimenting**? Does your organization
have an "R&D" department, even in retailing? Have you
tried anything like 18 new ideas within your field or related
fields?

For more on the history of Dayton's Department store; see
Dayton's: A Twin Cities Institution by Kristal Leebrick. For
more on the history and evolution of Target, *see On Target:
How the World's Hottest Retailer Hit a Bullseye* by Laura
Rowley.

Originally published on Hooversworld.com.com on August
2, 2016.

Gone But Not Forgotten

Chapter 11
Whatever Became of International Harvester?

With this newsletter, we begin a periodic series, "Whatever Became of?" As students of business history, we learn much from both success and failure. About 80% of the largest companies of America in the mid-twentieth century are no longer with us. Some of these enterprises were huge, employing tens of thousands of workers for decades. Some were household names. Here we present a very short history of one of those fallen giants, International Harvester. It is a story about the company that revolutionized American agriculture, but then was surpassed by a more agile, smaller competitor, Deere and Company.

Cyrus Hall McCormick was one of the greatest industrialists of the 19th century. Born in Virginia in 1809, he followed in his father's footsteps as an inventor of farm machinery, though the father's inventions did not meet with commercial success. At the age of twenty-two, McCormick invented a better reaper for harvesting grain, and patented it three years later, in 1834. Success came gradually as McCormick added elements to the reaper and improved it. But the Panic of 1837 drove his business into bankruptcy, and he spent the next seven years paying off debts.

Recovering from the loss, in the 1840s McCormick discovered greater needs for his machines on the bigger farms "out west" – in Ohio, Indiana, and Illinois. In 1847, He moved his business to Chicago, then an insignificant lake port, with a population of less than 30,000. (By 1900, Chicago reached 1.7 million people, probably making it the fifth largest city in the world.) McCormick continuously improved his machines, added other agricultural equipment, and expanded his factories. He and his brothers also developed the best marketing and distribution system in the industry, with over 10,000 dealers.

In the same era, wealthy Maine textile industrialist William Deering had founded Deering, Milliken and Company, still an important company today. But he invested in a farm implement company in Illinois, and by the 1870s had left the textile business and moved to Chicago, where he built the Deering Harvester Company. His innovations sometimes leapfrogged the McCormick machines.

With dozens of smaller competitors, the 1880s saw intense competition for the farmers' money. By the 1890s, both McCormick and Deering had massive Chicago factories. McCormick's plant on the south side covered over one million square feet and employed over 5,000 men. Deering's factory on the north side employed at least 7,000, though McCormick was a larger company in total.

After Cyrus McCormick died in 1884, his widow (twenty-six years younger than Cyrus) and his son Cyrus, Jr. took over the company and continued to build the business. William Deering was getting older and wanted to sell. The rise of trusts and attempted monopolies was all the rage in the 1890s, and the two companies made several efforts to merge, hoping to abate their deadly competition. But they could not agree on the value of the two companies and who would run any merged enterprise. Finally, in 1902, George Perkins of the House of Morgan was able to work out a compromise, and McCormick, Deering, and three smaller companies merged to form the International Harvester Company, with 85% of the U.S. market for harvesting equipment. The McCormicks owned 42.6% of International Harvester, the Deerings 34.4%, while Morgan and the smaller companies' owners held the balance.

(The McCormick fortune spawned many enterprises and philanthropies. Cyrus's brother Leander sold out to Cyrus, Jr. and his mother for $3.5 million around 1890. His grandson Colonel Robert McCormick took over the weak *Chicago Tribune* newspaper, ultimately making it into the newspaper with the highest advertising revenue in the world, with Sunday circulation reaching 1.5 million. The namesake McCormick Place is one of the world's largest convention centers. Deering's son James built a home near Miami, Vizcaya, now a beautiful art museum.)

Under the continuing management of the McCormick family in the first decades of the 20th century, the company entered the embryonic gasoline-engine tractor business and then the farm truck and highway truck businesses. The company continued international expansion, begun in the prior century. By 1909, International Harvester was the 4th largest industrial company in America, measured by assets. In 1917, it was larger than General Electric, Ford, or General Motors, and as large as all its farm implement competitors combined (four times the size of Deere). By the 1930s, "IH" had 44% of the U.S. tractor market with its Farmall brand, twice the share of competitor John Deere.

International Harvester had a reputation for building great, durable products, and an outstanding dealer network. Nevertheless, after World War II, the company began to rest on its laurels. The more agile and innovative Deere & Company passed it up to become the biggest U.S. maker of agricultural equipment in 1958. Even so, IH remained a strong #2, a giant *Fortune* 500 company, and the top American maker of heavy trucks.

By the mid-1970s, the company was no longer growing, was not as profitable as its competitors, and had a heavy debt load. It was ingrown and too satisfied. Xerox President Archie McCardell was hired – the first outsider chief executive in the company's history – to reinvigorate the "sleeping giant." The company spent heavily on new plants, innovative technologies, and new products. But IH's leaders did not listen to its customers, and even to its own experienced executives. The company took on more debt.

Then McCardell and his management team tried to convince the United Auto Workers (UAW) Union to accept concessions on work rules – IH had a tradition of agreeing to Union demands to avoid strikes, but now had less-favorable contracts than companies like Deere and Caterpillar. The workers called a strike and it drug on for five months, one of the longest strikes in UAW history. At the same time, inflation and interest rates zoomed, the economy collapsed, and farmers stopped buying. International Harvester lost about $500 million in six months, one of the biggest losses in corporate history at the time. Bankruptcy was narrowly averted.

McCardell was out, and his successors struggled to fix the broken company. In the mid-1980s, they sold the core farm equipment business, now ironically combined with long-time competitor J. I. Case and part of CNH Industrial, a Dutch-incorporated company controlled by Italy's Agnelli family. Their empire includes Fiat Chrysler and Ferrari.

The truck operations continued, and International Harvester was renamed Navistar, which continues today as a public company. Navistar makes heavy trucks and school buses, but has had its own struggles and the stock has remained essentially flat for years.

The lessons of International Harvester are manifold, including:

- No matter how many big companies are merged into a giant, leadership is never permanent.

- There are always agile, smart competitors ready to come along (the 182-year old Deere Company has only had nine chief executives in its history!).

- Being the largest in an industry and a long history of success can be the greatest enemies of future success (look at General Motors and Sears, Roebuck).

- Long-term success requires knowing your customers and your employees intimately, listening to them, and caring about them.

Originally published on AmericanBusinessHistory.org on October 24, 2019.

Chapter 12
Music for the Millions: The Wurlitzer Story

The Wurlitzer Company is one of the most interesting
companies we have studied. At their peak, their slogan was
"Music for the Millions." Here is the story of this formerly
great company, based on the excellent book *Wurlitzer of
Cincinnati* by Mark Palkovic.

The Founder

Rudolph Wurlitzer was born in Schoneck, Saxony,
Germany, in 1831, the first son of prosperous merchant
Christian Wurlitzer. Christian had suffered a great
disappointment when his father left his 2,000-acre farm to
his elder half-brother rather than to Christian. While this
was in line with German norms of primogeniture, Christian

did not think it was fair. Christian revolted by, in turn, leaving his general store to his youngest son, not his oldest, Rudolph.

Rudolph realized he would spend the next fifteen years building up his father's general store in a valley full of over one hundred violin and woodwind makers. But all his efforts would be only as a paid employee, until his kid brother was old enough to take over. Not an inviting prospect. So Rudolph told his father he wanted to migrate to America, as many other Germans were. His father did not take him seriously, as Rudolph had no money of his own.

Rudolph's uncle, the brother of his late mother who had favored Rudolph, loaned Rudolph 305 marks (about $80 at the time) to cross the Atlantic, which the young man did in 1853 at the age of twenty-two.

Arriving in New York, the five-foot four-inch Rudolph vowed to save 25% of anything he earned. But the money came hard as he worked long hours at low pay for a Hoboken grocer. Dissatisfied, he moved on to Philadelphia. Approaching a well-dressed man to ask for a job, he was rebuffed as a beggar, and a foreigner on top of that. This insult led him to go further west to the booming city of Cincinnati, which had a large German population.

Rudolph's first job in Cincinnati was as a porter for a dry goods store at four dollars a week. To save money, he slept in a packing crate. He then found a better job, eight dollars a week at the merchant and banking house of Heidelbach and Seasongood. The owners let him sleep in a loft at the office.

Young Rudolph learned English and picked up American ways faster than the other young employees and soon began a series of promotions, ultimately giving him the important position of Cashier (which is different in a bank compared with a retail store). Legend has it that Rudolph also traded in semi-precious stones and furs from the nearby countryside, selling them to dealers in Antwerp and Amsterdam. With the money he made, Rudolph paid back his uncle for the money lent him to come to America. And Rudolph also sought a way to make a more permanent and prosperous living.

While he could not play any musical instruments, Rudolph loved music and knew some of the finest instruments were made in the cottage industries around his German hometown. His own ancestors were lute and violin makers as far back as the seventeenth century. They used the choicest woods from the forests of Bavaria, the Alps, and the Carpathians. By the 1830s, over three hundred people in the area, including women and children, were making instruments.

At the same time, Cincinnati, one of the largest cities west of the Alleghenies, continued to boom. In 1856, the Democratic National Convention was held there, the first such convention held outside the original thirteen states. (James Buchanan was nominated, over the incumbent President Franklin Pierce.)

So, in 1856, Rudolph went to a music store owned by a man named Johnson. He noticed that the store had few woodwinds. The clerk told him they were very hard to come by. Rudolph took his $700 in savings and sent it back to Germany, ordering a shipment of musical instruments. When the goods arrived in Cincinnati, he calculated customs and freight costs, then doubled the total to arrive at a fair selling price. Rudolph then approached Mr. Johnson with the fine instruments. Johnson liked the instruments but refused to buy them because he said they had to have been stolen, in order to be offered at such a low price.

A stunned Rudolph Wurlitzer went back to the drawing board and "recalculated" his costs, pretending they were higher than they actually were. The proprietors of Heidelbach and Seasongood, where Rudolph still worked, vouched for his honesty to Mr. Johnson. Johnson bought the instruments at the higher, "more honest," price and Rudolph netted $1500 on his $700 investment.

Rudolph later joked that "From that time, my prices were REALLY honest." After that first deal, he quickly sent $7,000 back to Germany for more instruments (over $200,000 in 2020 money). He kept his old job, but also rented warehouse space in downtown Cincinnati for his burgeoning importing business.

Wurlitzer was able to offer such good value because he eliminated the many middlemen in the way instruments were exported from Europe, imported into America, and handled through distributors on both sides of the Atlantic. He realized he could sell as many instruments as he could get his hands on.

Rudolph was considered an amazing success back home, having prospered after only three or four years in the new country. He had also expanded the demand for all the instrument makers in the area.

In 1859, he became an American citizen. He tried to enlist for the Union in the Civil War but was rejected because of his short height. But he did get federal contracts to make trumpets and drums for the military. By that time, he had enough confidence to quit his old job and focus on the music business. His younger brothers began to join him in Cincinnati. In 1862, he added a retail store to his wholesale business, and in 1865 opened another store in Chicago, long before chain retail stores were common. But it would take one of his sons before the company developed a larger chain of stores.

In 1868, Rudolph Wurlitzer married Leonie Farny, whose family had emigrated from Alsace, France the same year that Rudolph came to America. Leonie was twenty-five and Rudolph was thirty-seven when they married. Between 1869 and 1883, six children were born, though one was lost before he was a year old. Surviving sons, in order of birth, were Howard, Rudolph H., and Farny. As Rudolph's business prospered, the family moved to a larger home, replete with a laundress, upstairs maid, and cook. All the children spoke English, French, and German.

Leonie Farny Wurlitzer's brother, Henry Farny, was a close family friend. He became a very successful artist, focused on the American West. Henry Farny was also a friend of Teddy Roosevelt's. He brought many other artists and cultural personalities into the Wurlitzer family circle.

Throughout the rest of the nineteenth century, Rudolph expanded the business. Starting in 1870, he made buying trips back to Europe about every other year, often with his wife and, when old enough, his children. He began publishing beautiful catalogs of all the instruments. By 1880, his line included hand-cranked reed organs from Paris and music boxes. In 1890, he incorporated the business with capital of $200,000, retaining most of the stock himself. By 1898, the catalogs reached 344 pages, including "pipe hand organs for street, saloon, and circus."

The Next Generation: Howard Wurlitzer

None of Rudolph's sons went to college. Each developed specific skills related to the music business. Howard, the oldest son, dropped out of high school at seventeen. By twenty, he was joining his parents on the European buying trips, which lasted months at a time. That same year, he was elected to the company's board of directors. By 1912, he was president of the company, at the age of forty. He would hold that job for the next fifteen years.

Howard was financially oriented and a very smart businessman, but he could be hard to deal with. He had no patience for inefficiency or carelessness. Some people liked him, but others hated him. When visiting Berlin, he noted how slowly everyone moved, how there was not "the rush and activity" of an American city. Howard was above all ambitious, desiring to grow the Wurlitzer company.

The second son, Rudolph H., became an expert on violins. Over time he amassed the world's largest collection of rare instruments, including over half of the Stradivarius violins known to exist. The company sold antique instruments under his leadership. Ultimately this became a separate company, run by his son and then his granddaughter, into the 1970s.

The third son, Farny, was twelve years younger than Howard and worked for him while Howard ran the company. Farny had a technical bent so his father sent him to technical school. Farny became the company expert in product development and manufacturing, complementing his older brother's strength in financial matters.

Their father, Rudolph, died in 1914.

The company continued to expand under Howard. Stores were added in New York in 1908, Philadelphia in 1910, and by 1912 Cleveland, Dayton, Detroit, Providence, Newark, Columbus, St. Louis, and Louisville. By 1916, the first California store, in San Francisco, was opened. Wurlitzer acquired interests in other musical instrument makers and opened offices in Europe in the 1920s.

In 1896, Rudolph and Howard had convinced music box supplier Regina Music Box Company to add a coin slot to their music box. These were sold to restaurants and taverns and were a big success. The Wurlitzer company became Regina's largest customer. In the same era, the company sold both Victor and Edison talking machines (phonographs).

An important figure in the company's history in this era was Eugene DeKleist. The German had worked for a French maker of carousel organs for merry-go-rounds. But the US tariff on these organs was high, and American carousel makers sought a more affordable domestic source for the organs. DeKleist then moved to North Tonawanda, New York, outside Buffalo, to establish an organ factory there in 1893. He tried to sell some to Howard, but Howard was only interested in ones with a coin operation feature, as another product to sell to bars and other businesses.

DeKleist then produced the coin-operated organs at North Tonawanda; they were a big success. The two companies continued to work together, in 1899 introducing the Tonophone coin-operated piano, in 1903 the PianOrchestra orchestrion with multiple instruments inside the box, and the Pianino in 1906. All of these products were immediate successes. These and automatic instruments called "photoplayers" were widely used by nickelodeons and then later by movie theaters showing silent movies. In 1916, the company claimed that two million people a day heard its instruments. Wurlitzer even made coin operated harps!

By 1908, DeKleist had become mayor of North Tonawanda and was losing interest in the manufacturing business. When the quality began to go downhill, Howard demanded that DeKleist sell out to Wurlitzer or Howard would start making his own instruments. The Wurlitzer company bought out DeKleist and dispatched Farny to live in the Buffalo area and run that operation, which became the company's largest factory. At its peak in the 1920s, almost 3,000 people were employed there.

Wurlitzer's huge success with the instruments made for use with silent movies led to the natural development of the theater organ. They were developed with the patents and help of Robert Hope-Jones from Britain, who had begun replacing air power with electricity in organs. At first called the "Wurlitzer Hope-Jones Unit Orchestra" in 1910, these magnificent instruments soon were tagged "Mighty Wurlitzers." By the time production ended in 1943, Wurlitzer had produced over 2,200 such organs, more than twice as many as any other manufacturer. (If you have a Windows computer, you can put a Wurlitzer theater organ on your computer with this free software: https://miditzer.org.)

At the same time, Wurlitzer continued making other instruments. In the 1920s, they bought the Melville Clark Piano Company of Dekalb, Illinois, to add more production capacity. Sold under the Wurlitzer name, pianos including player pianos became an important product. The company was one of the largest American producers, making a total of 2.8 million pianos.

Disaster Strikes

Prohibition had hurt their sales to bars in the 1920s, but the company continued to prosper. By 1927, they had 58 stores in California alone. Their coin operated instruments continued to sell, and their theater organs had been a huge hit, with production peaking in 1926. But two factors hurt the company badly by the end of the twenties: the rise of radio, hurting sales of pianos, and the introduction of movies with sound in 1927. Demand for theater organs evaporated. The company went into the refrigerator, radio, and furniture businesses to try to offset the losses.

Howard, still running the company but suffering from ill
health, saw no future in the business. Apparently the
family had internal disagreements about that future. So the
company bought out Howard's interest for $4.2 million in
1927, depleting the company's cash resources, and Howard
left the company. He died the next year.

As bad as things were, they got worse when the stock
market crashed in 1929 and the Great Depression began.
The Wurlitzer company was $4 million in debt and the
bankers took a more active role in the company's affairs.
They brought in the first outsider, RC Rolfing, in 1934. He
and Farny Wurlitzer then ran the company for the next
thirty years. In 1941, they moved the company's
headquarters to Chicago.

Rebound

Farny and Rolfing focused the company's efforts on music,
dropping the radios and refrigerators. With his knowledge
of phonographs and coin-operated instruments, in 1933
Farny had bought the patents for an "automatic
phonograph" and record changer from future Indiana
Senator Homer Capehart. Wurlitzer developed the
automatic phonograph concept, but at first resisted use of
the more popular term "jukebox" (named after juke joints,
which were considered low class).

In 1933, Wurlitzer sold 233 of the new devices. With the
repeal of prohibition, bars were back and demand
skyrocketed. In 1938, they sold 45,000 jukeboxes, which
were soon half the company's business. The famous Model
1015, introduced in 1946, sold 56,000 in the first eighteen
months on the market. Ultimately, the company
manufactured and sold over five million jukeboxes.

In the late 1940s, Farny led the company to experiment with

"electronic pianos" which were in fact not electronic, but were "electro-mechanical," still using hammers to hit metal bars. These pianos were smaller, lighter, and cheaper than regular pianos. The idea was to sell them to students and schools, hoping that the customers would later migrate to more expensive real pianos. These efforts led to the 1954 introduction of the Model 100 electronic piano, one of the first commercially successful electric pianos. Soon enough, rock and rollers and blues artists developed a taste for their unique sound, and demand grew. Ray Charles and many others played "Wurlis."

The Wurlitzer company was always committed to music education, usually offering lessons with the purchase of an instrument. With the new, cheaper electronic pianos, the company offered universities and schools a complete Music Laboratory. This set up allowed the teacher to listen to and talk to individual students, while the students wearing headphones could hear only their own instrument.

With these new products, Wurlitzer boomed in the 1950s and 1960s. After their struggles in the Depression, the number of stores had dropped as low as six in 1948, but by the 1970s the chain was back up to 49 stores.

The End

Despite this second burst of energy, the company spiraled downward. Japanese companies aggressively entered the American musical instrument business. The popularity of home pianos and organs went into decline. Farny Wurlitzer died in 1972 and RC Rolfing died two years later. Perhaps the will to live on had been sucked out of the company. But by 1985, a much smaller Wurlitzer was purchased by Cincinnati's competing piano maker Baldwin and was ultimately purchased by the Gibson Guitar Company. Today the last vestiges of the Wurlitzer name are on vending machines made in Germany by a former part of the company that was sold off years earlier.

Today, many Wurlitzer products are in high demand as collector's items. Even smaller music boxes can go for well over $10,000, and some of the other "automatic musical instruments" sell for four times that amount. We cannot help but compare this story to that of Brunswick, another midwestern firm built by German-American woodworkers, but a company that has figured out how to survive.

Originally published on AmericanBusinessHistory.org on December 5, 2020.

Chapter 13

Forgotten Industrial Giant: The Allis-Chalmers Story

Our business history articles often focus on the consumer products and services industries with which we all interact – from auto companies to department stores. Yet it's important not to forget the industrial companies that lie in the background, and make all this possible – U.S. Steel, Dow Chemical, Boeing, and many others. Some of these companies, like General Electric and Westinghouse, serve or served both industrial customers and consumers.

One of the most interesting of these was the Allis-Chalmers Company of West Allis, Wisconsin, just outside Milwaukee. This great company was one of the pioneers of the industrial age in America and around the globe. Allis-Chalmers built the engines that ran our factories: in 1900, they were perhaps the largest maker of steam engines in the world. Over time, they expanded into almost every type of engine and machine, using the slogan "Ours the Four Powers: Steam, Gas, Water, Electricity." The company made everything from giant turbines for power plants to the more familiar orange farm tractors. Allis-Chalmers was a continuous inventor and innovator in these fields.

Throughout the first half of the twentieth century, they were one of the one hundred largest American manufacturing companies. In the early 1950s, Allis-Chalmers' 30,000+ employees generated more annual revenue than IBM. The company was as big as the two largest pharmaceutical makers combined (American Home Products and Johnson & Johnson). It was also larger than 3M and Coca-Cola combined. Yet by the late 1980s, Allis-Chalmers had sold off its major business components, and in 1999 closed completely. Here is a very brief look at this formerly great company's history.

Edward Allis

Edward P. Allis was born in Cazenovia, New York in 1824. After graduating from Union College in New York state, he and his college roommate migrated to Milwaukee where they began a leather tanning operation in 1846. Ten years later, Allis decided to sell his share of the partnership, just before the "panic" (recession) of 1857. He waited out the financial crisis, getting back into business in 1861 by buying the Reliance Works, a troubled maker of flour mills and sawmills, at a bankruptcy auction. Reliance had declined from forty workers to twenty, but Allis saw opportunity in its plant and machinery. Profits rose during the Civil War. By war's end, Allis employed seventy-five men.

By 1871, Milwaukee's city leaders needed a new water system, including a 21-milllion gallon reservoir, pumping stations, and miles of pipe. Allis's Reliance Works was awarded the pipe contract, for 2,600 tons of iron pipe. Allis built a $100,000 pipe foundry, the first in the city, to fulfill the order. The financial burden led to the company's insolvency in the panic of 1873, but Allis prevailed and kept his company, now renamed Edward P. Allis & Company, intact and under his control.

Allis, who was primarily focused on the business and finance side of the works, began to hire the best specialized engineering minds he could find. He wanted to ensure that every product the company made was the best. In 1873, he hired George Hinkley, a specialist in sawmills. Hinkley perfected the commercial bandsaw, enabling much higher productivity in the booming lumber industry of the northwestern US.

In 1877, Allis added William Gray, an expert in flour mills. At the time, flour was milled using millstones, but Gray was interested in the new roller mill concept from Europe. Gray licensed this technology and improved on it. In addition to being more efficient, roller mills did a better job of turning the plentiful and cheap spring wheat found in the northwest states into flour, making it more competitive with the easier-to-mill winter wheat found further south. Gray, overcoming great skepticism, convinced the two leading flour millers of Minneapolis, Washburn-Crosby (later called General Mills) and Pillsbury, to give the new roller mills a try. Soon, the Minneapolis millers converted to roller mills and the city surpassed St. Louis as the nation's flour capital. The Allis company became the largest maker of flour milling machines and had trouble keeping up with the demand.

Allis's third great hire, his most important, was Edwin Reynolds in 1877. Reynolds had worked for George Corliss, builder of the giant Corliss steam engine that was all the rage at the 1876 Philadelphia Centennial Exposition, one of America's first great "world's fairs." Allis, unlike George

Corliss, promised Reynolds a free hand in developing better steam engines, which he promptly achieved. Reynolds engineered huge "blowing engines" which forced air into the blast furnaces used by the steel industry. Giant Carnegie Steel, the predecessor of US Steel, was soon using thirty-one of these engines.

The Allis company continually expanded, buying more land and building more factories. They created the city of West Allis. The company expanded into a dizzying array of products and parts, including gas engines. Over time, they established sales offices around the world, exporting literally tons of large machinery.

By 1889, when Edward Allis died at the age of sixty-four, his company had 1500 workers. It was the nation's largest maker of flour mills, a key competitor in sawmills, and most importantly, a giant in steam engines. While three of Allis's twelve children held executive positions, the company also had the talented executives and engineers that Allis had assembled, led by Edwin Reynolds.

Allis-Chalmers

In 1901, at the instigation of Edwin Reynolds, the Edward P. Allis Company put together a new company, Allis-Chalmers. The Allis company was merged with Chicago's Fraser & Chalmers, a major maker of mining equipment; the Gates Iron Works, also of Chicago, a maker of ore crushing machinery; and the Dickson Manufacturing Company of Scranton, Pennsylvania, which made blowing machines and air compressors.

While Reynolds had spent his life working on steam engines, he realized that electricity was becoming the nation's main motive force, and in 1904 acquired the Bullock Electric Company of Cincinnati. Thus Allis-

Chalmers had expertise and engineering leadership in steam, water, gas, and electric engines.

Surviving yet another fiscal crisis and bankruptcy in 1912-13, Allis-Chalmers again emerged as a strong company.

Allis-Chalmers continued to explore new product categories where its expertise could be applied. One of these was farm equipment, an industry dominated by the giant International Harvester Company created in 1902 by JP Morgan and the McCormick and Deering families. In 1931, Allis-Chalmers bought the faltering Advance-Rumely Thresher Company of LaPorte, Indiana. Advance-Rumely had a good name with farmers, the very successful OilPull tractor line, and a national network of dealerships. This thrust Allis Chalmers into being the fourth-largest maker of farm implements, after International Harvester, John Deere, and the JI Case Company of nearby Racine, Wisconsin. The company soon adopted bright orange as the color for its farm tractors to differentiate them from the competition. Their tractors added many innovations, including pneumatic rubber tires.

In the ensuing years, Allis-Chalmers was a major competitor in farm implements, construction machinery, and engines of every type. It contributed generators to Hoover Dam and many other big projects. The company even developed one of the first particle accelerators, the Betatron, developed at the University of Illinois in 1940.

Over time, Allis-Chalmers' fundamental strategic weakness began to take its toll. While the company seen as a whole was one of America's largest, it did not "dominate" any of its major markets. In power equipment, the company was smaller than General Electric and Westinghouse. Caterpillar, a smaller company in the 1950s, jumped into the lead in construction equipment. And in farm equipment, Allis-Chalmers was usually fourth biggest. Being number three or four meant higher distribution and marketing costs and lower factory productivity.

As hard as the company worked to stay alive, it all unwound in the 1970s and 1980s. Allis-Chalmers offloaded its construction equipment to a partnership with Italy's FIAT. They spun the farm equipment businesses off to a partnership with Germany's Deutz; this ended up as today's American company AGCO, a strong competitor. The power business was turned into a joint venture with the great German electrical company Siemens, becoming Siemens-Allis. Over time, Allis-Chalmers sold out its interest in all these partnerships and finally dissolved in 1999.

Yet even today, engines built by Allis-Chalmers continue to power factories and power plants all over the world and collectors prize vintage Allis-Chalmers' orange tractors. Over a period of one-hundred-and-thirty-eight years, Allis-Chalmers employed tens of thousands of people and followed an arc from dust to dust but left a lasting legacy of excellent engineering and products around the globe.

Originally published on AmericanBusinessHistory.org on February 22, 2020.

Chapter 14
Forgotten Giant: General Foods

For decades America's largest food company, General Foods was one of the most highly regarded marketing companies in the world. Formed in the roaring twenties by consolidating companies that led the way in convenience foods, GF became an industry giant. The company's growth enriched the founding Post family (including Marjorie Merriweather Post who pioneered frozen food and built Mar-a-Lago in Florida). By the late 1970s, General Foods was the second largest advertiser in America (after Procter & Gamble), filling the airwaves for promotions of products including Maxwell House Coffee, Kool-Aid, Jell-O, Post Toasties, Birds Eye frozen foods, and Log Cabin Syrup.

By 1985, the company was generating over $9 billion a year in revenue. Yet its acquisition that year by tobacco company Philip Morris (in the most expensive non-oil acquisition in history to that time, at $5.8 billion) meant the end of GF as an independent company. That deal was followed by years of mergers, split-ups, and spinoffs that have left the company in pieces. Rare for a dominant consumer products company, General Foods only existed under that name for fifty-six years. (Compare Procter & Gamble, 183 years old, and Colgate-Palmolive, 214). Here is a short summary of this great company's fascinating history.

The Amazing CW Post

Charles William Post was born in 1854 in Springfield, Illinois. He spent his early career inventing and selling agricultural equipment. He eventually moved to Fort Worth, Texas, where he developed real estate projects. Post's constitution was weak: he suffered from illnesses and pains his entire life. The stresses of his work led to two "nervous breakdowns" in 1885 and 1891.

The second breakdown led him to the Battle Creek Sanitarium of Dr. John Kellogg, in Battle Creek, Michigan. Dr. Kellogg's sanitarium was internationally known for rest, recuperation, and improved health. Many prominent and wealthy Americans went to Battle Creek. Key to Dr. Kellogg's methods were health foods and diets, including the avoidance of caffeine-laden coffee.

Taking a cue from Kellogg, in 1895 Post developed a warm cereal-based breakfast drink, Postum, as a healthy alternative to coffee. He created the Postum Company in Battle Creek that year, and two years later added Grape Nuts, which smelled like grapes and crunched like nuts but contained neither. Dr. Kellogg's younger brother William also saw the commercial potential in convenient health foods and started the now-famous Kellogg Company to make cereals.

The ever-innovative, ever-curious CW Post aggressively advertised Postum and his expanding line of products, which were a huge success. Post became one of the wealthiest Americans and traveled the world, collecting art and antiques. He bought over 200,000 acres of land in West Texas and developed a model city, Post, Texas.

He also took his little girl (and only child) Marjorie with him on many of his trips and adventures. Post ensured that his daughter learned history and culture. As Post built mansions, resorts, and mountain camps, Marjorie also learned design, interior decoration, and entertaining. Before she was twenty, Marjorie Merriweather Post had visited factories across America, learned how machines worked, learned the names of all the Postum employees, and learned her father's business ideals. Post even talked to her about how the Postum Company might expand by buying other good companies in the food industries.

In 1913, approaching sixty years of age, Post had appendicitis. He hired a custom train to rush him non-stop from Santa Barbara, California, to Rochester, Minnesota, to see the famous doctors the Mayo brothers. Post traveled in a private railroad car owned by his friends at the Santa Fe Railroad. The trip cost him $5,000 (about $135,000 in 2020 money). After a successful operation, he returned home. His depression and pain soon struck again. Post committed suicide in 1914. At the age of twenty-seven, Marjorie Post was the sole owner of the Postum Company, generating revenues of almost $20 million per year. This made Marjorie one of the wealthiest women in the world.

Marjorie Takes Command

In 1920, Marjorie married her second husband, New York stockbroker and yachtsman EF Hutton. The couple added a third daughter to the two girls from Marjorie's first marriage. This third daughter became known to the public as actress Dina Merrill. (EF Hutton's niece was "poor little rich girl" Barbara Hutton.) The family continued to build fabulous homes in New York City, on Long Island (mostly now part of Long Island University Post), in Florida (Mar-a-Lago, now owned by Donald Trump), and elsewhere. They traveled the world collecting more art and antiques. Their yachts got bigger, reaching an apex in 1935 with the 316-foot long Sea Cloud, the largest private yacht in the world when built (the ship still sails today and is the world's oldest operating ocean-going passenger ship).

Despite their incredibly full lives, Marjorie and Hutton focused their energy on the Postum Company and on how to expand upon its success. Following her father's ideas, in the 1920s Marjorie and her husband led Postum to buy Calumet Baking Powder, Swan's Down Cake Flour, Minute Tapioca, Jell-O, and Baker's Chocolate, which had built the first chocolate mill in America in the late 18th century.

Their most important acquisition was Cheek-Neal in 1925. Joel Cheek of Nashville had developed a system for vacuum packing pre-ground coffee. He tested it at Nashville's Maxwell House Hotel, where it was a hit, prompting Teddy Roosevelt to say the coffee was "good to the last drop." Maxwell House Coffee, and later Sanka and Yuban, were to become the most important single part of the company; an ironic twist given CW Post's highly successful opposition to coffee, which produced the funds to buy Maxwell House.

At about the same time that Postum bought Cheek-Neal and its Maxwell House brand, the Huttons were setting sail on their yacht from Gloucester, Massachusetts. The crew packed in food for the trip. At dinner, Marjorie noted how tasty, fresh, and juicy the goose was. Inquiring, she found out that a local man had developed a process to freeze food, and that the goose was actually a few months old. She unsuccessfully tried to convince EF Hutton that Postum should buy out the company and its food freezing process for two million dollars. EF was concerned that frozen food was a tough sell: consumers did not have home freezers, grocery stores did not have freezers, trucks did not have freezers.

Finally, in 1929, Hutton was convinced, and Postum bought the General Foods Company and its freezing process from Clarence Birdseye, for about ten times the earlier price. In June of 1929, the Postum Company adopted this more fitting name, becoming the General Foods Corporation. (General Electric had been founded in 1892 and General Motors in 1908, followed by General Tire, General Mills, and many other companies called "General.") General Foods would go on to make Birds Eye a household name, leading the way in frozen foods.

At the exact same time in that merger-filled era – June 1929 – another "food conglomerate" was formed. Called the Standard Brands Company, it was built on Fleischmann's Yeast, Royal Gelatin and Puddings, and Chase & Sanborn Coffee. For the next forty-plus years General Foods and Standard Brands would compete in multiple product categories, though General Foods was soon substantially larger. Another food giant created in the late 1920s was National Dairy Products, a consolidation of several dairies and ice cream companies. National Dairy's 1930 purchase of the Kraft-Phenix Cheese Company made the company #1 in cheese; the company was later renamed Kraft.

Marjorie Merriweather Post went on to two more husbands (including 1930s Ambassador to the Soviet Union Joseph Davies), more houses, more collecting, and a life of philanthropy. She remained active with General Foods and died in 1973 at the age of eighty-six.

The Long Growth

From its 1929 birth through the 1980s, General Foods was America's largest DIVERSIFIED food company. (In the early years, meatpackers Swift and Armour were larger, and for most of the 20th century, National Dairy Products/Kraft was also larger.) With solid revenues generated by low-priced products, the company never lost money in the Great Depression (the lowest points were about $100 million in sales and $9 million in profits).

The demand for convenience foods was accelerated by the entry of women into the workforce, especially during and after World War II, playing right into General Foods' hands. Jell-O, Maxwell House, Post Cereals, and other General Foods brands were #1 or close in their categories. The company added Kool-Aid, Oscar Mayer, Orowheat, and Entenmann's Bakery to its portfolio. Known for innovation, General Foods created instant coffee, Tang (the drink that went to space), Cool Whip, and many other new products. General Foods spent up to $100 million a year on research and development.

In 1958, revenues reached one billion dollars for the first time. The business expanded internationally in the 1950s and boomed in the 1960s. Above all else, General Foods was a prominent and successful marketer, by the late 1970s ranking as America's second largest advertiser after Procter & Gamble. In 1983, the company opened a 500,000 square-foot headquarters complex, designed by top architects Roche/Dinkeloo, in Rye Brook, New York. General Foods was the world's largest coffee producer, generating over a quarter of the company's revenues. The company became #1 in coffee in Sweden, #1 in chewing gum in France. Old archrival Standard Brands was about half the size of General Foods. These numbers tell the growth story better than words can:

Year	General Foods Revenues ($MM)	General Foods Net Income ($MM)
1924	24	4
1929	128	19
1935	107	12
1937	133	9
1949	475	27
1958	1009	48
1967	1652	99
1970	2282	119
1980	5960	256
1984	8600	317

The Great Shuffling

Then, in the 1980s, the world changed. The 1980s were full of big deals in the food industry. Everyone seemed to be buying and selling companies. New names like Conagra and Sara Lee rose to prominence.

Tobacco giants RJ Reynolds and Philip Morris shared several problems: public perception as being tobacco-only companies; a declining market for tobacco products; mountains of cash and available credit from their enormously profitable tobacco businesses; and no need to use that capital to invest in tobacco. In 1985, Reynolds bought Nabisco, which was about 75% the size of General Foods (Nabisco had acquired Standard Brands in 1981).

That same year, Philip Morris made a surprise and plentiful offer for General Foods: $5.8 billion in cash, the largest non-oil merger in history up to that time. General Foods management and Board of Directors tried to find other buyers to bid up the price, but no one could beat the Philip

Morris offer. Philip Morris had risen to be considered one of the best marketing companies in America due to its success in building Marlboro cigarettes (passing up old leaders Camel and Winston) and Miller Beer, a smaller brewer that Philip Morris converted into a leader.

In 1988, Philip Morris also bought the giant Kraft company. Twelve years later, in 2000, Philip Morris bought Nabisco (including Standard Brands) for $18.9 billion. Philip Morris – today named Altria – consolidated its giant food businesses under the Kraft Foods name. Philip Morris became the largest consumer products company in America, passing long-time leader Procter & Gamble. Kraft, Nabisco, Standard Brands, General Foods, Oscar Mayer, and hundreds of top brands were now part of the same company.

As is the case in many – perhaps most – mergers, anticipated "synergies" did not come about. Great old brands got lost in the huge company. Layers of management piled up. New CEOs had new ideas. Leadership and the organizational structure changed frequently. Priorities shifted too often; innovation slowed. In the end, all these huge deals did not work, at least not for the brands and food companies (the deals may have worked fine for the brokers who put the deals together). The net result today, the result of stories too long to tell here, is that the great products of General Foods (and of Nabisco, Kraft, and Standard Brands) are today scattered over the landscape, with many owners. The principle owner of the old General Foods brands is now Kraft Heinz, a public company that resulted from more mergers. Kraft Heinz, which has struggled in recent years, is controlled by Warren Buffett's Berkshire Hathaway and Brazil's 3G Capital group (who also control the world's largest brewer, Anheuser-Busch Inbev). Many of the brands are also owned by international powerhouse Mondelez.

In studying this history, we cannot help but comment on brands and their management. General Foods was on top of the world. It has been said (by us), "If Kool-Aid had been well run, there might be no need for VitaminWater." While any such statement is highly speculative, the reality is that many of those great brands have lost supermarket shelf space to upstarts.

The last thirty years have not been pleasant for a lot of great old brands. Few companies or factories can remain focused when they have a new owner every few years. On the other hand, companies which love and nourish their brands have, overall, prospered. Church & Dwight (the maker of Arm & Hammer products), Procter & Gamble, Colgate-Palmolive, Hormel (with its trusty Spam), John Deere (since 1837, with only 9 or 10 leaders in 183 years), Mars, and others come to mind.

We cannot help but wonder what the world would be like had General Foods continued its tradition of independence, innovation, and leadership. Perhaps we would still be seeing Jell-O ads on television every evening, even if the products were all new. Perhaps Procter & Gamble would not have purchased Folger's Coffee and then succeeded in taking the coffee lead away from Maxwell House (Folger's is now owned by the JM Smucker Company).

This article just scratches the surface of these stories. Many books and articles can readily be found on Marjorie Merriweather Post and her homes and yachts, the deals of the 1980s, Post Texas, the battling Kellogg brothers, and many other elements of this article.

Originally published on AmericanBusinessHistory.org on October 23, 2020.

Chapter 15
From Milk Duds to Samsonite: The Beatrice Foods Saga

In setting the stage for this story, I interject myself, because "I was there."

Setting the Stage

The year is 1975. I am two years out of college, a junior securities analyst for institutional investor Citibank in New York. My veteran analyst boss Pete Wetzel and I are on one of our field trips to Chicago. We sit in an office at 120 South LaSalle Street, in the heart of Chicago's financial district. The office is neither fancy nor large. Across the desk from us sits William G. Karnes, one of Pete's favorite Chief Executive Officers (CEOs) of the hundreds he has studied.

As Pete asks Bill Karnes about the recent performance of each major part of Karnes' company, Beatrice Foods, the amiable and patient Karnes flips through the pages of a fat black binder. Each page tells the story on one of the company's over 400 "profit centers." Bill Karnes replies, "They were doing well but stumbled a bit last month.," or "That operation set another record last quarter." Like other company veterans, Karnes pronounces the company's name "bee-AT-russ" after the small Nebraska town where it all began in 1894.

Beatrice Foods has acquired hundreds of small companies in the food and other industries, all over the world. In one day, Karnes bought three small food companies in Indiana as he drove around the state. Few if any companies in American history were more "acquisitive." The company's 400 plants produce Meadow Gold ice cream and butter, Clark bars, Milk Duds, Eckrich meats, Mario's olives, La Choy Asian foods, Dannon yogurt, Airstream trailers, and Samsonite luggage, among hundreds of other brands. Over two hundred new products are introduced each year.

As of 1975, Beatrice has also racked up one of the most astonishing records in US business history. Annual revenues reach $4 billion, two years ahead of the company's own projections. *Fortune* magazine rates it not only one of the best-run American companies, but also among the 40 largest US industrial companies, bigger than Boeing, 3M, Coca-Cola, and the rapidly rising Xerox. Perhaps more telling, Beatrice now generates 14% more revenues and 36% more profits than perennial food giant General Foods. The company is closing in on the largest food company, Kraft, and will soon enough pass them.

Return on equity is an exceptional 16%. For the twenty-three years that Bill Karnes has been in charge, the company has reported increased sales, profits, and earnings per share every single quarter, four times a year like clockwork. Those profits flow from hundreds of small factories employing 64,000 people in every nook and cranny of the world. Over the last ten years, since 1965, Beatrice's stock return has been 7th best of the 50 largest companies on the *Fortune* list, even beating IBM.

The company is a masterpiece, demonstrating the outstanding management of a complex and diverse business.

The next year, Bill Karnes retired. Within ten years, Beatrice Foods would be no more, torn apart and then virtually forgotten in the dustbin of business history. Here is the story.

Beginnings

George Haskell, born in Iowa in 1864, was one of five children who grew up in an orphanage after their father died when George was four years old. By the time he was twenty-five, he had worked his way up from bookkeeper to secretary of Nebraska's Fremont Butter and Egg Company. In that year, 1889, he opened a branch of the firm in Beatrice, Nebraska. After the Fremont Company went bankrupt in the Depression of 1893, in 1894 Haskell and co-worker William Bosworth set up the Haskell & Bosworth Company in the Beatrice branch of their former employer. The new firm dealt in poultry, eggs, butter, and produce. They gradually expanded the butter and cream business. In 1898 they incorporated their small firm as the Beatrice Creamery Company. Bosworth left the company the next year.

Under George Haskell, the company continued to grow. Dairy farmers brought milk to the creamery, where the cream was separated and the skimmed milk returned to the farmer. After this time-consuming process, the milk was often too sour to be useful. Haskell began to finance cream separators for the farmers so they could do the separation on the farm, and only bring him the cream. This process also saved the farmers from making two trips to town. By 1905, Beatrice had financed over 50,000 cream separators for farmers in Nebraska and Kansas. In 1898, Beatrice had churned 940,000 pounds of cream – by 1904, that figure was over ten million pounds.

In 1905, Beatrice acquired the Continental Creamery of Topeka, Kansas, along with that company's "Meadow Gold" brand name, one of the first trademarked butters. This became the primary brand used by Beatrice. Meadow Gold was the first butter to be sold in a sealed package, the first butter to be advertised in a national magazine, and the first ice cream established as a national brand.

The company headquarters was moved to Chicago in 1913 and continued to be run by George Haskell until his death in 1919. After two interim leaders, Haskell's nephew Clinton H. Haskell ("CH") served as company President from 1928 to 1952.

Stage Two

By the time forty-year-old CH Haskell took over, Beatrice was a major dairy products company, generating annual sales in excess of $50 million and profits of $1 million. The year before, in 1927, financiers were putting together a giant national combination of dairy companies, National Dairy Products. Beatrice's board of directors almost sold the company to National, but decided the price offered was not high enough. National soon bought Kraft Cheese, and later the company was renamed Kraft, for many years the nation's largest food company outside of giant meatpackers Swift and Armour. But Beatrice remained independent in the shadow of the giant.

In his twenty-four years of leadership, CH Haskell continued to expand Beatrice. He did this both through growing the existing business and by buying more companies. Ice cream and milk companies from Denver to Brooklyn were added to the mix. When Beatrice bought Detroit's AF Thibideau Company, it became the biggest egg processor in America. By 1930, the company had 157 plants in operation, making it the third-largest dairy company after National and Borden and number one in butter. Between 1927 and 1932, Beatrice's milk production rose from under a million gallons a year to twenty-seven million gallons. Ice cream grew from a half-million gallons to almost ten million.

CH Haskell also began to diversify Beatrice away from being only a dairy company. In 1943, he bought the LaChoy Asian foods company, which became a great success and the leader in that field. Beatrice also began to operate frozen food warehouses and wholesaling, becoming a major distributor of frozen foods, which were booming during this era. Throughout this early history, Beatrice focused on food quality and purity, as well as innovating in packaging and advertising. The Meadow Gold brand rose in prominence. In Haskell's last year as President, 1952, sales reached $229 million and profits $3.9 million. In that year, milk and cream were 32% of sales, butter 22%, ice cream 16%, and poultry and eggs 6%.

The Arrival of Bill Karnes

Born in 1911, William Karnes' mother died when he was five, so Karnes was raised by his two aunts in Chicago. After graduating from the School of Commerce at the University of Illinois, he earned a law degree at Northwestern University. Bill Karnes joined Beatrice as a law clerk upon graduation at $110 a month in 1936. Three years later, he was promoted to head up the company's new Employee

Relations Department, to help the plants deal with wage and labor issues. The twenty-five-year-old Karnes quickly became adept at settling strikes and other labor problems. He settled many difficult labor conflicts, including one at which famed teamsters union leader Jimmy Hoffa was present. People who met him instantly liked and trusted Bill.

He was also an incredibly hard worker, doing "whatever it took" to get the job done. When one of his associates was later asked why the company was so successful, the man said, "That's simple. We work half days. 6 AM to 6 PM."

By 1943, the thirty-two-year-old Bill Karnes was made a vice president of Beatrice. His responsibilities included putting new pension and health insurance plans in place. Beginning in 1945, he started working on finding good acquisitions to ensure Beatrice's continued growth. For nine years, he worked directly with and learned from CH Haskell. On March 25, 1952, Bill Karnes was named President of Beatrice, largely because of his ability to work with a wide range of people and their personalities. He would lead the company for the next twenty-four years.

Karnes' first step was to surround himself with the best managers in the company. After selecting his senior officers, he began to look for growth opportunities. Realizing the rapid growth of the western United States, in 1954 he bought Creameries of America, with twenty-five milk and ice cream plants in Texas, the western states, and Hawaii. This was the biggest acquisition in Beatrice's history up to that time. Beatrice continued to buy small dairy products companies across the US, many of them in the rising South. The company also purchased the premium Louis Sherry ice cream brand in New York City.

Beatrice also expanded its operations in food warehousing and distribution and in non-dairy products. The frequency of acquisitions accelerated over the years. Key to the company's continuing success were Bill Karnes' management and acquisition philosophies.

The Beatrice Way, as developed by Bill Karnes

Above all else, more important than any high-level strategy or sophisticated management system, Bill Karnes believed in people. Find the right people, put them in charge of a single plant or division, and let them run it. This meant that Beatrice was extremely "decentralized." While the company developed research, legal, human relations, and other central support teams for the plants, all key business decisions were made at the plant level. Karnes wanted decisions made as close to the customers as possible. Plant managers were given responsibility for results, but also the authority that enabled them to achieve those results. Plant managers received a base salary and two percent of the plant's profits. Monthly reports to headquarters were limited to a few simple pages of numbers. Under Karnes, the company grew to enormous size, but never had as many as two hundred employees at the corporate headquarters in Chicago.

Every year at Christmas, Bill Karnes visited the company's numerous plants and offices in the Chicago area and shook the hand of every single employee. He was known to stand up at a divisional sales meeting with two hundred salespeople present, and name each one, name their spouse, and tell something of that person's accomplishments. Annual awards and recognition for the best performers at all levels of the company were part of the Beatrice way of life, including a "Hall of Champions" in the hallways of the headquarters.

Those who worked most closely with Karnes said he was

"an extremely sensitive person." He rarely raised his voice, never swore, and never used fear or intimidation as a management tool. He suggested his managers ask rather than order, to lead by example. He would only promote people who had proven their ability to get along with others, those who could tolerate differences of opinion. Karnes almost always promoted from within, rarely going outside the company for talent. He liked a broad mix of personality types, education levels, and ages. His door was always open to any employee.

Bill Karnes often cited a Chinese proverb, "If you want a crop for a year, grow rice. If you want a crop for ten years, grow trees. If you want a crop for a hundred years, grow people."

In reviewing the company's many acquisitions, it is apparent that sometimes Karnes bought a company mainly to get its excellent management. Many executives of acquired companies went on to greater responsibility within the Beatrice organization.

While Beatrice made hundreds of acquisitions, under Karnes it never did an "unfriendly" deal. Never once in its over 400 acquisitions was the company sued by minority stockholders for not making a fair offer.

When Bill Karnes found a company he thought would be a good fit with Beatrice, he sometimes spent years romancing the owners, convincing them to sell. Any time he considered buying a company, he first met with the owners and managers and talked business philosophy at length. He had to make sure that they shared the same ideals – that, in today's lingo, they shared the same "culture." Karnes only bought companies that were profitable and well-run. He would not buy a company unless the management agreed to stay on or had trained able successors.

Equally important, under Karnes, Beatrice focused on companies which had good growth opportunities, in the right market niches or fastest growing parts of the country (or later, parts of the world). Most of the companies Bill Karnes bought were small, generating under twenty million dollars a year in revenue, often just three to six million. He looked at their future more than their present, then funded expansion into new territories and new products. Beatrice took regional brands and made them national. The company introduced over two hundred new products a year. The company's growth thus stemmed both from adding new companies and from expanding the ones it had already bought ("Internal" or "organic" growth).

Karnes had no interest in commodity businesses, like sugar and coffee, and gradually reduced the importance of plain fluid milk at Beatrice. Studying the incredibly long list of brands and companies owned by Beatrice at one time or another (shown at the end of this article), it can be seen that Beatrice was perhaps "the king of the niches." Over time, the company entered more niches, in a staggering array of industries, though food was always at the core, representing at least 75% of Beatrice's annual revenues.

Throughout his acquisition sprees, Bill Karnes did not take on debt, paying stock for the companies he bought whenever possible. Those sellers who kept their stock were amply rewarded over the years. Only when he began to buy overseas companies which would not accept American stock did he begin to allow the company to take on a modest amount of debt.

The Beatrice Way at Work: Food

In the late 1950s and into the 1960s, Beatrice expanded its specialty (non-dairy) foods operations, building on the success of what it learned from owning LaChoy since 1943.

(Under Beatrice ownership, LaChoy grew from sales of $1.8 million to $135 million.) Acquisitions included Clark candy bars, Jolly Rancher candies, Milk Duds, Mario's olives, Liberty maraschino cherries, Gebhardt's chili, Fisher nuts, "After Dinner" mints, Mother's cookies, Vlasic pickles, and Rosarita Mexican foods. A national market was created for Shedd Spread, a leading margarine. Bakeries making the franchised Butterkrust and Sunbeam breads were added. 1976 witnessed the addition of Krispy Kreme doughnuts and Martha White cake mixes. Beatrice became a major bottler of RC Cola, Canada Dry, 7-Up, and Dr. Pepper.

One of the most significant acquisitions was the Peter Eckrich company of Fort Wayne, Indiana, a major regional producer of cold cuts and packaged meats. Beatrice rapidly expanded Eckrich from four states into most of the rest of the nation. Sales tripled in the first six years under Beatrice. Eckrich leader Donald Eckrich went on to become one of Beatrice's top executives.

These food acquisitions were supplemented by buying the John Sexton company of Chicago, a major food distributor that served restaurants across the nation.

By the time Karnes retired in 1976, these many small acquisitions had grown the company's specialty food operations to $2 billion in annual sales and over $100 million in operating profit.

Beatrice also continued to expand its frozen and cold storage warehousing and distribution operations. At the peak, the company had over one-hundred-and-fifty million cubic feet of cold storage space around the United States.

A typical, successful example of Karnes' foresight and acquisition strategy was a small company owned by Joe Metzger. Metzger had been born in Switzerland but then moved to Spain, then the US in 1942. In America, he met an old friend, Daniel Carasso, who had fled wartime Paris. Carasso's Greek father had founded a yogurt company in Barcelona and later in Paris, naming it Danone after his son Daniel. Joe Metzger and Daniel Carasso purchased a small yogurt factory in the Bronx and renamed the product Dannon, an anglicization of Danone. While Daniel returned to France after the war to take over the family yogurt business there, he remained a partner in the US business run by Joe Metzger and his son Juan. In 1947, Dannon started adding preserves in the bottom of the yogurt and sales in the New York metropolitan area began to rise, though it took until 1952 to turn a profit.

The Metzgers were obsessed with product quality. The yogurt was delivered to stores in their own trucks, and their drivers would pick up any yogurt past its expiration date. By the time Bill Karnes arrived on the scene in 1959, sales had risen to $3 million a year, all in the Northeastern US. It took a great deal of convincing to get the Metzgers to join Beatrice. They were concerned that the company would force them to use its distribution system and use preserves from one of the other Beatrice divisions. But Bill Karnes promised them that they could still run their company as they always had, just with more capital so they could expand beyond the Northeast. As part of Beatrice, after 1959 Dannon led the way in introducing yogurt to America and became the dominant US brand. Juan Metzger also played an important role when Beatrice later began to buy food companies around the world.

While a few Beatrice divisions exported their products to other countries, the company did not have a factory outside the US until it opened a condensed milk plant in Malaysia in 1961. As Beatrice gained experience in different nations, the company gradually acquired more and more international businesses. Not only did Bill Karnes stick to his proven formula of decentralization, but he also required that each operation be managed by local people, not executives imported from America.

By the 1970s, Beatrice was buying up ice cream companies all over Europe. A major success was Tayto, the largest potato chip company in Ireland. Candy and snack food companies in Venezuela, Colombia, Peru, Guatemala, Honduras, and Panama were added to the mix. Holanda ice cream became the number one brand in Mexico. Beatrice became a powerhouse in the Caribbean and added more companies from Canada and Australia. By the late 1980s, the International Food division was generating $2.5 billion in annual sales and an operating profit of $147 million.

Beyond Food

Bill Karnes' appetite for great niche companies with growth potential was not limited to the food industry. When he found strong brands with good managements and great future potential, he applied his standard process of getting the know the people, romancing them, and then allowing them to keep running their businesses.

The long list of non-food acquisitions included: Melnor, the leader in lawn sprinklers; World, the number one maker of hand dryers for restaurant bathrooms; Taylor, the largest maker of commercial ice cream freezers; Culligan, the water softener market leader; Samsonite, the king of the luggage industry; Vogel-Peterson, the coat rack "giant;" Stiffel, America's largest maker of high quality decorative lamps; Silex, maker of coffee brewers for restaurants; and Airstream, the famous maker of trailers. These names just scratch the surface: the list is almost endless (see it at the end of this article).

The company also ventured into highly technical niches, often chemical industries that stemmed from Beatrice's other activities. One division developed a system that could turn anything into a powder form – even wine and cheese. This company provided powders that made food processing easier, making ingredients that went into everything from pizza to cake mixes. Customers included almost every major American food manufacturer. Other divisions produced everything from printing inks to tanned leather to reinforced engineering plastic compounds provided to Boeing and others in the aerospace industry.

In virtually every case, Beatrice turned a small or regional company into a national force. In some cases, Beatrice took a national brand and make it stronger, or made it an international brand.

By the early 1980s, annual sales of these non-food products, from 99 companies operating 350 factories, totaled $2.3 billion with operating profits of $250 million.

In this diverse empire of 9,000 products from 400 food and non-food companies in 27 countries, only a small Canadian dairy operation branded its products as "Beatrice." Most customers never heard the company's name, only dealing with the decentralized operations, each with its own brand and reputation. Bill Karnes liked it that way.

Following the age-65 retirement rule that he had put in place, William G. Karnes retired as Chief Executive Officer (CEO) of Beatrice in July, 1976.

The Peak

From March of 1952 when Bill Karnes took over through February of 1982, after he retired, Beatrice posted 120 consecutive quarters in which profits were higher than the year before, a record equaled by few if any other companies in business history. During the years in which Karnes led the company, annual sales rose from $235 million to $5.7

billion in 1976. Net income rose from $4 million to $206 million. The company's return on equity was over 17%, among the highest of any company that size, and the debt-to-equity ratio only 23%, below most companies. Throughout his reign, dividends were also consistently increased and the stock rose in value, having split five times. Business magazines published extensive articles about the miracle of Beatrice and its unusual leader.

While it took over eighty years for Beatrice to reach its peak, it took less than ten years for it to reach its end as an independent company.

The Demise

In the initial years after Karnes retired, sales and profits continued to rise, perhaps out of momentum as his policies and attitudes remained intact. But problems soon began to arise in the company's management. Upon Karnes' retirement, William Mitchell became Chairman and Wallace Rasmussen was named President and CEO. Both were company veterans and should have understood the importance of working with others, but they did not get along. Within fourteen months, Mitchell was out. Rasmussen, who was more of a "tough guy" than Karnes, ruffled feathers. Many veterans left the company or retired, depleting the management ranks. When it came time for Rasmussen to retire at 65, he tried to change the rules and increase the mandatory retirement age, which the board of directors agreed to, but then changed its mind.

The dowdy headquarters were moved to a shiny new building, taking up four-and-a-half floors compared to the one-and-a-half floors required by Karnes' lean team.

At the same time this was taking place, the Beatrice board was restructured to include more "outside directors," people who were not executives of the company. The Beatrice board had always consisted primarily of insiders who knew the business. Experts in corporate governance advocated more outsiders on corporate boards, to ensure that management did not line its own pockets. The Securities and Exchange Commission endorsed this trend, and Beatrice went along. The change had the effect of reducing the number of board members imbued with the Beatrice culture.

Wallace Rasmussen refused to name a successor, putting the board in a difficult spot. A committee composed only of outside directors selected Richard Voell to take the top spot, effective January 1, 1980. When this was announced internally, several key executives told the board they would quit if Voell got the job, so the board changed its mind and appointed James Dutt as CEO. Also in 1980, a somewhat discouraged Bill Karnes also left the board of directors.

Dutt brought a new attitude to the leadership of Beatrice. He kept a cartoon on his wall that said, "All those opposed, signify by saying 'I quit.'" Dutt drove the organization hard. He began to dismantle the decentralized structure of the company, giving more power to central management. Key decisions were no longer made in the field, as the 430 plants now reported to 28 much larger "business units." By 1985, the headquarters staff had swollen to 750 people, about five times the size it had been under Karnes. Dutt brought in many outside consultants, something Karnes only did for highly specialized or technical tasks. Dutt's consultants imagined broad new strategies. The "old school" ideas of Bill Karnes were replaced by the latest and trendiest ideas for managing a company. To meet with James Dutt, employees had to submit a written request.

Dutt declared that Beatrice would become more modern, a "unified marketing company." He publicly stated his goal of becoming the world's premier marketer of food and

consumer products, implying that Beatrice would become
the marketing equal of Nestle, PepsiCo, Coca-Cola, and
Procter & Gamble. The corporation's name was changed
from Beatrice Foods to the Beatrice Companies and a new
logo was designed. For the first time, Beatrice began a $30
million advertising campaign promoting the Beatrice name,
a "brand" that few customers had ever heard of.

Dutt also sold off some of the company's best operations,
including Shedd's, Krispy Kreme, and Dannon yogurt, in
order to buy companies he found more appealing. More
company veterans left the company, including Donald
Eckrich, who had risen in the ranks. Between 1980 and
1985, 39 of the top 58 executives retired, resigned, or were
fired. Over 800 people throughout the company took early
retirement. Morale at the company plunged. James Dutt
aggressively recruited executives from outside the company,
people unaware of the Beatrice Way and the company's
traditions.

At the same time, in the quarter ended in June of 1982,
Beatrice reported its first drop in quarterly earnings in
thirty years, declining 36% from the year earlier. Beatrice's
stock was no longer as strong, and rumors began to
circulate that the company might be acquired. To fend off
the sale of the company, Dutt decided to buy a very big
company, theoretically making Beatrice bigger and harder
to buy.

In 1984, Beatrice ended its long history of avoiding too
much debt by borrowing in order to buy Esmark for $2.7
billion. Esmark, descended from the formerly giant Swift
meatpacking company, had become a "conglomerate" of
unrelated businesses, including Wesson oil, Max Factor
cosmetics, Avis rental cars, and Playtex intimate apparel.
As a result of the transaction and taking on Esmark's debts,
Dutt's ego may have been satisfied, but Beatrice's debt
stood at $4.5 billion, with interest rates of 12-14%. By 1985,

the company's debt-to-equity ratio was 199%. More companies were sold off to reduce the heavy debt load.

The giant company now had 123,000 employees worldwide, but the Beatrice Way was long gone. In 1985, earnings per share declined 18%. The business press was now writing severely negative stories about Beatrice, something the writers had not done for over thirty years.

The board of directors finally said, "enough is enough" and fired James Dutt in August of 1985. He had run Beatrice for six years. Desperate, the board convinced the seventy-four-year-old Bill Karnes to return to the board of directors and chair an important committee. He brought with him a new CEO (but longtime Beatrice executive) who understood the company's heritage, William Granger.

Karnes and Granger tried to bring the company back to its roots. A secretary came to Karnes' office to tell him that the limo was waiting to take him to the company's Gulfstream jet, which would in turn take him to a board meeting in New York. (Under Karnes, Beatrice had never owned any company aircraft; now the company had eight airplanes.) Bill Karnes told her, "No, I am taking the elevator down to the street and walking a few blocks to the transit system, where it will cost me 45 cents to get to O'Hare airport, where I will get a coach seat on a commercial flight." He arrived in New York before the other board members.

But it was too late to save the mess that Beatrice had become. The company was embattled and again the target of potential buyers. Private investing firm KKR made an offer for the whole company, which Karnes initially opposed. But when he and the board studied the alternatives – and KKR raised its offering price – they ultimately decided it was the best thing to do for Beatrice shareholders.

On April 17, 1986, KKR purchased Beatrice for $6.2 billion in the largest leveraged buyout (debt-financed deal) outside the oil industry up to that time. Major parts of the combined Beatrice-Esmark empire were quickly sold off to reduce the debt that KKR incurred. Famous brands were cast to the wind, with many diverse buyers. Samsonite, for example, has had five different owners since 1986. Continuity of management was lost. The Beatrice Way was history.

Lessons?

It is rarely easy to assess the causes of decline at a big corporation. Often, as in the cases of General Motors, Sears, and IBM, we can point to four or five key factors and management mistakes. Given its track record and stewardship of top niche brands, the fall of Beatrice is perhaps harder to understand. No union strikes, technological changes, or major foreign or domestic competitors entered the Beatrice picture. Beatrice's troubles were of its own making.

Perhaps Bill Karnes did not embed his "DNA" as deeply in his managers as he hoped and believed. Obviously, some of them like Warren Rasmussen and James Dutt really did not "get it," even after having spent years at the company. Maybe their egos overtook their common sense once they rose to the top. Or perhaps Bill Karnes, a true "servant leader," was just an unusual freak in the business world, "irrelevant" to modern corporate practice. We'd like to think not.

For those of us who love business history, the great story of Beatrice, with such a sad ending, also makes us treasure those companies which have been able to "stay the course" over many decades. Those companies which, year after year, stay true to their initial vision and which still carry the

"DNA" of their founders are worthy of our attention and admiration. While they may make for less exciting headlines, we would point to such examples as UPS, Target, the Walt Disney Company, Coca-Cola, PepsiCo, FedEx, Home Depot, Caterpillar, Deere, Procter & Gamble, Johnson & Johnson, Colgate-Palmolive, and many others.

We at the American Business History Center continue to be entranced by the human saga that is business. Few things are as fascinating as the rise, fall, and sometimes even rebirth of great businesses. As they arc through their cycles of life, they affect hundreds of thousands of employees, suppliers, customers, stockholders, and communities. We hope you continue to enjoy the diverse stories we present.

List of Beatrice Companies and Brands

The following brands and companies were owned at one time or another by Beatrice. Some of the larger (and often "less fitting") ones like Avis were part of the acquisition of Esmark, after Beatrice's glory days, reflecting a departure from Karnes' philosophy of finding smaller niches and industry-leading companies.

(This list was compiled from the Internet and may contain spelling errors.)

- Absopure distilled and spring water
- Acryon leisure and household products
- Adams International snack food machinery
- Adisa snack foods
- A.H.Schwab children's play products
- Ailiram biscuits and confections
- Airstream
- Allison leisure apparel
- All-Pro leisure apparel
- Almay hypo-allergenic cosmetics
- Altoids
- American Hostess ice cream
- American Pickles
- Antoine's food products
- Aqua Queen garden equipment
- Argosy recreational vehicles
- Arist O' Kraft cabinets

- Armitage Realty Co.
- Arrowhead bottle water
- Artic ice cream
- Assumption Abbey wine products
- Aunt Nellie's food products
- Avan recreational vehicles
- Avis car rental
- Banner painting equipment
- Barbara Dee cookies
- Barcrest beverage mixes
- Barrons table specialty meats
- Beatreme dairy products and flavorings
- Beatrice dairy products
- Becky Kay's cookies
- Beefbreak meat specialties
- Beeforcan meat specialties
- Beneke bathroom accessories
- Best Jet painting equipment
- Bickford food products
- Bighorn specialty meats
- Big Pete specialty meats
- Bireley's orange drink (Asahi Soft Drinks)
- Blue Boy ice cream
- Blue Ribbon condiments
- Blue Valley Creamery Company
- Body Shaper plumbing supplies
- Bogene closet accessories
- Boizet specialty food products
- Bonanza mini-motorhomes
- Bonkers cat treats
- Bosman barbecue equipment
- Boquitas Fiestas snack foods
- Bowers candies
- Bredan butter
- Brenner candy
- Brookside wine products
- Brown Miller condiments
- Bubble Stream plumbing equipment
- Burny Bakers food products
- Butterball
- Butterchef Bakery
- Buttercrust baked goods
- Buxton leather accessories
- Byrons barbecue
- California Products beverage mixes
- Callard & Bowser confections
- Camofrio sausage, luncheon and specialty meats
- Campus Casuals sport clothing
- Captain Kids food products
- Cartwheels travel bags
- CCA Furniture accessories
- Chapelcord school and religious apparel
- Charmglow barbecue grills and outdoor products
- Checkers beverages
- Chicago red wine products
- Chicago specialty plumbing tools and supplies
- Chipy snack foods
- Choky hot chocolate
- Churngold condiments
- Cincinnati Fruit condiments and fountain syrups
- Citro Crest beverage mixes
- Clark candy
- Classic travel bags
- Classy Crisps
- Cook n' Cajun barbecue equipment
- Colonial cookies
- Costello's food products
- Country Hearth baked goods
- County Line cheeses
- Cow Boy Jo's meat specialties
- Cremo milk and ice cream
- Culligan
- C.W. pickles
- Dannon yogurt
- Danskin bodywear
- David Lau Food products
- Davy Jones candy
- Dearborn brass home improvement equipment
- Decora cabinets
- Dell condiments
- Delmar interior design
- Delta Food products
- Denyer-Dans specialty meats
- Derby tamales
- Dixie Lily food products
- Doll oriental foods
- Dopp travel bags
- Doumak marshmallows

- Eckrich
- E.R. Moore school and religious apparel
- Europe food bars
- Everain garden equipment
- Excello painting supplies
- Farelon school and religious apparel
- Fashionarir travel bags
- Fiesta specialty foods
- Fireside marshmallows
- Fisher nuts
- Flavor Ripe specialty food products
- Flee Bags travel bags
- Flygon electrical barbecue equipment
- Fortsmith Folding tables and chairs
- Food Producers International (FPI) specialty foods
- Franprix food distribution
- Gambils food products
- Gebhardt Mexican foods
- GFI specialty meats
- Givenchy hosiery
- Gladiola food products
- Gold Medal beverages
- Good & Plenty
- Gourmet ice cream
- Grandmother Joshua specialty products
- Great Bear bottle water
- Grove Crest beverage mixes
- Guangmei snack foods
- Guasti wine products
- G & W pizzas
- Halston Orlane fragrances and skin care products
- Handee Ram Rod plumbing supplies
- Handiform closet accessories
- Happy Daz school and religious apparel
- Harmon Kardon high-fidelity components
- Hart skis
- Hawaii's Own fruit drinks
- Heckman furniture
- Holiday Homes mobile homes
- Holland dairy products
- Holanda ice cream and ice cream stores
- M.J. Holloway's candy
- Homemaker leisure and household products
- Hotel Bar butter
- Hot Foot leisure and household products
- Hunt's
- Indiana moulding and frame-furniture
- Irwinware bar accessories
- Jacobsen mobile homes
- Jacks snack foods
- Jax furniture accessories
- Jetstream garden equipment
- Jhirmack hair care products
- John Hancock outdoor furniture
- Johnston's yogurt
- Jolly Rancher
- Jubilee specialty food products
- Kalise ice cream
- Keller's butter and eggs
- KeyKo condiments
- Kleen Stream plumbing products
- Kneip specialty meats
- Kobey's
- Krispy Kreme
- La Choy
- Lady Betty condiments
- La Menorquina ice cream
- Lambrecht pizza
- Lara Lynn food products
- Latums baked goods
- Liberty condiments
- Light 'n' Fresh baked goods
- Lignoflex food products
- Liken interior design
- Little Brownie cookies and baked goods
- Little Pete plumbing supplies
- Longhorn food products
- Long Life aseptic dairy
- Loomcrafted interior design products
- Lords candy
- Louis Sherry ice cream, frozen deserts
- Lowrey's specialty meats

- Luxuria leisure and household products
- Ma Brown jams, jellies, pickles
- Magnolia bathroom accessories
- Manhattan mobile homes
- Marionette condiments
- Mario olives
- Mark Force Vatco travel accessories
- Martha White
- Max Factor cosmetics
- Max H. Kahn curtains
- Meadow Gold
- Melnor garden equipment
- Migros food distribution
- Milk Duds
- Mills wine products
- Molly Bushell confections
- Monticello sport shirts
- Monzini collection sport shirts
- Moorewear school and religious apparel
- Morgan Yacht Company
- Mother's Best food products
- Mountain High yogurt
- Mt. Ida olives
- Mug Old Fashioned Root Beer
- Murray's food products
- Nat Nast sportswear
- New Yorker mobile homes
- N-Rich non-dairy creamer
- Now and Later
- Nuttall's confections
- Olive Products condiments
- Olympian sportswear
- Omega travel bags
- Optima & Wonderloom school and religious apparel
- Orville Redenbacher's
- Ovenmates household goods
- Ozarka Spring Water Company
- Palmeto baked goods
- Pan Free beverage mixes
- Payco ice cream and novelties
- Patra fruit juices and drinks
- Pauly natural cheese

- Pepi's meat specialty products
- Pernigotti confections and snack foods
- Peter Pan
- Phoenix candy
- Pico Grande wine products
- Pik-Nik
- Pitegoff painting supplies
- Playtex
- Plum De Veal veal products
- Premier is ice cream
- Princess House closet accessories
- Pyramid modular homes
- Rainbo food products
- Rainwave garden equipment
- Reasor modular homes
- Reber food products
- Record food distribution
- Red Tulip candy
- Reddi wip whipped cream
- R.F. specialty meats
- Richardson candy
- Rid-O-Ray electrical barbecue equipment
- Robert's cookies
- Rosarita
- Round the Clock hosiery
- Royal Crest yogurt
- Rusty Jones
- Samsonite patio furniture, hand and soft side luggage
- Sanson ice cream
- Savoy confections and biscuits
- Sexton Foods
- Shedd's
- Smith Kendon Confections
- Stew Starter/Soup Starter
- Stiffel Lamps
- Stute jams and fruit juices
- Swift Ice Cream
- Swift meats
- Swiss Miss
- Switzer licorice
- Tayto snack foods
- Thermicold storage
- Treasure Cave blue cheese
- Tropicana
- Van Camp confections
- Viva low fat milk and cottage

- cheese
- Waterloo Industries tool boxes and chests
- Webcraft specialty printing and paper products
- Wesson
- Wilson specialty meats
- World Dryer hand dryers

This story is largely based on the fascinating book *Beatrice: From Buildup Through Breakup*, by Neil Gazel (1990).

Originally published on AmericanBusinessHistory.org on March 19, 2021.

Chapter 16
Uneeda Business History: the Nabisco Story

From its founding in 1898 at the height of the trust era, the National Biscuit Company quickly rose to become the largest of the big branded food companies. By the 1920s the company was far larger than such well-known companies as HJ Heinz, Campbell Soup, Kellogg, Hershey, and Wrigley. Few companies did more to innovate in the modern mass marketing of groceries than "N.B.C." with its famous logo and red triangle. But late in the twentieth century, Nabisco went through no less than seven different ownership structures. Yet, through it all, Oreos, Premium Saltines, Nilla Wafers, and Chips Ahoy not only live on, but are stronger than ever in their history. Here is their story.

Consolidating an Industry

Following in the footsteps of John D. Rockefeller's Standard Oil Trust, the late 1890s were the heyday of industry consolidations. In virtually every industry from thread to tin cans, Wall Street financiers and lawyers worked to create new companies that would dominate, if not monopolize, their industries. The idea was to buy up enough competitors to get control over pricing and end ruinous price wars. Hundreds of such trusts were set up. Many, perhaps most, failed when some firm outside the trust realized the profits to be made by "busting" the cartel, through lower prices, better products, or other innovations. Nevertheless, the organizers sometimes made millions by floating new stock issues in the big new companies.

In this context, a group of biscuit and cracker bakers came to the Chicago law office of Adolphus W. "AW" Green in 1890. They needed help "consolidating" their industry.

Green was a most unusual fellow. Born in 1843, AW was the last of eleven children of a Boston Irish family. His father died and his mother took in boarders to make ends meet. Despite the family's hardships, AW's mother was able to put all her children through school. None stood out as much as AW. Like his mother, he loved books and read continually. She also inspired in AW a love of literature, the arts, and the classics. The bright, serious boy made it into the prestigious Boston Latin School, then graduated from Harvard at the age of twenty, in the top quarter of his class. Off he went to find his fame and fortune in New York City, hoping to become a lawyer. At the time, many young men became lawyers by clerking at a law firm rather than attending law school.

But first AW Green went to work at the Mercantile Library of New York City, a private library funded by the city's wealthy business leaders as a source of knowledge for their employees. Surrounded by his beloved books, with time to visit museums and attend the theater, Green was soon made head librarian. In 1868, the contacts he made at the library led the twenty-five-year-old Green to a job as clerk for a top law firm. Green worked hard and studied hard. He learned from the top attorneys in the nation, and easily passed the bar by the time he was thirty.

Desiring to start his own law practice, AW Green followed Horace Greeley's advice, "Go West, young man." In 1873 he arrived in Chicago, the great American boom town of the era. Following the great fire of 1871, the city was rebuilding, open to new ideas and new faces. But it was still a rough, dirty city, and Green was at first repulsed, missing the high culture of New York that Chicago had little use for. Yet Green prospered, adding young partners to his law firm. He began to work for some of the most powerful business leaders in Chicago. His reputation as a top business lawyer spread. In 1879 he married, and over time had eight children.

It was into Green's successful law office that the biscuit and cracker bakers came. They wanted his help in forming a trust, a combination that would bring together many bakers, allow them to get stock in the new company, and lessen competition. As he did throughout his life, AW Green studied everything he could about the biscuit and cracker industry. He soon became an expert on the business.

AW found that every city of any size had one or two cracker bakeries. Using old-fashioned, labor-intensive production methods, these local bakeries delivered wooden barrels and boxes of crackers to stores in horse-drawn wagons. The industry's first product had been "hardtack" or "pilot biscuits." These hard, almost indestructible, long-lasting biscuits had proven key to the sustenance of sailors and soldiers far away from the kitchens of home. Over time, the bakers added various cookies and crackers to their product lines. Most of them had well-known local brands, usually sold only within several miles of the bakeries. (Bread bakeries were – and are – a separate industry, producing a perishable product with a much shorter shelf life and therefor even smaller trading areas.)

The cracker barrel had become the symbol of the country general store. Old-timers sat around the barrels sharing the town gossip. But the person who bought the last crackers, at the bottom of the barrel, often found soggy crackers, insects, and rodent droppings there. According to legend, when one store owner was accused of having rats in his cracker barrel, he replied, "That's impossible, because the cat sleeps there."

Green saw that the industry was falling behind in an era of continuous new inventions. The railroads together with the rise of mass magazines led to a national market for products. Procter & Gamble had launched its first great brand, Ivory Soap, in 1879. Coca-Cola, Heinz, and other national brands were developing fast. Grocery store chains, led by the Great Atlantic and Pacific Tea Company, were rising as well. AW did not believe that the old industry structure of small bakeries around the nation could survive the changing world without consolidating.

So in 1890, the forty-seven-year-old Green helped this group of bakers incorporate the American Biscuit and Manufacturing Company. ("Biscuit," the British term, was considered classier than crackers.) Among the forty bakeries in thirteen states included in the combine were Dozier of St. Louis, Sommer-Richardson of St. Joseph, Missouri, (with its well-known Saltines), the Loose brothers of Kansas City, and Langeles of New Orleans. The largest was Bremner of Chicago, with eight ovens. The new company was the largest cracker baker in "the West."

Despite his newfound cracker baking expertise, Green wanted to continue to practice law, and had little interest in running a cracker trust. He helped other local cracker bakers form smaller combinations.

At the same time, the opportunities in the industry attracted the attention of another Chicago lawyer, William H. Moore, five years younger than Green. But unlike Green, Moore was more interested in building businesses and making investments than practicing law. He had become one of the top trust creators in America, over time helping create the Diamond Match Company, the American Can Company, and steel combines that ultimately formed part of US Steel.

Working with the largest cracker bakers in "the East," Moore in that same 1890 created an even larger Biscuit trust, the New York Biscuit Company. The company was backed by top Chicago investors including Philip Armour of meatpacking fame, railway car builder George Pullman, merchant Marshall Field, and Abraham Lincoln's son Robert. Bringing together eight companies with twenty-three bakeries in ten states from Maryland to Maine, this company with almost one-hundred-and-forty ovens was now the biggest in the nation. Soon after its founding, the biggest baker in the nation, Kennedy of Cambridgeport, Massachusetts, joined the New York Biscuit Company. The Kennedy firm also had a major plant in Chicago, in the heart of American Biscuit's territory.

In 1897, troubles at the Diamond Match Company led William Moore to resign his leadership position with New York Biscuit.

War and Peace

These two "industry giants," American and New York,

battled each other for the next several years after their 1890 foundings. They expanded in each other's territories, American building a large bakery in the heart of New York City. Price competition was intense and neither company was satisfied.

After unsuccessful attempts at a cease fire or merger, the two companies finally agreed to combine, creating an even larger cracker trust, the National Biscuit Company, in 1898. The National Biscuit Company, known as "N.B.C.," incorporated yet a third cracker group, the United Baking Company. The massive new trust controlled over half of the cracker and cookie business in America, with 114 bakeries and over 400 ovens, producing 360 million pounds of crackers a year.

The promoters, including Green, received $6 million in new stock, with Moore and his brother getting about $4 million of that. But the Moore's were out of the management picture, and the new board, made up of bakers, asked Green to be the President of N.B.C. He had no interest in running the company, preferring his law practice, and turned down the offer. Yet he agreed to chair the Board of Directors and serve as General Counsel.

Green's N.B.C.

Nevertheless, AW Green could not keep his eyes (or his hands) off the National Biscuit Company. Soon enough, he was running the show – and that is a great understatement. At the age of fifty-five, when many men of the era might have retired, Adolphus Green began a new career, while still running his law firm.

With no hobbies outside his family, his books, and his love of high culture, the somber, tightly wound Green ran the company with an iron hand.

AW Green was hell-bent on making N.B.C. a success. Deeply understanding both the cracker industry and the changes sweeping the nation, he insisted the company develop a brand name and a product which it could ship anywhere in the nation, a product that would not go stale too soon and could be shipped long distances. Soon after the company was founded, he focused on the soda cracker, the biggest seller.

AW left no stone unturned as he sought his ideal product. The design had to be right, the recipe had to be perfect, it had to be packaged and sanitary, not sold by the barrel, and it needed a great name. Working with the nation's first great advertising agency, N.W. Ayer, he picked the name "Uneeda Biscuit."

AW never delegated much authority, making every detailed decision himself. He told the bakeries how to make the product, he made up manuals for selling the new crackers. He approved every label, every font, every capital letter on the package. His people developed the revolutionary "In-er-Seal" package which kept the crackers fresh, inventing new machines to make and fill the packages.

Green decided to avoid the traditional method of distributing grocery products through wholesalers. He instead created agencies across America, with their own horse-drawn, highly decorated wagons, delivering the N.B.C. products directly to retailers.

Against all advice, Green kept the price of the crackers low, a nickel a package. His bakers told him he would lose money at that price, but he was immovable.

Working with ad agency Ayer, Green developed a character for his products, a boy in a yellow rain slicker, indicating that N.B.C.'s crackers stayed dry even in damp weather.

In coming up with a trademark and logo for the company, Green studied his books and discovered an old Venetian printer's mark that he liked, an oval with a double cross above it. This became the N.B.C. symbol, on every package. (We at the American Business History Center have noted that most great business creators were perfectionists, but we have not studied anyone more obsessed with details than Adolphus W. Green).

Before the end of N.B.C.'s first year in business, Uneeda Biscuits hit the market in their new, carefully-designed packages. Green spent more money in advertising the product than had ever been seen in the cracker business — $7 million in the first ten years. He plastered cities and countryside with signs and ads.

Green tolerated no mistakes. "Uneeda Cadets" were sent out into the field to buy up any old Uneeda Biscuits that were no longer fresh. The company, led by an attorney, sued competitor after competitor to stop the use of such names as "I-Wanna" and "Uwanna" Biscuits.

By 1900, *Americans were buying ten million packages of Uneeda Biscuits a month*. People wrote songs and poems about the crackers, and they were seen in numerous movies as the symbol of the good American life, available to all. The company was making over $3 million in annual profits on sales of $35 million, one of the few highly successful trusts. Green drove the company harder and harder, building the biggest cracker bakery in the world on West Fifteenth Street in Manhattan. He took steps to make the bakeries better places to work, adding benefits and even stock purchase programs for his employees. He continually toured the company's agencies and bakeries in his private railroad car.

But if an executive put their feet on their desk, wore a loud tie, or forgot to wear their suit jacket at all times, they could be fired on the spot. Perhaps no one really liked AW Green except for his family and his stockholders.

AW had few friends and lost others, but he did not seem to care. The bakers in the trust had expected to continue to run their bakeries independently, with their own brands, still sold in boxes and barrels. Seeing their independence disappear, some of the bakers left the trust to form competing companies. Most prominent among the departures were the Loose brothers of Kansas City, who in 1902 formed Loose-Wiles Biscuit Company, which became N.B.C.'s distant second-place competitor. (Loose-Wiles was renamed Sunshine Biscuit in 1946.)

In 1906, Green moved the company's headquarters from Chicago to New York, to be near the financial markets and the company's giant New York City bakery, which employed about 6,000 workers.

In 1912, four years after competitor Loose-Wiles had introduced the "Hydrox" sandwich cookie, N.B.C. introduced its clone, named "Oreo." Green may have picked the name based on an ancient Greek word for hill. Despite Green's best efforts, the company still made hundreds of different products, many still sold in bulk rather than neat packages. But when he saw a product worth packaging and promoting nationally, as he did with Oreos, Barnum's Animal Crackers, and Fig Newtons, he pursued it.

Adolphus W. Green effectively ran N.B.C. until the day he died, in 1917, at the age of seventy-four. At the time, his company was by a substantial margin the biggest food company in America after the giant meatpackers Swift and Armour, and the largest company dedicated to branded food rather than bulk food. Dividends had been paid stockholders year-in and year-out.

Phase Two

Upon Green's death, the top job at N.B.C. passed to one of his young lawyers, Roy Tomlinson, continuing a tradition of legal leadership. For the next twenty-eight years, until 1945, Tomlinson ran the company.

Interestingly, despite losing control early on, William H. Moore had never lost interest in the company. He and his two sons served on the Board of N.B.C., helping Tomlinson lead the company. Moore's grandson later became a key company executive.

While easier going and more relaxed than Green, Tomlinson was still aloof. But he had inherited a great, profitable company and kept it rolling along. Despite a reputation of becoming fat, lazy, and stodgy during this era, N.B.C. made some major moves.

Continuing their emphasis on advertising, when radio came along in the 1920s, N.B.C. was among the first to sponsor national radio programs. Advertising on the dominant National Broadcasting Company, the use of "N.B.C." became confusing. The National Biscuit Company then began to refer to itself as "Nabisco," previously only used as a brand on sugar wafers.

Another intriguing character enters the picture here. Henry Perky was like Green an attorney, born in the same year, 1843. He became obsessed with health food, studying the breakfast cereal giants Kellogg and Post of Battle Creek, Michigan. After many various and unsuccessful jobs, in 1895 he patented a process for shredding wheat grains into a breakfast food. By 1901, his Shredded Wheat was a huge seller, and he built a $2 million showcase factory next to Niagara Falls in New York State. Over 100,000 people a year toured the immaculate, spectacularly lit Shredded Wheat factory. Perky later sold out his interest, and in 1928 Nabisco bought the Shredded Wheat Company for $35 million in Nabisco stock. Nabisco also bought the maker of Milkbone dog biscuits.

As profitable and big as Nabisco was, the 1920s saw another rush of industrial combinations and mergers. In the food industry, Post's daughter Marjorie Post and her husband E.F. Hutton created General Foods out of Postum cereal, Maxwell House Coffee, Birdseye frozen foods, and other brands. Cincinnati's yeast kings, the Fleischmanns, merged their yeast company with Royal Baking Powder to form Standard Brands. Standard Brands acquired Chase & Sanborn Coffee, going head-to-head with General Foods. By the 1950s, both companies were bigger than Nabisco, though Nabisco was still larger than Heinz, Kellogg, and other big names in the branded food industry.

The Great Depression hit Nabisco hard, but the dividends kept flowing and most of the 20,000 workers took pay cuts but kept their jobs.

In 1934, the company introduced the distinctive tasting "Ritz" cracker as a premium product, but a treat anyone could afford. Five million were baked in the first year. Within three years, 29 million Ritz crackers were baked each day, making it the world's best-selling cracker.

In the 1930s, Nabisco also developed the "NAB" line of small packages for use in the newly popular vending machines. Cheese peanut butter crackers and other items were soon found in hundreds of thousands of vending machines in bars, gas stations, offices, and factories across the land.

Throughout his twenty-eight-year reign, Tomlinson kept the dividends flowing but invested little in the bakeries or new technologies. Corporate policy was to do things because "That is the way we have always done them."

Nabisco used two-story "reel" ovens, which used a Ferris-wheel like system to bake the products as the wheel rotated the goods down into an oven on the floor below. In the meanwhile, other bakers had moved to "band" ovens which moved the products in a continuous line, up to 300 feet long, and was more efficient and faster than the old reel ovens. By 1945, half of the ovens at Loose-Wiles/Sunshine were band ovens, but Nabisco had very few. They would not fit into Nabisco's old, multi-story urban bakeries. But why change? The company still made money. And it had never borrowed a penny, making it one of the most conservatively financed big companies in the nation.

Wall Street analysts and reporters grumbled about the company being stodgy and asleep. Until Nabisco found a new leader.

Phase Three

In 1945, upon Tomlinson's retirement, Nabisco predictably chose another lawyer, George Coppers, to be the next President. Despite having worked decades for the company, Coppers had new ideas. Over the next twelve years, Nabisco spent tens of millions building new, one-story bakeries using band ovens. The largest one was at Fair Lawn, New Jersey.

Unlike his two predecessors, Coppers listened to his colleagues and applied their suggestions. His door was always open. But he had no patience for doing things just because "They had always done them that way." Most of Tomlinson's management team retried or was fired, replaced by younger, more energetic leaders.

Coppers also led the company into a major international expansion, especially successful in Europe. He presided over the company until 1960. His successor, Lee Bickmore, was the first salesman to run Nabisco.

By 1965, Nabisco was generating annual profits of $38 million on revenues of $627 million. While National Dairy Products (later renamed Kraft), General Foods, Borden, Standard Brands, Ralston Purina, and Beatrice Foods were larger in revenues, Nabisco made more profit as a percent of sales than any of them. Only the phenomenally profitable Campbell Soup had a higher profit rate.

In 1966, Nabisco introduced Chips Ahoy!, which went on to great success.

When Bickmore retired in 1972, Nabisco had become a billion-dollar company.

The Merry-Go-Round

For eighty-three years, Nabisco had been a strong, independent, highly focused company with little diversification beyond its core crackers and cookies. It dominated the industry, far larger than Sunshine or the third-place company, United Biscuit, which was renamed Keebler in 1966.

But, in 1981, leadership made the big decision to merge with the slightly larger Standard Brands, now a very diversified food company, including Planter's Peanuts and Baby Ruth candy bars. Standard Brands had a younger, more aggressive management, and generated $3 billion a year in sales. Nabisco was slightly smaller, doing $2.5 billion. Nabisco's superior direct-to-store delivery system was paired with Standard Brands' big product line. Nabisco shareholders owned slightly over half of the combined company, Standard Brands slightly less than 50%. Nabisco's chief was named CEO of the combined company. Standard Brands' CEO Ross Johnson was given the number two spot, Chief Operating Officer, of the new company, now called Nabisco Brands.

Later in 1981, the new company also bought Life Savers for $250 million.

Only four years later, in 1985, tobacco company R.J. Reynolds, looking to diversify beyond cigarettes, bought Nabisco Brands for $4.9 billion. At the time, Nabisco Brands was making profits of over $300 million a year on revenues exceeding $6 billion. The ambitious Ross Johnson was made CEO of the even bigger new combine, RJR Nabisco.

Johnson was "flashy," wearing gold chains and building an "air force" of ten corporate aircraft. But the great brands of Nabisco kept turning out the profits. The company attracted the attention of corporate buyout experts KKR, who took the company private for $24.9 billion in 1988, in the biggest leveraged buyout in American history up through that time.

Johnson at first fought the deal but left with a $50 million severance package. Nabisco was not listed on the stock exchange for the first time in over eighty years. The battle for control of RJR Nabisco was so intense that two books, *True Greed* and *Barbarians at the Gate*, were written about it. Bestseller *Barbarians at the Gate* went on to be made into a tv movie starring James Garner as Ross Johnson.

But the thrill-ride of changing owners was not over for Oreos and Ritz crackers. The private company, saddled with billions of dollars of debt due to the leveraged buyout, struggled. In 1999, KKR took the company public again and got out of the deal, taking a huge loss. The tobacco business was separated and the company was again primarily a food company, keeping the brands of Nabisco and Standard Brands.

This company attracted the attention of the biggest tobacco company, Philip Morris (later renamed Altria), which also wanted to diversify away from tobacco. In 2000, Philip Morris bought Nabisco for $14.9 billion. The tobacco company had already bought giants Kraft and General Foods, making it the nation's largest food manufacturer by a huge margin.

Yet Philip Morris, despite its legendary marketing powers demonstrated by the victory of Marlboro cigarettes over Camels and Winstons, found out that, like RJR, smoking and food did not mix. In 2006, they spun out Kraft Foods as a separate, public company. This new Kraft Foods controlled all of the Nabisco brands and bakeries.

With an enormous array of great brand names including Kraft cheese, Oscar Mayer wieners, Jell-O, and Oreos, this company proved too big and complex to prosper. Or at least Wall Street analysts thought it would be more profitable if broken up. In 2012, it was split into two public companies, Kraft Foods taking most of the traditional US brands and Mondelez International taking much of the international business and all the snack items, mainly Nabisco. Since then, Kraft Foods, controlled by the 3G Capital Group of Brazil and Warren Buffett, has struggled. Mondelez has done better.

Today, Oreos, the world's best-selling cookies, generate over $3 billion in annual sales. Nabisco cookies and crackers, along with international brands, represent almost half of Mondelez's $26 billion in annual sales. PepsiCo's Frito-Lay dominates in salty snacks (e.g., Doritos and potato chips) while Nabisco rules in cookies (and still sells a lot of crackers).

And thus, in a relatively short period of 31 years, from 1981 through 2012, Oreos and Ritz have been overseen by seven successive owners and companies.

Lessons?

Without the obsessive Adolphus W. Green, we probably would have never heard of Nabisco. While Uneeda Biscuits faded away with the passage of time, Green's focus on packaging, branding, making pure products, and advertising them live on at Mondelez International.

Too often, great brands have become mere "portfolio" components for big companies which try to do too much, try to promote too many brands. Like Nabisco, they change hands over and over. Yet, even if these brands go through the ownership roller-coaster, some are strong enough to survive and even prosper.

This helps us understand why great marketing companies keep and nurture powerful brands – for example, Coca-Cola or Procter & Gamble's stewardship of Tide detergent.

Fig Newtons and Premium Saltines could have gone the way of Adams gum, the Gold Dust Twins, Sapolio, Ipana and Pepsodent toothpastes, or other storied brands of the past. But perhaps because of the strong foundation laid by AW Green, or perhaps just because people love the cookies, Nabisco's heart and soul seem to have survived the turbulent seas, floating along and printing money for their owners.

Originally published on AmericanBusinessHistory.org on September 12, 2021.

Chapter 17
Tech Wars: RCA and the Television Industry

From the telegraph to the modern age, high technology has seen continuous innovation, followed by the rise of numerous competitors, then consolidation into fewer companies, and finally decline. Here is one of our favorite stories.

The advent of television rivals the automobile, airplane, telephone, personal computer, and Internet in its impact on the lives of people. Few technologies touch as many people on a daily basis around the globe as much as TV and its descendants cable, satellite, and streaming.

By the 1920s, when radio first rose to prominence, inventors and researchers were already working on radio's natural child, television. Major companies including General

Electric and Westinghouse began to bring together vacuum tube and the other technologies required to make television a reality, but it was the Radio Corporation of America (RCA) that led the way. At the 1939-40 World's Fair in Flushing Meadow, Queens, New York, RCA premiered television, thrilling the millions of visitors to the Fair.

To understand television, we need to first take a glimpse at the evolution of radio.

Radio Wars

RCA itself was born out of efforts to consolidate (monopolize?) the radio industry just after World War I. Engaged in patent battles over the emerging technology of radio, General Electric convinced competitors Westinghouse, American Telephone & Telegraph, and United Fruit (which used ship-to-shore radio on its banana boats) to merge their radio interests into one powerful company which they controlled: RCA. This effort had the support of the US government, particularly the Navy, which wanted to ensure that future radio inventions were American, not controlled by the British Marconi Company which was the "first-mover" in radio. Thus, the British were forced to sell their American operations and related patent rights to the newly formed RCA in 1919.

But RCA soon achieved independence from GE and its other owners under the brilliant leadership of David Sarnoff, a Russian Jewish immigrant who had started with the Marconi Company at the age of fifteen. Under RCA control, Sarnoff created the National Broadcasting Company (NBC), the dominant network in the early years of radio. In order to get music to play on his network, Sarnoff also bought the Victor Talking Machine Company, the leading maker of phonographs and records, with large manufacturing facilities in Camden, New Jersey. When the massive Rockefeller Center mixed-use complex opened in Manhattan, it was in large part "Radio City." The tallest building was named the RCA building, opened in 1933, and the company had its NBC studios in Rockefeller Center at "30 Rock," where they remain today.

In a pattern common to new consumer electrical technologies, radio took off rapidly. The first commercial radio station, Westinghouse's KDKA in Pittsburgh, came on the air in 1920. Within five years, over 600 stations were in operation.

Sales of radio receivers to consumers rose from $50 million in 1923 to $207 million in 1926 and $366 million in 1929 (over $5.5 billion in 2021 dollars). While RCA was a leading maker of those receivers, with a market share of 15-20%, it dominated the more complex manufacture of the tubes and other components, as well as collecting patent royalties from other makers. Again in a typical pattern, there was a "goldrush" into the new technology: over 600 companies assembled and sold radio receivers in the 1920s. Continuing in the normal pattern, there was a shakeout: competition and the Depression wiped out most of the early radio makers like Atwater Kent and Grigsby-Grunow as well as later entrants. Only 18 radio manufacturers and assemblers remained in business by 1934.

In addition to RCA, the largest of those surviving radio makers were Philadelphia's Philco and Chicago's Zenith. Smaller competitors included Motorola (which specialized in car radios) and Crosley.

Television Comes Along

Immediately after its 1939 World's Fair premiere, RCA tried to sell television receivers to the public. But there were few programs to watch and the tiny sets were expensive, so this time the market did not take off. Nevertheless, all those in the radio industry knew that television would succeed sooner or later.

With their experience in radio, Philco and Zenith were quick to follow RCA into the television business. These competitors, along with the second major broadcast network Columbia Broadcasting System (CBS), skirmished with RCA over the technical standards for television, but RCA's system won out when the National Television System Committee (NTSC) adopted the RCA approach.

Then, as the nation converted to war production, the manufacture of television sets was banned by the government in 1941. Technical innovations developed during the war like radar made TV better, but the war put TV on hold.

After adjusting to peacetime production, establishing more TV stations, and developing more programming, television was again ready to roll by the end of the 1940s, beginning in New York City. (If you watch the wonderful 1948 film noir *The Naked City*, shot live in the streets of New York, you will see apartment residents hanging out of their windows, sitting on fire escapes, talking to neighbors. Just a year later, such scenes became nearly impossible to film, as TV drew people indoors.)

In 1948, about 800,000 television receivers were sold. Two years later, 1950 sales were 7.5 million and remained at 5-6 million per year for the next decade. Another goldrush was on. As in radio, RCA made tons of money on the patents flowing out of its large research laboratories and by making the picture tubes and other key components. Radio receiver brands General Electric, Westinghouse, Philco,

Zenith, and Motorola all entered the TV set fray alongside

RCA.

These natural competitors from the radio industry were joined by other brands. One was Fort Wayne, Indiana's Magnavox, a maker of radio speakers and other parts. Another name was DuMont. Inventor Allen DuMont of New Jersey had actually produced the first all-electronic TV in 1938. DuMont made television sets and set up a broadcasting network; both efforts failed and ended in 1956.

An important new name was Admiral, a late entrant into the radio industry and the brainchild of aggressive Chicago entrepreneur Ross Siragusa. The company used plastic cabinets instead of the wood used by other makers, bringing out the 10-inch Consolette TV in 1949 at a price of only $249.95, a hundred dollars less than competitors (but even then, the Consolette cost almost $3000 in 2021 dollars). Admiral Corporation's revenues tripled between 1948 and 1950.

Sears, Roebuck and Montgomery Ward also sold large numbers of TVs made by various manufacturers. Yet another competitor was Sylvania, the maker of lightbulbs and one of the few makers of TV tubes, competing with RCA.

Sears, Ward's, GE, Westinghouse, Philco, and Admiral also offered an array of "white goods" (laundry and kitchen appliances) in addition to "brown goods" (such as televisions, radios, and phonographs). RCA even dabbled in these fields, buying an interest in white goods leader Whirlpool.

The Rise of Color TV

These many companies produced black-and-white television sets throughout the 1950s, with Zenith becoming the largest maker, producing over a million sets a year. At the same time, all realized that color TV would come along sooner or later.

RCA and its labs spent $130 million developing its color system, which narrowly beat out a system proposed by rival CBS. While both color TV's (costing over $1000) and color broadcasting (very rare) had been available since the mid-1950s, color did not take off until the early 1960s. By 1962, a million color sets were in use, generally selling for $6-700 ($5-6000 in 2021 dollars), over three times the price of a black-and-white television.

At first, RCA held as much as 70% of the market for color television sets, but the other producers quickly joined the fray. By 1964, RCA's share fell to 42%, followed by Zenith at 14%. Yet RCA made most of the picture tubes and other components, earning a profit of $35 on each picture tube that it sold to its competitors.

With this history and its outstanding research labs, in the 1960s RCA was the world's largest producer of consumer electronics and the most technologically advanced company in the industry. But the company was not to remain on top.

The Collapse of the American Consumer Electronics Industry

In 1964, US makers produced 94% of the color TVs sold in the United States. In 1975, that percent had dropped to 67% and by 1987, just 17% (vs. Japan's 42% share). Today, the RCA brand is a minimal vestige of its former self.

As business historians, our top question is, how and why did RCA lose its leadership and ultimately disappear from the industry? Were the Japanese companies Sanyo, Sharp,

Sony, and Matsushita (Panasonic) just cheaper than the American makers? Or better?

As it turns out, there was more to the story than just Japanese prices and intelligence. According to eminent business historian Alfred Chandler in his excellent book *Inventing the Electronic Century: The Epic Story of the Consumer Electronics and Computer Industries*, much of the blame lies with the US government and with RCA management itself.

Despite being initially formed with the full backing of the Federal government, RCA's dominance of the industry continually attracted the attention of Federal trustbusters (the Federal Trade Commission and the Anti-trust division of the Justice Department). In 1958, the government forced RCA to offer its patents royalty-free to its American competitors, though foreign companies had to pay full royalties. As is so often the case when legislators and regulators bear no burden or responsibility when things go wrong, there were unintended consequences to this action.

Without the ability to invent new things and profit from them for the life of a patent, RCA had little incentive to keep pioneering and innovating in consumer electronics, as it had done for decades. At the same time, to continue the company's important royalty revenue stream, RCA aggressively peddled its technologies to Japanese firms including Sony and Matsushita and to European companies led by Philips of the Netherlands. (Philips bought Magnavox in 1974, giving the company strong US distribution.) The entire American television industry was thus weakened both by fewer new innovations and by more foreign competition.

At the same time, RCA management began to lessen its focus on consumer electronics. In 1968, David Sarnoff's son Robert took over the reins of the company from his father, though David remained a major influence in decision-making. Losing its patent edge over competitors in consumer electronics, RCA pursued two initiatives: (1) to take on IBM in the mainframe computer business; and (2) to become a "conglomerate."

The conglomerate idea was all the rage on Wall Street in the 1960s. Promoted by investment bankers who profit most when companies are bought and sold, the idea was that any good management team could run any kind of business and that operating totally unrelated businesses enabled companies to diversify away from the risks of being in only one industry. Litton Industries, Beatrice Foods, International Telephone & Telegraph (ITT), LTV, Gulf & Western, and many others became giant conglomerates, buying up everything from hotel chains to insurance and typewriter companies. In RCA's case, the company bought a carpet maker, car rental leader Hertz, the makers of Banquet frozen dinners, and top American book publisher Random House, among others. The Radio Corporation of America had no expertise in any of these fields.

Neither of these strategies worked. RCA's 601 mainframe alone cost $100 million to develop but only sold four units. After such huge losses, RCA sold its computer business to rival UNIVAC.

The conglomerate concept ultimately proved unsound. When the conglomerate builders retired or died, their successors gradually sold off the diverse businesses and returned to focusing on whatever industry had the greatest opportunity or what they were best at. (General Electric belatedly became a conglomerate by rapidly expanding into financial services under CEO Jack Welch and is still recovering from that era of diversification.)

In this context, RCA failed to keep moving ahead in consumer electronics, while the foreign companies kept innovating. The company's efforts to pioneer in tape-based video recording fell behind those of a small company named Ampex. Ultimately, the Japanese Victor Company (JVC), controlled by Matsushita, developed the highly successful VHS system. Initiatives in the laserdisc field were equally unsuccessful against the Japanese. In CDs and DVDs, Philips and Sony led the way.

In this process, the other American makers of consumer electronics were sold out or buried by foreign competitors. Admiral was purchased by Rockwell and Philco by Ford; both new parent companies lost interest in the consumer electronics businesses. Some of the brand names have lived on after being purchased by new companies which saw value in the old brands. For example, one can still buy Westinghouse televisions online, though that great company is now long gone and split into many pieces. Selected niche American companies, as in high fidelity audio systems, live on. (Apple's "designed in California, made in Asia" approach is a very different, unique story.)

Ironically, in 1986, RCA was purchased by its founding parent General Electric for $6.3 billion, without the government stopping the deal. GE kept the gem of the company, NBC, but by 1988 had sold off its television and consumer electronics businesses to the French Thomson company (also ironically descended from Boston's Thomson-Houston, a forerunner of GE). Thomson later parted with these operations and brands. The historically strong RCA Victor record business was sold to the German Bertelsmann empire. The RCA building in Rockefeller Center became the GE building, and is now the Comcast building (current owner of NBC).

And thus, RCA's glorious history of innovation, changing the lives of millions, came to an ignominious end. Yet consumer electronics marches on, in the hands of such current leaders as Apple, Samsung, LG, and Huawei. But given the ever-evolving nature of technology, how long will these companies stay on top?

Before Zoom: The Author, Seated Left, Defers to Big Sister Alice on TV Choices, 1956, While Awaiting Arrival of the Personal Computer and the Internet

Chapter 18

Gone with the Wind: Amazon Spends $8.45 Billion but Doesn't Get the Best of M-G-M

In order to bolster their Amazon Prime Video streaming service, Amazon is buying the legendary M-G-M, probably the most famous of the great movie studios, for $8.45 billion. This will be the second biggest acquisition in Amazon's history, exceeded only by its $13.7 billion 2017 purchase of Whole Foods Market. Metro-Goldwyn-Mayer, with its roaring lion logo, produced such blockbusters as Gone with the Wind, the Wizard of Oz, and Ben-Hur. Yet Amazon will get none of those films from the studio's glory days, as detailed in this brief version of M-G-M's convoluted history.

Beginnings

Our story begins with New Yorker Marcus Loew, who has made money from a life in the fur business. Known as an easy, amicable fellow, he begins to invest in income-producing real estate such as apartments. Loew with his neighbor and lifelong friend, fellow fur maker Adolph Zukor, then begins to put penny arcades into vacant spaces in New York City. Later they start showing 5-10-minute films in nickelodeons. The two men merge their entertainment businesses and grow wealthier from them. Zukor's daughter later marries Loew's son.

Zukor watches audiences' reactions to films closely and decides that they might sit still for a long movie – say 20 minutes – if it had a good story. He sells out his interest in their partnership to Loew and goes into movie production in 1912. Largely through his efforts, feature length movies come about, against strong opposition from those making money off short films, including Thomas Edison. Zukor's movie production and distribution company evolves into Paramount Pictures, which he controls. Marcus Loew, on the other hand, likes the theater ("exhibition") business and builds large movie houses around New York City. Zukor owns no theaters.

Back in 1906, Marcus Loew had brought two brothers into his company. Nicholas "Nick" and Joseph Schenck emigrated from Russia when they were young and ended up powerful forces in the film industry. After delivering newspapers and other odd jobs, the brothers get a beer concession at the Fort George amusement park on a high point in upper Manhattan. With the profits, they add rides and amusements there, where Marcus Loew is a frequent customer. The two later build Palisades Amusement Park across the Hudson River in Fort Lee, New Jersey. Nick Schenck becomes Marcus Loew's right-hand man in the operation of his theater circuit.

As we swing into the post-war boom and the beginning of the roaring twenties, the motion picture industry becomes big business. Producers fight to get their pictures into the top theaters in the biggest cities and the theater owners fight over which pictures they get first. Adolph Zukor realizes he needs to control his own cinemas, so he goes on a buying and building spree. Marcus Loew wants to ensure he has a steady flow of films for his theaters. He decides to put together a movie production company. The two old friends move into each other's turfs.

The Creation of Metro-Goldwyn-Mayer

Marcus Loew first plans to buy two smaller film companies. The first is Metro Pictures, a producer and distributor of pictures. (Film distribution companies decide which films go to which theaters, pay for all advertising and printing the films, and usually receive 25-35% of the box office receipts on top of the advertising costs.) Metro's future does not look good in 1920, when Loew makes his move, eight years after Zukor has entered the movie production side of the business.

The other firm Loew pursues, four years later, is Goldwyn Pictures in 1924. The eight-year-old studio has been created by Samuel Goldfish, Broadway producers the Selwyn brothers, and a few friends. Its name comes from the combination of Goldfish and Selwyn. The company's logo is a roaring lion, which the new company keeps. Goldfish runs the studio and has high quality standards but cannot afford major stars; the company struggles. Goldwyn

Pictures has gone public, but in 1923 the stock drops about 60%. Marcus Loew has found a bargain. Samuel Goldfish by then has legally changed his name to Samuel Goldwyn, and soon leaves the company to produce movies on his own.

As Loew is creating Metro-Goldwyn, he comes to believe he needs someone stronger to run the total operation. He picks former Boston area theater owner Louis B. Mayer, a former producer at Metro who has left to make pictures on his own. Also joining our story is Irving Thalberg, who at age twenty-one has run production for the smaller Universal Pictures studio. In 1923, Mayer hires this "boy wonder" of Hollywood, then twenty-three-years-old.

These operations, wholly owned by Loew's, Inc., are merged into Metro-Goldwyn in 1924 and renamed Metro-Goldwyn-Mayer in 1925.

Marcus Loew and Louis B. Mayer make a great pair. Loew stays out of the spotlight and remains in New York, running the company. Louis B. Mayer runs things with an iron hand in Hollywood. He is happy to be the public face, frequently out with stars and starlets for the photographers. While Mayer ultimately goes on to much greater fame than Marcus Loew, the two are in continual communication and Loew calls all the financial and budget shots.

Loew takes good care of Mayer and his associates. Loew's pays Mayer $1500 per week, Thalberg $650, and their associate Robert Rubin $600. Within a year, Mayer's salary is increased 67% and the twenty-five-year-old Thalberg's pay is tripled (equivalent to annual salaries in 2021 dollars of $2 million and $1.5 million, respectively). In addition, the three get twenty percent of any profits their pictures make, with Mayer receiving over half of that profit pool.

But only two years later, in 1927, Marcus Loew dies at the

age of fifty-seven. Nick Schenck is now the head of Loew's, Inc.

The Glory Years

Nick Schenck and Louis B. Mayer form the oddest of partnerships. They apparently strongly dislike each other, but nevertheless make a lot of money and some great movies while in partnership. Mayer has to take orders from Schenck in New York but in Hollywood he is seen as a star-maker. Behind his back, Mayer refers to Nick Schenck as "Mr. Skunk."

As the 1920s progress, Schenck's M-G-M and Zukor's Paramount are the largest studios in the nation and own hundreds of theaters. M-G-M promotes itself as "having more stars than heaven," including Ramon Novarro, Buster Keaton, John Gilbert, Norma Shearer, Greta Garbo, Joan Crawford, and Lon Chaney. Top directors included King Vidor, Marshall Neilan, and Erich von Stroheim. With additional talent in set and costume design, the studio employs 4500 people.

Two other firms of the era are worth mentioning because they show up later in our story.

In 1919, a group of superstars create their own movie production company in order to escape the grasp of the industry giants and have more artistic freedom. Mary Pickford, her husband Douglas Fairbanks, Charlie Chaplin, and pioneering director DW Griffith form United Artists. Nick Schenck's brother Joe joins that organization as President. The upstart company makes good profits as long as Pickford and Fairbanks are active but goes into decline after World War II.

Another smaller studio was that of the four Warner

brothers. Their studio leaps into the big time when it, along with William Fox's studio, led the way into sound "talkies." Warner Brothers leads the way in 1927 with The Jazz Singer starring Al Jolson. (Both M-G-M and Paramount add sound cautiously, in part because of the cost of re-equipping their larger theater chains with new projection and sound equipment.)

The twenties were also the time of the rise of the great picture palaces across America, palatial venues for watching movies. Paramount, Loew's, Fox, and Warners all participate in building these massive beauties.

In 1929, competitor William Fox, enriched by his early move into sound film, buys control of Loew's (and thus M-G-M) from Marcus Loew's family and Nick Schenck, who gets a multi-million dollar bonus for engineering the deal. But Mayer and his Hollywood team are outraged, only learning of the pending merger when it is announced in the newspapers. When the stock market crashes (and Fox is critically injured in a car wreck), the deal falls through, but the relationship between Schenck in New York and Mayer in Hollywood is further strained.

When the Great Depression hits, movie attendance takes a sharp decline. Ticket prices drop. Foreign bookings, always important to the industry, dry up (and even more so during wars). Adolph Zukor has built his empire with debt and complex stock deals: Paramount collapses into bankruptcy, Zukor losing control.

Following the conservative financial management tradition of Marcus Loew, M-G-M remains profitable and survives under Nick Schenck and his Hollywood team. Despite Thalberg's early death at thirty-seven in 1936, M-G-M produces a string of classic movies, most famously both the Wizard of Oz and Gone with the Wind in 1939. Gone with the Wind, one of the most expensive films produced to date, is a huge blockbuster. The movie's cumulative ticket sales through 2021 (If adjusted for inflation) total over a billion dollars, ranking it as the biggest box office success in history.

The movie industry's top players generate these revenues in 1938 from production, distribution, and exhibition (theaters):

Loew's	$108.9 MM
Warner Bros.	$102.2 MM
Paramount	$100.9 MM
20th Century-Fox	$ 58.2 MM
RKO	$ 56.3 MM
Columbia	$ 20.1 MM
Universal	$ 18.6 MM
United Artists	$ 11.7 MM

For Loew's and M-G-M's leaders, the cash keeps flowing. In 1937, the three highest-paid executives in any company in America are reportedly Louis B. Mayer at $1.2 million, Rubin at $750 thousand, and Nick Schenck at $540 thousand (in 2021 dollars, equal to about $22 million, $14 million, and $10 million).

The Decline

In 1948, the federal government determines that these companies are "too powerful" and forces them to separate their production businesses from their theater chains. Paramount has the largest chain, over one thousand movie theaters. Paramount lawyer Leonard Goldenson takes over the new company that owns the Paramount theaters and

uses their cash flow to buy the ailing ABC TV network,
turning it into a major competitor to industry pioneers NBC
and CBS. Ultimately ABC leaves the theater business and is
acquired by the Walt Disney Company.

Loew's smaller theater chain also becomes an independent
company, separate from M-G-M. Control of the Loew's
theaters is bought by New York's Tisch brothers in 1959.
They proceed to leave the theater business and turn Loew's
into a conglomerate of diverse businesses, today a $13
billion (revenues) company focused on energy, finance, and
hotels.

Worse than the loss of profits from their theaters, the
movie studios have to deal with a new phenomenon in the
late 1940s and early 1950s: television. The future looks
bleak for the movie industry; stock prices drop. The
companies try to woo customers back to theaters with
expensive blockbusters, but most do not sell enough tickets
to cover their enormous production costs. M-G-M's 1959
epic Ben-Hur is an exception, raking it in at the box office,
but still not enough to make the company successful.

Louis B. Mayer hangs in there with M-G-M until 1951, when
his conflict with Schenck finally results in the two men
parting ways. Nick Schenck retires from M-G-M in 1957,
having run the company for thirty years. A new guard tries
to revive the company, but its glory days are long past. As
the 1960s and 1970s proceed, Paramount, Fox, Warner
Brothers, Universal, United Artists, and others, including
upstart Walt Disney Productions, fare better.

The Wheeler-Dealer Era

In the following decades, the M-G-M story gets complex
beyond recognition. Hundreds of articles and books have
been written about these dealings, each with their own

drama. Here we only outline the key developments.

As television rises, broadcasters and others begin to see the value in the classic films. The "vault" or libraries of old films begin to be bought and sold for tens of millions of dollars. The buyers reap millions in "syndication" rights for television. Warner Brothers sells off some of their older films in 1956, M-G-M starts licensing or selling films to television stations and networks that same year, and Paramount follows in 1958. M-G-M is offered $10 million for one TV showing of *Gone with the Wind*, but passes on the offer, preferring to make money by showing the movie in theaters every few years. The movie companies also go into the production of television series for the networks, M-G-M producing *Dr. Kildare* and *The Man from U.N.C.L.E.*, among others.

M-G-M's *Dr. Zhivago* is a 1965 success, but hits are few and far between. The major studios of old struggle to achieve consistent profitability. United Artists, still backing independent producers rather than owning a physical studio, achieves success with the James Bond series and other films.

The 1960s and 1970s become the "conglomerate era" on Wall Street, with upstart companies (and some older ones) buying up company after company in unrelated industries. Corporate raiders begin to circle M-G-M. High-flying conglomerate Gulf & Western buys Paramount in 1966 and San Francisco's Transamerica financial company buys United Artists the following year. In 1969, parking lot and funeral home operator Kinney National Services buys Warner Brothers, renaming itself Warner Communications.

In the midst of this, in 1967, heir to and President of the Seagram liquor company Edgar Bronfman acquires control of M-G-M, with help from magazine publisher Time, Inc.

Gone with the Wind: Amazon Spends $8.45 Billion but Doesn't Get the Best of M-G-M

In an effort to turn around the company's declining fortunes, Bronfman and the board of directors choose Louis Polk, Jr., to head M-G-M in 1969. Polk, still in his thirties, has been chief financial officer of General Mills. He brings with him a team of financial analysts and planners, with a goal of "rationalizing" the movie industry. Their efforts are cut short when another big figure arrives on the scene, desiring to own M-G-M.

That figure is none other than a real gambler, Kirk Kerkorian. Kerkorian has made his fortune in the airline business, but then sells it and uses the proceeds to build casinos in Las Vegas. He sees M-G-M as a powerful, well-known brand that he can put to better use. By the end of 1969, Kerkorian replaces Bronfman in control of M-G-M. Kerkorian begins building the biggest casino hotel on the strip, the M-G-M Grand (today named Bally's casino, later succeeded by an even more humongous M-G-M Grand, one of the largest hotels in the world). While M-G-M continues producing films and TV shows, and is profitable, two-thirds of those profits come from the hotel and casino operations. In 1980, Kerkorian splits the company into two publicly held corporations, one with the casinos and the other, Metro-Goldwyn-Mayer Film Company, in the entertainment business.

In 1981, this new M-G-M, under Kerkorian, buys United Artists from Transamerica for $380 million. This transaction contains a bit of irony, given that United Artists was first created to get out from under the thumb of the big studios like M-G-M. The business has become all about owning libraries of films that can be sold or licensed to others. The company now owns large libraries of M-G-M, United Artists (including the James Bond films), and even some Warner Brothers films that United Artists has acquired over the years. In 1982, Kerkorian renames the company MGM/UA Entertainment.

In 1985 and 1986, another towering figure enters our story. Maverick Atlanta cable broadcaster Ted Turner wants more films to show on his Turner Broadcasting networks and stations. Turner buys MGM/UA for $1.5 billion but takes on too much debt to finance the transaction. He sells the UA part back to Kerkorian for $300 million to recoup cash. He also sells off M-G-M's valuable California real estate. When the dust settles, Turner Broadcasting ends up with the M-G-M and Warner Brothers film libraries and Kerkorian keeps the United Artists libraries and the rights to the lion logo, one of the most recognized in the world. Kerkorian's entity emerges with the name MGM/UA Communications Company. But the Wizard of Oz and Gone with the Wind are now owned by Turner.

This new MGM/UA has a few hits including Rain Man, with Dustin Hoffman, but the company is bleeding red ink, over $40 million a year in losses in the late 1980s. Management is a revolving door under Kerkorian, with new executive after new executive trying to turn the company around.

So, in 1990, Kirk Kerkorian sells MGM/UA to Italian Giancarlo Parretti's Pathe Communications for $1.3 billion, a nice profit from the $300 million he had paid four years earlier. Parretti buys the company with funding from giant French bank Credit Lyonnais. But Parretti turns out to be a fraud and a crook, draining MGM/UA of resources. He has also bribed Credit Lyonnais officers in order to get his loans. Parretti ends up in prison and the bank forecloses on the renamed MGM-Pathe in 1992. That year, the company posts a $271 million loss. Credit Lyonnais pumps $2 billion into the company, trying to turn it around, with little luck.

Kirk Kerkorian, always looking for an interesting deal and knowing the company's history, buys MGM back from the French bank for $1.3 billion in 1996 with partners and outside financing. With Kerkorian's support, the company buys several film libraries for over $800 million in 1997 and

1998. As a result, the company, again named Metro-Goldwyn-Mayer, owns the largest film and TV library in the world, despite not owning the classic M-G-M pictures which Ted Turner has purchased.

(The Turner evolution is almost as convoluted as MGM's. In 1996 he sells Turner Broadcasting to Time Warner, the result of a merger between magazine publisher Time, Inc. and diversified entertainment company Warner Communications, owner of Warner Brothers. After an ill-fated merger with AOL, Time Warner is eventually purchased by AT&T, the former Southwestern Bell Telephone Company, in 2016. But that does not work out too well, either, with AT&T announcing it is spinning out those operations and merging them with the Discovery Networks into a new company in 2021. The new company, entitled Warner Brothers Discovery, will continue to own the classic films of both Warner Brothers and Metro-Goldwyn-Mayer.)

Throughout these years, the old film studios continue to change hands. Rupert Murdoch gets control of Fox, Sumner Redstone's Viacom controls Paramount, and Japanese giant Sony gets Columbia Pictures.

In an effort to get more material for their emerging Blu-Ray disc technology, Sony puts together a consortium of investors (and big lenders) to buy MGM and its huge film library from Kerkorian for $1.6 billion in 2004. The company becomes a private corporation once again, with no shares available to the public on the stock market. Despite some successes, especially the continuing James Bond series, revolving leaders fail to make MGM prosper. Failing to find a buyer and beset by enormous debt, the great, historic MGM files for bankruptcy in 2010. It emerges from bankruptcy owned by the creditors and a new group of managers from independent film production company Spyglass Entertainment.

Under the new team's leadership, MGM continues to make new deals and soon becomes profitable again. The company buys a majority stake in the company that produces such TV shows as The Voice, Survivor, The Apprentice, and Shark Tank. Making the most of their library, they sign distribution and licensing deals with others, including Sony.

Which brings us up to 2021, when Amazon agrees to acquire the company for a total of $8.45 billion, including the assumption of debt. While the great films of Mayer and Thalberg are not in the deal, being owned by Warner Brothers Discovery, Amazon gets an enormous library of 4000 movies and 17,000 TV programs. They also get the lion and his roar.

Conclusion

At the American Business History Center, we have studied many companies, but few have had the dizzying complexity of the tumultuous MGM story, even after we've omitted many details and great movie titles. One thing is clear: great art, even in film, has lasting value. While movie theaters, retail chains, big companies, and even tall buildings come and go, classic films from every era retain or increase their value decade after decade. Who knows how much these old films will be valued at in another century?

For the full details on all the events described in this story, see the excellent book *MGM* by Tino Balio (2018).

For a complete history of the movie industry, see the "Videos" section of the American Business History Center website.

Originally published on AmericanBusinessHistory.org on June 5, 2020.

Industry Battles

Chapter 19
Battle of the Giant Watchmakers

Every industry tells a story of competition: the rise and fall of companies. Technological industries often see more "changing of the guard" than more stable businesses like food, soap, and beverages.

One of the first high-tech industries in America was the watch business. This pocket-sized scientific instrument was (and is) one of the wonders of the modern world. The top watchmakers' products were in every pocket or on every wrist for over one hundred years. The great innovators rose to fame, becoming household words. But today the greatest of them are long gone. Here is a quick look at the history of the American watch industry and its leading companies.

In America before the Civil War, watches were for rich people. Primarily imported from England and Switzerland, a decent pocket watch could easily cost $30-40 ($800-1000 in 2020 money; the cost of a high-end smartphone, which has supplanted the watch for many people). Besides, most people did not need a watch: farm life could run on sunrise and sunset alone. "Clock time" was not required for people's lives.

Clock time was also extremely complex, as each city set its time by when the sun was overhead, at high noon. When it was noon in New York City, it was 12:02 in Albany, 11:56 in Philadelphia, and 11:50 in Baltimore.

Needless to say, this made many aspects of life difficult. High among the challenges was catching your train when you connected from one railroad to another. The Pennsylvania Railroad, the nation's largest, ran on Philadelphia time. If you were headed westward, you would change trains in Chicago, where each railroad ran on its own time.

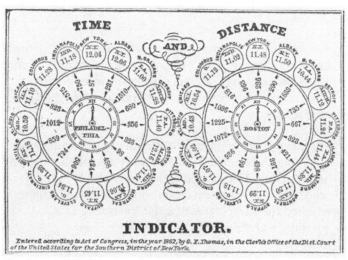

1862 Time in US Cities

The confusion between city times was finally resolved in 1883 when the railroads led the US to adopt standardized time zones.

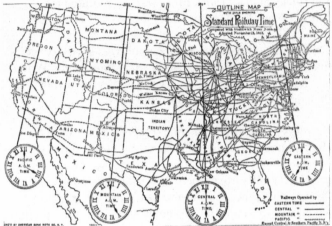

Map of time zones into which the US was divided after the adoption of Standard Time on 18th November 1883. Dated 19th century.

The military needs of the young nation also called for more and better timekeepers. Few soldiers had accurate watches. Thousands may have died in Civil War battles because troop movements could not be coordinated based on precise timing.

Throughout the 19th century, America was becoming more industrial and more urban. No longer did people ride their horse on their own schedule; they increasingly rode scheduled trains and streetcars. Businesses and factories required their employees to arrive "on time." Clock-watching increasingly became a national habit.

These pressures led to the need for more accurate timekeeping devices and for more watches of every quality. Watches were needed by everyone, not just the rich.

Waltham: The First Great American Watch Company

Americans bought high quality English watches as well as Swiss watches, which covered the range from the best to lesser quality watches. These watches consisted of hand-made parts: the core timekeeping "movement," the watch case (sometimes gold), the dial and hands, etc. Often the local jeweler would buy the parts and assemble them to meet the specific needs of each customer. When parts broke, the jeweler or watchmaker would have to make new ones. The whole process was cumbersome, labor-intensive, and thus expensive.

New England was the cradle of American industry. Giant textile plants used the most advanced machinery. The federal arsenal at Springfield, Massachusetts had pioneered interchangeable parts, each precisely machined. The clock-making industry, centered in Connecticut, had gradually replaced handwork with machine-based factories.

In 1833, the twenty-one-year-old Aaron Dennison of Boston had spent three years as a jeweler's apprentice and invented an automatic cutter to automate part of the watchmaking process. Dennison spent the next several years learning about watchmaking and dreaming of mass-producing watches by machine.

Finally, in 1849, Dennison was able to convince Boston clockmakers and investors to put up about $40,000 to try his idea of making watches (at least in part) by machine. While a factory was built in Roxbury, Massachusetts, Dennison went off to England to study watchmaking. In order to achieve his goal of machine-made watches, Dennison and his partners had to invent and make their own machines, including measuring devices that could differentiate distances down to thousandths of an inch.

The Roxbury plant was not big enough, so the factory was moved to Waltham, Massachusetts, a rural town of about 5,000 people. In 1854, production began with ninety workers producing thirty watches a week. The company's first product failed and the company struggled. Dennison was better at inventing than at running a business. By 1857, the company was broke and purchased at auction for $56,000. The new owner, Royal Robbins, then improved the manufacturing process and increased production. Annual Waltham watch production rose from three thousand in 1857 to eleven thousand in 1861. This was perfect timing to help meet the needs of the Civil War. Waltham's "William Ellery" watch sold well at $13 ($400 in 2020 money). Waltham produced over 70,000 watches each year in the mid- and late-1860s. (The company operated under different names before settling on the Waltham Watch Company.)

Over the next twenty-five years, the Waltham Watch Company was a growing, profitable business. The company found ways to organize production and increase their output by tenfold, then by a hundredfold. Their American watches were more durable, more accurate, and less expensive than Swiss or English watches. By 1875, Waltham was making over 100,000 watches each year, employing thousands of workers. The company won awards at the 1876 Philadelphia Centennial Exposition. But by then, another major watch company had risen to compete with Waltham.

Elgin: The Second Great American Watch Company

Former Chicago mayor Benjamin W. Raymond and other Illinois investors were approached by JC Adams of the Waltham Watch Company about starting watch production in the Chicago area. The United States, especially the frontier west, was booming. In 1864, this group founded the National Watch Company. They built a plant on 35 acres of land donated by the nearby city of Elgin, Illinois (population 3-4,000). They hired seven of Waltham's top people, offering them $5,000 a year salary ($95,000 now), a $5,000 signing bonus, and one acre of land to build their homes on. As the company's watches were commonly called "Elgins" or "Elgin-made," the company was ultimately renamed The Elgin Watch Company.

The Elgin Company built extensive factories and began production in 1867. The first watch, the "BW Raymond," sold for $117 ($2200 now). Over time, the main factory in Elgin became the world's largest watch factory. In the early 20th century, the company built an observatory to determine perfect time by the stars and opened a watchmakers' school. Employment reached as high as 4,500 workers.

By 1876, Elgin was producing 100,000 watches a year, matching Waltham's output. That year, Elgin dropped its prices by 30-40%, requiring Waltham to lower its pricing. The two industry giants continued to battle for leadership in a back-and-forth war for the next fifty years. As time passed, the machinery became better and the products more accurate. Precision tolerances fell from thousandths of an inch to ten thousandths of an inch and beyond. With bigger production runs, costs (and prices) fell. (A pattern repeated in almost all advancing technologies like automobiles, computers, and software.)

Waltham and Elgin were not without competition. In 1892, the Hamilton Watch Company of Lancaster, Pennsylvania, was created; this smaller producer was known for its railroad watches and often was ranked third largest. Other makers included the Illinois Watch Company (which made watches for Sears, Roebuck and Montgomery Ward),

Hampden, New Haven, South Bend, and several others. All

were dwarfed by Waltham and Elgin.

Challenges for the Watch Giants

Despite creating badly needed products, always making them better and cheaper, the two huge producers faced numerous and repeated challenges.

In the period between the Civil War and World War II, America faced numerous financial "panics" (recessions or depressions). 1893, 1907, and 1921 were among the worst panics. Since watches were an expensive product, and old ones could be repaired for continued use, watch demand dropped precipitously at these times. Production and employment at Waltham and Elgin fluctuated dramatically. Investment capital for new machines was scarce or expensive.

For example, between 1891 and 1892, Waltham's production dropped from one million watches to 400,000; Elgin fell from 440,000 to 120,000. By 1903, each company was producing a million watches a year, and in 1907 Waltham made two million, a level not reached by Elgin until twenty years later, by which time Waltham had dropped back to 500,000.

Another challenge was the Swiss. They continued to export movements and finished watches to the US. When tariffs were high, the Swiss watches and parts were smuggled in. Having been almost run out of the American market by Waltham and Elgin in the late 19th century, they were back in force by the 1930s.

Yet the biggest challenge to Waltham and Elgin came from another American idea: the Dollar Watch.

Waterbury/Ingersoll: A Third Major Competitor

In 1896, the Waterbury Clock Company (dating from 1854) began manufacturing "dollar watches" for salesman Robert Ingersoll and his brother. Dramatically increasing access to decent watches, these were an immediate success. Eventually morphing into one company, named Ingersoll for a while, then Waterbury Clock, this company was by 1905 producing three million watches a year, toppling Waltham and Elgin in units produced but not in dollar value. The company's slogan became "the watch that made the dollar famous." Other companies also produced dollar watches, including the Western Clock Company under the brand "Westclox."

Ingersoll teetered near bankruptcy in the Great Depression but was saved when they licensed Mickey Mouse from Walt Disney, selling huge numbers of Mickey Mouse watches.

Three Smaller Competitors

Among the dozens of companies making watches, a few others are worthy of mention because of their role in the industry's later history.

Joseph Bulova emigrated from Bohemia to New York and in 1875 started his watch company on Long Island. Bulova made his movements and key parts in Switzerland (in a plant now owned by Rolex). The Bulova Watch Company assembled the finished watches at their US factories. The company was an excellent marketer and may have risen to the number one US position in the 1950s as Waltham and Elgin went into decline.

German immigrant Dietrich Gruen started the Gruen

Watch Company in Cincinnati, Ohio, in 1894. Like Bulova, Gruen made his parts in Switzerland and assembled them in the US. Gruen was famous for innovative, unique watch designs.

The Benrus Watch Company was founded in 1921 by Romanian immigrants, the three Lazrus brothers. The company name was a contraction of BENjamin LazRUS. Starting out as a New York City watch repair shop, Benrus evolved to assembling Swiss-made parts into finished American watches, the same system used by Bulova and Gruen.

These three companies helped improve the Swiss watch industry by sharing American ideas of mass production. They also proved more durable in the mid-20th century than industry pioneers Waltham and Elgin.

Challenges of the New (20th) Century

In addition to Swiss competition, dollar watches, and economic cycles, the new century brought additional challenges.

The first was the wristwatch. Initially seen as too dainty for men, that changed in World War I. Called "strap watches" for men to differentiate them from the feminine "wristwatches," these became popular among soldiers for their easy access and convenience. Perhaps more importantly, they were critical for the emerging group of airplane pilots, who could not afford the time to reach into their pocket and open the case every time they needed to check the time. Gradually, wristwatches took a greater share of the watch business.

Waltham and Elgin were still selling tons of pocket watches. Elgin moved into wristwatches, but Waltham, which had been through multiple management changes, could not afford the new machinery to make the ever-smaller and ever-thinner wrist watches. In 1927, Elgin produced two million watches, but Waltham had fallen to 500,000.

The smaller competitors, including those using Swiss parts, were more agile in converting to wristwatches. Hamilton, Bulova, Gruen, and Benrus each had their turns as industry leaders, at least among the top four US companies in the first seventy years of the twentieth century.

A major post-war recession in 1921 almost wiped out both Sears, Roebuck and General Motors. It was even tougher on the watch industry, resulting in many factory closures. The Great Depression of the 1930s was even worse, and longer lasting.

Added to these pains were those nettlesome Swiss. In order to get machinery and other products from the Swiss, the US government lowered the tariffs on Swiss watches and parts. The Swiss watchmaking industry also limited the sales of their advanced machinery to the US. The Swiss and their American assemblers gained market share.

Yet perhaps the real blow to Waltham and Elgin was World War II. For starters, the US government made them stop making watches. All these watch companies were major defense suppliers, focusing on bomb fuses and other timing devices.

But the cruelest blow was that the Swiss, remaining neutral throughout the war, never stopped making watches and never stopped shipping them into the US.

By wars' end, Waltham and Elgin were no longer in shape to compete. Their tired machines were best for making pocket watches, not wristwatches. Their labor forces were tired and had lost their enthusiasm. More agile competitors who were often better marketers rose to the fore.

Waltham went bankrupt in 1949. The manufacture of consumer watches continued until 1958, when the ghost was finally given up, after 101 years. Like other brands in this story, the name Waltham continues to be used by manufacturers, including Asian companies, which are unrelated to THE Waltham Watch Company.

Emerging a bit stronger after the war, Elgin continued to make watches at its huge plant until the 1960s. A new plant was opened at Blaney, South Carolina, which promptly renamed itself Elgin, SC. Five years later, even this plant was closed. Elgin was out of the watch business by 1968, lasting 104 years.

But One Company Transitioned to the New Era

In 1940, Norwegian shipping magnate Thomas Olsen and his friend Joakim Lehmkuhl fled Hitler and landed in the US. They were looking for investments and wanted to help the war effort. This search led them to buy the old Waterbury Clock Company (with its Ingersoll brand); Waterbury soon became one of the largest makers of timing fuses and other similar material for World War II.

After the war, under Lehmkuhl's leadership, the company continued its interest in making affordable watches. Now named US Time Company, this company came out with the "Timex" wristwatch. This watch used advanced metal alloys to lower costs and increase durability. Instead of an openable case that allowed the watch to be repaired, the case was sealed and could not be opened. The watches were meant to be disposable, though they lasted a long time and were very accurate.

Timex was well-marketed and became a huge hit. Famous newsman John Cameron Swayze was featured in television ads proclaiming "Timex – takes a licking and keeps on ticking" as the watches were put through punishing tests onscreen. Millions were sold, and by the 1960s the American watch industry had a new dominant player.

The Evolution of the Watch Industry

The history of the industry after World War II is a complex story, worthy of a future post on our part.

Major new innovations came along quickly. In 1960, Bulova introduced the "Accutron" tuning fork watch, far more accurate than any other timepiece. In 1970, Hamilton produced the $2100 Pulsar, the first digital watch.

The advent of digital watches, replacing the mainspring and works with a vibrating quartz crystal, gave rise to two Japanese powerhouses, Citizen Watch and Seiko. Today Citizen is probably the largest watchmaker in the world based on units sold, though the big Swiss makers are larger in dollar terms due to their higher prices. Citizen's portfolio of brands includes Bulova. Other Japanese companies, including Casio, also became significant watchmakers.

The Swiss answered the digital challenge with the "Swatch," yet another "disposable" watch concept. Today the Swatch Group, controlled by the children of Lebanese immigrant Nicolas Hayek, generates about $8 billion in annual revenue, including such time-honored names as Longines, Omega, Rado, and Tissot. Swatch also owns Hamilton.

Patek Philippe and Rolex of Switzerland and other luxury watchmakers are also billion-dollar companies.

Good old Timex, now based in the Netherlands but still owned by the Norwegian Olsens, continues to prosper and includes the Guess, Versace, and Ferragamo brands. In the late-1980s, their Ironman Triathlon watch was an enormous success.

Yet competitive challenges continue. By dollar volume, the Apple Watch may now be the biggest watch in the world. The global race to make the most complex, the most beautiful, the most accurate, and the most innovative timepieces continues unabated.

Sources: There is a wealth of information on the history of each of these companies, and on the history of the components and technologies involved. Research on the Internet will lead to many collectors' sites full of company and product history. A good place to start is the National Association of Watch and Clock Collectors, which also operates a museum in Columbia, Pennsylvania. For the full story of clocks, watches, and the role of time in our lives, David Landes' *Revolution in Time* and Alexis McCrossen's *Marking Modern Times* are both excellent. For a detailed look at the American watchmakers before 1930, Michael Harrold's *American Watchmaking* is outstanding.

Originally published on AmericanBusinessHistory.org on September 25, 2020.

Chapter 20
How Baking Powder Changed the World of Horse Racing and Auto Racing

May is a critical month in the world of sports. The first Saturday in May brought the 145th running of the Kentucky Derby. And around Memorial Day, the Indianapolis 500 comes along....historically the most attended single-day event in sports. Three years ago, the 100th running brought out about 500,000 people. The bleachers and grandstands alone seat about 250,000! Both races are great American traditions.

But how many know their connection to an everyday kitchen product, baking powder?

During and immediately after the Civil War, New Englander Eben Horsford's Rumford Baking Powder pioneered the industry, making it easier to bake bread.

In 1873, another company, the Royal Baking Powder Company, was set up in Manhattan. Royal began to advertise heavily and create recipes and cookbooks. Under the Hoagland brothers, Royal's sales rose from $350,000 in 1876 to $3 million in 1888, at which time the company was spending the huge sum of $300,000 per year on advertising. By 1917, the Royal Company had $30 million in assets, bigger than Coca-Cola, H.J. Heinz, or Campbell Soup. The company was phenomenally profitable and led the industry, which drew many competitors.

With his new, "better," formula, William Wright entered the fray with his Calumet Baking Powder in 1889. With colorful packaging and even more aggressive advertising, Calumet passed Royal in sales by the early 1920s, and in profits in 1927.

The 1920s were an era of corporate mergers and acquisitions. With support from big New York banking houses including J.P. Morgan and E.F. Hutton, two "food conglomerates" were created: General Foods (from the Postum cereal empire) and Standard Brands (formed around Fleischmann's yeast). In 1928, Wright sold Calumet to Postum, soon renamed General Foods, America's largest food company after the big meatpackers like Swift and Armour and National Dairy Products (later renamed Kraft). In 1929, Standard Brands bought Royal. The competition was now turned over to deep-pocketed giants. The owners who sold out were rich.

Calumet's William Wright had bought a Kentucky horse farm in 1924 and renamed it Calumet Farm. When he died in 1931, he left $55 million to his son Warren, who threw his full energies into thoroughbred racing. Between 1941 and

1991, Calumet-bred horses won a record nine Kentucky Derbies, including Triple Crown winners Whirlaway and Citation. Calumet Farm was later sold and went into decline but is on the comeback and remains one of the most famous names in racing.

Meanwhile, giants General Foods and Standard Brands ran big ad campaigns for Calumet and Royal baking powders. They thought they "owned the market." But there was a thorn in their side.

For years, Terre Haute, Indiana's regional wholesale grocery firm Hulman & Company had marketed Clabber Girl baking powder in Indiana and neighboring states. By the 1930s, the founder's grandson, Anton "Tony" Hulman, Jr., was out of college and helping run the business. Tony thought Clabber Girl had no future as a regional product....he needed to "go national." While the New York behemoths General Foods and Standard Brands were distracted by their big product assortments, Tony focused on baking powder. Over time, he won. Today, Clabber Girl has about two-thirds of the U.S. market, and now also owns the Royal brand in America.

But Tony Hulman, like his father, also loved speed and racing. In 1945, he bought the Indianapolis Motor Speedway for $750,000. The historic but dilapidated facility had not been used during the War. His advisors told him not to buy it, or, if he did, to tear it down and put the huge tract of land to better use. Tony didn't listen. Today both the track and the entire growing IndyCar racing series are owned by the Hulman company and his heirs.

Who would've guessed that those little cans of baking powder would propel so many cars and horses to record speeds? History is made in strange ways!

(Since this article was written, the Hulmans sold the Indianapolis rack and Indycar series to automotive entreprenuer Roger Penske.)

(For the complete details about the baking powder wars that shaped American consumer marketing and advertising, see the great book *Baking Powder Wars: The Cutthroat Food Fight that Revolutionized Cooking*, by Linda Civitello.)

Originally published on AmericanBusinessHistory.org on May 25, 2019.

Chapter 21
Who Makes Our Balls?

Our weekly newsletters tend to cover big industries like retailing and automobiles. But we also find smaller, niche industries fascinating. Here is a look at who makes the balls used by America's major team sports, with as much history as we could discover.

As we investigated three great American brands and their history – Rawlings, Spalding, and Wilson – it became clear that these are both among the most beloved and most unloved brands. Beloved because most of us have used those products and know their names. They are old brands, seen in most American households at one time or another. Unloved because their owners seem to buy and sell them over and over again and never keep them very long. Today it looks like they may have more stable ownership, but only time will tell. Certainly their pasts are extremely convoluted, as you will see in the following paragraphs.

Baseball and Rawlings

Before 1876, pitchers made their own baseballs. That approach had obvious weaknesses. Then, in 1876, Boston Red Stockings pitcher A.G. Spalding started making standardized balls, and went into the ball business full-time. Spalding's company became *the* source for major league balls. Spalding also acquired the Reach brand, which they used on some products, including baseballs. In 1929, the A.G. Spalding company went public.

In 1955, Spalding bought another key sporting goods maker, Rawlings. Rawlings was founded in 1887 as a sporting goods store in St. Louis by brothers George and Alfred Rawlings. They also published a catalog to reach a broader audience.

When Spalding (the second-biggest sporting goods maker) bought Rawlings (fourth biggest), they started having their baseballs made by the Rawlings division. But the federal antitrust folks did not like Spalding owning former competitor Rawlings. Moving at their usual snail's pace, the feds took until 1963 to force Spalding to sell Rawlings. Rawlings was purchased for $10 million by private investors and returned to being a private company.

At the same time, Spalding liked supplying the MLB with baseballs, but Rawlings had the baseball production skills. So Spalding signed a contract to have the newly independent Rawlings keep making baseballs for it, to be sold to the teams with the Spalding brand on them.

When this contract expired in the mid-1970s, MLB still wanted the Rawlings balls. So, from 1977 on, the league has used Rawlings balls. Today the Rawlings factory in Costa Rica makes over two million baseballs a year. (Rawlings is also a major producer of baseball gloves.)

Who has owned Rawlings since 1963? After the private owners, try this for craziness:

- In 1967, Rawlings was bought by conglomerate Automatic Sprinkler Company of America (later named A-T-O, then called Figgie International after CEO Harry Figgie).

- In 1994, Figgie spun out Rawlings as an independent public company.

- In 2003, the K2 ski company bought Rawlings for about $70 million.

- In 2007, the diversified consumer products company Jarden bought K2.

- In 2015, the even more diversified consumer products company Newell Rubbermaid bought Jarden.

- In 2018, a partnership of MLB and Seidler Equity Partners bought the Rawlings business for $395 million.

So does anyone love this poor old company, handed from one owner to the next to the next, lost inside giant diversified companies? And who the heck is Seidler Partners, do they even care about baseball or will this just be another buy-and-sell deal?

Surprise, surprise! Seidler is run by the two Seidler brothers, Peter and Robert. Their grandfather just happened to be Walter O'Malley, the legendary owner of the Brooklyn and then Los Angeles Dodgers from 1950 to 1979. Today the Seidler family is a major investor/owner in the San Diego Padres. Perhaps old Rawlings, owned by MLB and baseball lovers like the Seidler brothers, has found a lasting home after all.

Yet, in the intervening years, think what it must have been like for the people working at the company. How many new forms, new reports, new strategies, and different cultures they must've dealt with. None of that makes it easy on a company, its employees, its suppliers, or its customers. Dealing with change can be hard enough, without the excess challenges of being part of yet another company every few years. It can be a real circus.

Back to Spalding

What became of our friend Spalding?

Not only did they have a nice run with MLB from 1876 to 1976, but they also made the basketballs for the National Basketball Association from 1983 to 2019. In May of 2020, it was announced that the NBA was switching to Wilson for their balls – more on Wilson in a minute.

We last left Spalding in 1963, when they were an independent public company, having recently lost their Rawlings division. So now try this circus of ownership:

- During the 1960s, Spalding stock was bought up by public company Dunhill International, a diversified company with interests in tobacco (Dunhill), bank notes, and infant feeding and bottle products (Evenflo).

- In 1967, Dunhill was merged with muffler maker AP Parts and renamed Questor Corporation.

- In 1982, Questor "went private," dropping off the stock exchange.

- In 1984, parts of Questor (Spalding and Evenflo) were bought by the sons of Venezuelan supermarket operator Diego Cisneros. The Cisneros group renamed these businesses the "Spalding and Evenflo Company."

- In 1996, pioneer private equity firm Kohlberg Kravis Roberts (KKR) bought Spalding and Evenflo from the Cisneros group, possibly for as much as $1 billion. Two years later, KKR broke Evenflo and Spalding into two separate companies. As is often the case in private equity deals, both companies were saddled with more debt.

- In 2003, after many efforts to restructure Spalding and reduce its heavy debt load, KKR sold Spalding to athletic apparel and t-shirt company Russell.

- In 2006, Warren Buffett's Berkshire Hathaway bought Russell for about $600 million. Buffett saw it as a good addition to the Fruit of the Loom company, which he had purchased in 2002 after it had gone bankrupt. Mr. Buffett seems to have a passion for longstanding brand names which he thinks have potential, even if they have been mismanaged in the past. Today Spalding is part of Fruit of the Loom, which in turn is part of Berkshire Hathaway.

So there you have another company literally "footballed" around by owners. But, like Rawlings, maybe Spalding finally has a good owner, an investor known for buying and holding rather than flipping what he buys for short-term profits.

What about Wilson?
What about footballs?

Wilson Sporting Goods has made the balls for the National Football League since 1941 and still provides the NFL with about 25,000 game balls a year. As noted above, they just picked up the NBA ball contract. Based on our research, it appears that Wilson has been a bigger company than either Rawlings or Spalding for most of its life. But if you were expecting a straight-forward, simple history in this industry, think again.

Our story begins with the 1853 founding of the wonderfully named meatpacker Schwartzchild and Sulzberger Company. By the 1890s, this was a major company in an industry led by giants Swift and Armour. In 1913, seeking ways to use the by-products of their slaughterhouses, they started the Ashland Manufacturing Company to make violin strings, tennis racket strings, and surgical sutures. This led them into the tennis racket business.

But Schwartzchild and Sulzberger expanded too quickly and got into financial trouble. Their bankers recruited Thomas Wilson, a veteran of the meatpacking industry, to take over the company in 1915. He soon renamed the company Wilson & Company. Wilson (the man) saw a future in sporting goods and expanded that part of the business. For the next fifty years, Wilson was the third-biggest meatpacker, although only about one-quarter to one-third the size of Swift and Armour. Behind Wilson in the meat rankings were Cudahy, John Morrell, Hormel, Hygrade, Rath, and Oscar Mayer. In the early 1950s, Wilson was one of America's fifty largest companies.

Then, yet another circus of ownership begins:

- In June 1967, Texas wheeler-dealer Jimmy Ling's

LTV (for Ling-Temco-Vought) conglomerate bought Wilson & Company, including the sporting goods operation. At the time, Wilson was twice the size of LTV.

- Six weeks later, LTV took Wilson Sporting Goods public as a separate company, offering the public a one-half interest in the company and keeping half.

- In 1970, snack and beverage giant PepsiCo bought Wilson Sporting Goods.

- In 1985, PepsiCo sold Wilson Sporting Goods to private equity firm Wesray Capital, run by former Treasury Secretary William Simon.

- In 1989, Wesray sold Wilson Sporting Goods to the Amer Group, a Finnish conglomerate that distributed Toyotas and sold cigarettes in Finland.

- Over time, Amer morphed into Amer Sports, focused on sporting goods, including Wilson and the French Salomon brand (skis, snowboards, etc.).

- In 2019, Chinese sportswear giant Anta bought Amer for about $5 billion.

And thus, after a third ring in our circus of conglomerates and private equity players, we find both the NFL and the NBA buying their balls from a Chinese-owned company!

The end????

P.S. In case you wondered, both MLS and FIFA soccer (foot?) balls have been made by the big German sports company Adidas for decades. Hockey pucks have been made by a small Canadian company, Inglasco, since the 1980s. These are two islands of stability in this complex, ever-changing industry history.

When we finally get sports up and going again, we look forward to seeing Rawlings making home runs, Spalding in our homes and gyms, and Wilsons going through the goalposts.

Originally published on AmericanBusinessHistory.org on June 4, 2020.

Chapter 22
The American Bicycle Industry: A Short History

There are an estimated one billion bicycles in the world today, almost half of them in China and another one hundred million in the United States. About one hundred million new ones are manufactured each year, over half in China and many others in Taiwan, around Asia, and in the Netherlands and Germany. The United States, despite buying fifteen to twenty million new bikes a year, is no longer a major factor in bicycle production. But it used to be. What follows is a brief look at the history of this once-vibrant American industry.

The Rise of the Bike

First developed in Europe, the bicycle took years to reach

"perfection," to be safely rideable by the average person. In the 1860s, a very brief fad for high-wheeled "boneshakers" spread across the nation, but was reserved for professional riders, acrobats, athletes, and a few brave consumers.

In 1876, thirty-three-year-old Boston civil war veteran Colonel Albert A. Pope, the owner of a factory that made parts for the big New England shoe industry, attended the Philadelphia world's fair. Pope was impressed by the latest British bike, the Ariel "ordinary" or "penny-farthing." The wooden-framed high-wheelers on hard tires rode a bit more smoothly than the old boneshakers. Seeing a future for bicycles, in 1878 Colonel Pope hired the Weed Sewing Machine Company to make bikes, under the brand "Columbia."

Colonel Pope's Pope Manufacturing Company later acquired Weed in order to focus on producing Columbia bikes in Hartford, Connecticut, where the company ultimately became one of the city's largest employers. The Colonel began buying up bicycle patents in order to ensure his company's leading position. By 1888, the factory was turning out 5,000 high quality bicycles a year.

Still, bikes were used only by the brave. Riding was limited to special schools and riding rinks. It was more about entertainment than about transportation.

A Rideable Bike

That all changed when the British Rover company brought out their "Rover" safety bike, invented in the 1870s but fully developed in the 1880s. The Rover was the first modern bicycle, with equal-sized 26" wheels, allowing much easier mounting and permitting the rider's feet to reach the ground. Major American producers Pope, Overman, the Western Wheel Works, and Gormully and Jeffery soon made safety bikes. (While Pope's Columbias were the most famous bicycles, many of the others were manufactured in the Chicago area, which became the center of the industry.)

(Many automakers, including Henry Ford, began with bicycles. Gormully and Jeffery's bike brand was the "Rambler." The company later started making automobiles, was then bought by former General Motors President Charles Nash and renamed Nash, eventually along with Hudson becoming the American Motors Company. British Rover also moved into motorcycles, then autos, and its descendant company still makes Land Rovers under the ownership of the Indian Tata family empire. The Indian motorcycle company first made bicycles and competitors Harley-Davidson and Iver Johnson also made bikes. Wilbur and Orville Wright were bicycle builders before they took to the air.)

The safety bike was not only far easier to ride but was also much lighter and faster than the old-fashioned ordinaries. Bicycles were no longer limited to athletes and the brave.

The first American safety bike was produced by Overman in 1887. Pope and other companies followed in 1888. The new design took over the market: by 1890, only ten percent of the bicycles produced by the Pope company were ordinaries.

Over time, more improvements were made to the bicycles: a stronger tubular steel frame, the addition of shock absorbing springs and systems, and perhaps most importantly, pneumatic tires filled with air rather than the old solid rubber tires. Separate parts makers, like the "saddle king," Arthur Garford, made important contributions. Connecticut's Torrington Company made spokes for the wheels and many other parts and the New Departure Company (later part of General Motors) made ball bearings, assembled into finished bikes by Albert Pope and his competitors. The British Dunlop company led the way in better bicycle tires but was soon followed by the big American tire companies including Firestone.

The First Boom

The American bicycle industry did not truly take off until the 1890s. In 1890, American companies built about 30,000 bikes. In 1892 the number was 60,000 (of which Pope made about one-third) and in 1894 100,000. But then, as the impact of the economic depression that began in 1893 subsided, a new boom hit the industry. Five thousand people rode their bikes to work every day in downtown Chicago.

Production rose to over 400,000 in 1896 and then more than 900,000 a year in 1898 and 1899. (We have been unable to ascertain how many of those bikes Pope produced, but the firm was always among the three or four biggest producers and may have made as many as one-third of the bikes sold in America at the time.)

With this big rise in popularity, the bicycle manufacturers, often led by Colonel Pope, fought local laws limiting when and where bicycles could be ridden on city streets. The makers also lobbied for better roads and more paving, years before the automakers joined the fight. Pope continued to invest in the business, building a new headquarters, expanding factories, and adding plants to make steel tubing and tires. He fought many patent battles in his efforts to dominate the industry. Colonel Pope also developed a fabulous estate for his family outside Boston.

At the same time, the ever adventurous and increasingly rich Pope, with major east coast investors including the well-known Whitneys, got into the booming electric car industry, becoming a significant producer.

The 1890s, like the roaring 1920s and the conglomerate era of the 1960s, was a time of many big business deals and mergers. John D. Rockefeller's Standard Oil Trust inspired other business leaders to consolidate their industries in order to eliminate competition and "rationalize" the industry. "Trusts" were formed in industry after industry.

Baseball player, manager, and sporting goods entrepreneur A.G. Spalding, backed by eastern capitalists, decided the bicycle industry was ripe for the creation of a bicycle trust. In 1899, this group formed the American Bicycle Company (ABC), made up of about fifty companies which produced at least 60% of the bikes in America. The idea was to buy these companies up with stock rather than cash. But it turned out that many bike makers feared that bikes were just a fad, as they had been thirty years earlier, and wanted out of the business. So they demanded cash. In the final event, the sellers got some cash and some securities, but the company was heavily in debt because it had to come up with more cash, which proved difficult.

Colonel Pope sold his company to the new ABC bicycle trust, receiving some cash but also a lot of the riskier securities (stocks and bonds). Approaching sixty years of age (considered old at the time), Pope was ready to spend less time running businesses. In 1899, he also sold his interest in the electric car company to his eastern investor partners.

The End of the Boom

Then, almost as suddenly as it had risen, the bicycle fad crashed. By 1904, total US bike sales dropped 75% to 250,000. The ABC was busted, dropping from a three-million-dollar annual profit at its peak to zero, with tons of debt on its balance sheet. The securities held by Colonel Pope and the other bicycle makers approached worthlessness. In 1903, the Colonel stepped in, re-negotiated the capital structure of the company, and took control. He renamed the ABC the Pope Manufacturing Company, which again re-entered the car business with the Pope-Hartford and Pope-Toledo automobiles.

Pope's empire had peaked. As the booming auto industry consolidated, with only the strongest surviving, the Pope brands failed (the Toledo plant later became famous for making Jeeps under the Willys-Overland company). While Columbia bicycles remained the best-known bicycle brand, the industry flatlined for the next thirty years. Adults no longer bought bikes: they were relegated to the toy sections of retail stores and only sold for children, at much lower average prices.

Colonel Albert Pope died at the age of sixty-six in 1909. His once-powerful bicycle company went through bankruptcies and ownership changes. In 1916 it was renamed the Westfield Manufacturing Company after its Massachusetts factory town, still selling bikes under the Columbia name. The company was purchased in 1955 by parts-supplier Torrington (later bought by big machine tool producer Ingersoll-Rand) and then by lawn-mower producer MTD (which agreed to be acquired by Stanley Black & Decker in 2021). In the bike boom of the 1970s, Westfield's production reached 600,000 bicycles per year, but the company was bankrupt again by 1987. Under still other owners, production in the US finally ended in 1991. The brand, now made overseas, is still marketed by toy maker Ballard Pacific.

Another significant manufacturer in this era was the Homer P. Snyder company, whose bikes were distributed by the D.P. Harris Hardware company under the Rollfast brand. At their pre-World-War-II peak, Westfield (Columbia) and Rollfast sold 75% of the bikes in America, under their own brands and under the private label brands of retail chains.

The Rise of Another Great Brand and More Booms

Arnold, Schwinn, and Company was founded in Chicago in 1895 by German immigrant bicycle maker Ignaz Schwinn with backing from meatpacker Adolph Arnold, who later sold out to Schwinn. Not one of the largest manufacturers, Schwinn didn't join the ABC in 1899, remaining independent. By 1916, the company had produced a cumulative total of a million bikes.

The Great Depression of the 1930s was at first no help to the industry, with annual sales of bikes in America staying below 300,000 per year through 1933. Then, with new streamlined designs, fat "balloon" tires for easier riding, and better marketing, often led by Schwinn, demand again took off, crossing 500,000 in 1934 and reaching a record 1.2 million by 1936.

This new boom attracted two existing manufacturing companies to the industry. Miamisburg, Ohio's Huffman Manufacturing Company had been founded in 1924 to make supplies for gas stations. In 1934, they entered the bicycle business. Cleveland's Murray Ohio Company, founded in 1919 to make auto parts, also entered the bike business in the 1930s.

These two companies focused on inexpensive bicycles sold under store brands (private labels) for the largest retail chains, leaving the top end of the market (and independent bicycle dealers) to Schwinn. Big customers for Huffman and Murray were Sears, Montgomery Ward, Western Auto Stores, and the retail outlets of Firestone, Goodyear, and Goodrich. These mass retailers sold most of the bikes in America. Murray and Huffman became huge producers, and later introduced their own brands, Murray and Huffy. Both companies ultimately built large new factories.

In 1950, yet another bicycle maker, the Cleveland Welding Company, with its Roadmaster brand, was bought by big bowling, boat, and sporting goods producer AMF in 1954. AMF had begun life in 1900 as the American Machine and Foundry Company with a pioneering cigarette-making machine. AMF became another big American bike producer.

For a while, the demand for bikes continued to grow, though they continued to be mainly for children. The post-World-War-II baby boom accelerated this demand.

Then, in the 1960s and 1970s, business again took off. Low-riding, banana-seat "hot rod" bikes like the Schwinn Sting-Ray became popular, as well as BMX dirt bikes. But also "English racers," often made by the British Raleigh company, came into the market. Adults got back into bikes. All the American bike makers jumped into the game, adding handbrakes (instead of coaster brakes) and sophisticated gearing systems for three-speed, five-speed, and ten-speed bicycles. US bike sales were 3.6 million in 1961, 7.5 million in 1968, and 15 million by 1973.

The boom made the cover of Fortune magazine, which in the spring of 1974 reported these estimated 1973 bike production numbers:

- Murray Ohio 2.4 million

- Huffman 2.3 million

- AMF 1.75 million

- Schwinn 1.465 million

- Stelber Industries .625 million

- MTD (Columbia) .6 million

This boom, too, ended abruptly, with sales dropping in half to 7 million bikes in 1975.

The Decline of Bike Manufacturing in America

Such ups and downs are difficult for a manufacturing company to manage, especially when they are so unexpected and unpredictable. Brands and companies continued to change hands, to be bought and sold.

The big retailers pressured the makers to keep their prices low, and Asian manufacturers with low labor costs began to come onto the scene. In the 1980s even top-quality maker Schwinn moved their production to Taiwan and China. Despite efforts by the American industry to get high tariffs on imported bikes, in 1996 the government determined that "Chinese bikes were no material threat" to the US industry and eliminated bike tariffs.

The once-great Schwinn company went into decline. This was in large part due to mis-management by the fourth generation of the Schwinn family, which controlled the company until it went bankrupt and the brand was sold in 1992 (and bankrupt again under new owners in 2001).

Today, most of the classic brands mentioned above (and well as many private label bikes) can be found in stores, but they are primarily owned by Asian companies and Canadian marketing company Dorel Industries (including the Schwinn, Mongoose, and Cannondale brands). The bikes themselves are primarily built in China. The world's largest maker of bikes is Taiwan's Giant Manufacturing Company (founded in 1972) with annual revenues of about two billion dollars.

More recent decades have seen the rise of two large

American high-end bike companies, Trek and Specialized, which are today among the world's largest sellers of bicycles. But their bicycles are also made in Asia. After a severe decline, US bike manufacturing has begun to grow again, up to about 500,000 bikes out of the 15-20 million that are sold in the USA every year. Mass marketers still sell huge numbers of bikes, particularly for kids, but the average prices of Trek and Specialized bicycles are much higher, generating billions of dollars in revenue.

Conclusion

It is something of a puzzlement to us why the bike industry has seen so many booms and busts. This pattern is not common for such basic consumer products which are so affordable relative to the value they provide society. Yet today the global bicycle industry continues along, making more bikes every year. Bicycle use by adults, particularly in Europe and Asia but also in American cities, is on the rise. New rural bike paths and urban bike lanes are being created around the world. The bicycle continues to be one of the most efficient forms of transportation ever devised, converting human energy to motion. And the great old names like Columbia, Schwinn, and Huffy still exist in name, if not with the same potency as in their glory days.

Originally published on AmericanBusinessHistory.org on August 21, 2021.

Chapter 23
The Tortuous Saga of the First Wonder Drug: Aspirin

Ancient Remedies

The Mesopotamian Ur III tablet, dating from about 3500 BC, mentions the willow tree (Salix in Latin) as a medicinal remedy. Centuries later, additional references are found in Egyptian papyrus documents. Throughout history, doctors in many parts of the world knew that eating the bitter-tasting bark of the willow tree had medicinal properties, including relief from fever. Many of the various concoctions derived from it caused intense stomach distress, and in some cases liver damage.

The German Chemists

Fast forward to the second half of the nineteenth century. The British had the best wool. Cotton, silk, and other fabrics came from around the world. These fabrics were dyed using ancient, rare, and expensive raw ingredients like the Phoenician Murex sea snails for the purple of royalty. In the late 1850s, nineteen-year-old British chemist Henry Perkin was trying to synthesize quinine in the laboratory when he noticed a purple color. He named it mauve. It was the first synthetic dye. Soon everyone from Napoleon III's wife the Empress Eugenia to Britain's Queen Victoria were wearing clothing colored with Perkin's mauve dye.

Friedrich Bayer, son of silk weavers from Barmen, Germany, was inspired by Perkin's discovery. In 1863, the thirty-eight-year-old Bayer and a friend founded Friedrich Bayer and Company to pursue synthetic dyes.

While not the source of the best fabrics, Germany's universities had become the world's most advanced centers for the study of chemistry. Germany's industrial resources also included coal, which meant that the country had plenty of coal-tar, key to the aniline chemicals used in synthetic dyes.

Bayer and Company grew slowly, until, after the founders died, Carl Rumpff took over in 1881. He raised capital to expand the firm by selling stock to the public. He used the capital to substantially increase Bayer's research efforts, funding chemistry PhD candidates and post-doctoral students if they would spend a year working on new dyes. One of those chemistry students, a particularly ambitious one, was twenty-three-year-old Carl Duisberg, hired in 1884. After failing to find a synthetic way to make indigo (still today the color used on blue jeans), Duisberg succeeded in synthesizing Congo red in a way that did not violate existing patents. Rumpff soon charged Duisberg with finding new products that the company could make from the coal-tar used in making dyes. Other German chemical companies had discovered the potential of medicines, particularly fever-reducing pharmaceuticals, from coal-tar. Duisberg began to pursue these leads.

The Rise of Carl Duisberg and His Prized Innovation

In 1890, Carl Rumpff died. The ever-ambitious Duisberg, now twenty-nine, became the head of Bayer. He also married Rumpff's niece. Duisberg then began assembling the best chemists he could hire and built huge new laboratories and factories at Leverkusen, Germany. Duisberg moved into a mansion adjoining the factories. Bayer's research focused on pharmaceuticals and pharmacology. It was in these buildings that we return to the story of willow bark.

Combing through forty-year-old scientific journals and studying history, Carl Duisberg's men began to focus on synthesizing the active ingredients in willow bark. Earlier attempts by others had resulted in products which upset the stomach and risked the liver. Bayer researchers found it difficult to eliminate the harmful elements. Finally, after a great deal of testing and clinical trials, his people were convinced of the safety and fever-reducing efficacy of their pure, synthesized acetylsalicylic acid (ASA). After much internal debate, the name "Aspirin" was chosen as a short and memorable name. The product came to market as a prescription drug in 1899. Doctors quickly wrote the company, saying that Aspirin had many more uses than anticipated, helping not only with fever, but with headaches, toothaches, and other aches and pains. The first "wonder drug" had been created. Demand for the powder (later pressed into pills) exploded. Bayer was in the big time now, and highly profitable.

(Within weeks of perfecting Aspirin, the same Bayer researchers also discovered a "non-addictive" alternative to the pain-killer morphine, which reportedly gave patients a "heroic" feeling. Bayer thus named the "safe" new drug Heroin.)

Duisberg focused his energies on managing Aspirin, the company's big new success. Because other companies made ASA (though not as pure as Bayer's), he could not patent it in Germany. The company did trademark the name Aspirin. For a few years, Bayer was awarded a patent in Britain, but this was overturned after an extended patent fight. The trademarked brand-name Aspirin became as important as having a patented manufacturing process.

Among major markets, only in the United States was Bayer awarded both a patent and a trademark, good through 1919. But the American customs duties (tariffs) on German drugs were high. Copiers, usually with vastly inferior products, flooded the market with ASA. So that he could sell Bayer Aspirin in the US at a lower price, Duisberg created an American subsidiary and built a pharmaceutical factory in Rensselaer, New York.

At the same time, America was flooded with quack (and often dangerous) "patent medicines," which were heavily advertised in newspapers and magazines. With names like Brane Fude, Lydia Pinkham's Vegetable Compound, and Bardwell's Aromatic Lozenges of Steel, these fakeries were the bane of the medical field. Journalistic exposes of their risks led to the passage of the Food and Drug Act of 1906. Thereafter, doctors could only prescribe drugs approved by the government, drugs could not be advertised to the public, and drugs could only be prescribed by their chemical names – usage of brand names was forbidden.

Prescriptions for Aspirin now read "acetylsalicylic acid." Desperate to differentiate its product, the American Bayer company began stamping its Aspirin pills with the letters B-A-Y-E-R spelled out vertically and horizontally in the form of a cross. Despite the FDA regulations, patients learned to ask for Bayer Aspirin. The little white pills, especially those sold in America, continued to be a financial blessing for the Bayer company. Having studied John Rockefeller's creation of the Standard Oil Trust, Duisberg also began to seek ways to limit the "ruinous competition" between Bayer and the other big German chemical and drug companies, primarily BASF and Hoechst.

Dark Times

Then came the ultimate snag in the efforts of Duisberg and his company: World War I.

After failed efforts to keep America neutral by Woodrow Wilson, German Americans, and German companies like Bayer, the US entered the war in 1917 on the side of Britain and France after a German U-boat submarine sank the British ocean liner Lusitania, killing many Americans.

The US government soon took steps to seize all "alien assets" in America, including the factories, patents, and trademarks of the Bayer Company. Bayer's American executives – almost all imported from Germany – took extreme steps to avoid seizure of the company's assets. They worked with German spies and the German embassy and tried to restructure the business to save it for their German owners through a complex, clandestine ownership structure. These efforts were found out, resulting in (to say the least) bad press. Other American makers of ASA advertised their products as made in America, not by the evil enemy.

Despite all his "best" efforts to avoid the seizure, Carl Duisberg was losing his golden egg. The US government seized Bayer's US assets.

On December 12, 1918, the American "Alien Property Custodian" put the American assets of the Bayer Company up for sale at auction. A wide range of chemical companies and Wall Street investors expressed interest. Bidding started at one million dollars. As the numbers rose, chemical giant DuPont dropped out. At $5.3 million, only two bidders were left. Big Wall Street firm Paine Webber's last bid was $5,305,000. For $5,310,000, Bayer's American business was sold to the most unlikely and insignificant of bidders, a company called Sterling Products.

Enter William Weiss

Sterling Products had been founded in 1901 in Wheeling, West Virginia by two small-town pharmacists who had grown up together in Ohio: William Weiss and Arthur Diebold. The two men wanted to jump on the patent medicine boom, the same trend that the Food and Drug Act attempted to quash only six years later. Their first product was a quack analgesic, Neuralgine, which they sold from the back of a horse-drawn buggy. Weiss was great at selling and marketing.

Carl Duisberg the expert chemist had spent his life demanding the finest ingredients and the highest purity of product. He was aghast that his "baby" had fallen into such low-life hands. But there was nothing he could do about it.

With their patent medicine business under siege, Weiss saw the value of Bayer Aspirin, obviously valuing it higher than even giant companies like DuPont did. Weiss took the leadership role at Sterling. (His partner Diebold left and later founded a future competitor, American Home

Products, eventually renamed Wyeth and even later acquired by Pfizer.) William Weiss quickly put his selling skills to work on Bayer Aspirin.

But Weiss and Sterling had a problem: they knew how to sell, not how to manufacture. Especially not how to manufacture a complex product using precise chemistry. In the scandals and seizure, Bayer's American executives and chemists had lost their jobs and many had been deported. Few were left who knew how to run the big Aspirin factory in Rensselaer.

The ever-inventive Weiss then secretly reached out to "the enemy" – he wrote letters asking Duisberg for help. Duisberg at first ignored him, but finally met with Weiss, who he viewed with caution at a minimum and more likely alarm. After three years of tense negotiations, an agreement was finally reached. Bayer of Germany would give Sterling the technical assistance it needed. In return, Bayer would receive 50% of the profits Sterling made on Bayer products sold in the US, and 75% of any profits Sterling made on these products in Latin America. Of course, these agreements were in contravention of the requirements laid down when Sterling acquired Bayer's American operations from the government. But nobody was supposed to know about the deal between Bayer and Sterling.

Weiss then happily went about selling Bayer throughout the Americas with great success. His energy and imagination were endless. In small villages south of the border, he would put a movie projector on the back of a truck, and Bayer Aspirin would sponsor weekend movies for the locals. In the United States, he created enemies at the FDA and among doctors and pharmacists by heavily advertising Bayer Aspirin, which became a non-prescription, over-the-counter product. Nevertheless, patients demanded it and Sterling Products was happy to meet that demand.

In the meanwhile, back in Germany, Carl Duisberg was finally able to achieve his Rockefeller-inspired goal of limiting competition among the German chemical companies. He pulled off a merger with BASF, Hoechst, and several smaller firms to create a giant cartel, IG Farben, which Duisberg headed. This was one of the largest industrial companies in the world. By the end of the 1920s, Sterling Products was surreptitiously sending over a million dollars a year in profits to IG Farben. After Duisberg's death in 1935, this notorious firm went on to produce the gas for the concentration camps and anything else the Nazis desired for their war efforts. (The cartel was later broken up into its original pieces.)

Unhappy Endings?

Unsurprisingly, this state of affairs did not end well for Weiss. The American Justice Department uncovered the dirty dealings, and in 1941 William Weiss was banned from working at Sterling Products for life. Yet Sterling Products continued to successfully sell their wonder drug, Bayer Aspirin. In the post-war period, the "great analgesic wars" raged, Bayer Aspirin competing with American Home Products' Anacin and Bristol-Myers' Bufferin and Excedrin. American television audiences were inundated with clever (and sometimes dishonest) advertising. All three companies made a great deal of money. Shares in the companies boomed. Later on, Johnson & Johnson's Tylenol (acetaminophen), American Home Products/Wyeth's Advil (ibuprofen), and eventually Aleve (naproxen) entered the achy competition.

After changing hands twice in the 1980s and 1990s, in September 1994 the American rights to Bayer Aspirin were acquired for one billion dollars by the German Bayer Company, no longer part of a cartel and now allowed to do business in the United States.

From ancient Egyptian remedies through wars, epidemics, and an overdose of scandal, the bark of the willow tree and the little white pill with the cross on it has persisted, and even found new uses. Carl Duisberg's dream of ameliorating American headaches has come full circle.

(This article only touches on some of the high points of this convoluted story. Two excellent and fascinating books tell the complete story: *The Aspirin Wars; Money, Medicine, and 100 Years of Rampant Competition*, by Charles Mann and Mark Plummer, focuses on Bayer in the US and the competitive battles of the 1950s and 1960s, while *Aspirin: the Remarkable Story of a Wonder Drug*, by Diarmuid Jeffreys, covers the full German and international story of the drug. Both books include most of the stories told above, plus many other details on the executives, scientists, scandals, lawsuits, government agencies, spies, ailments, and science involved in this strange, amazing saga.)

Originally published on AmericanBusinessHistory.org on April 3, 2020.

Chapter 24
Gas Station Wars: Rockefeller to Dinosaurs to Tigers in Tanks

In the twentieth century, no industry created more giant American companies than the petroleum industry. In 1917, big oil represented six of the fifty largest American companies. By 1955, eleven oil companies made the top fifty industrial firms in *Fortune* magazine's annual list; seven were in the top twenty. And in 2019, with a list expanded to include financial services, transportation, retailing, and many other industries, oil companies made up five of the top fifty and nine of the one hundred biggest American companies. (2020 was an aberration because of

Covid, which caused the big oil companies to lose money

and drop in revenue.)

No other industry has gone to the ends of the earth and to the bottoms of the oceans that the oil industry has, ever searching for more petroleum. From its outset, the industry has been a global business, as reflected in the story that follows.

The oil industry is built around four critical parts:

- Exploration and Production (finding and drilling crude oil wells)

- Transportation and storage (tanker ships, pipelines, trucks, storage terminals)

- Refining ("cracking" the crude oil into components including gasoline, kerosene, aviation fuel, lubricants, and petrochemicals)

- Marketing (filling stations, convenience stores with gasoline)

Marketing is the part that touches the lives of most Americans. Our use of gasoline skyrocketed in the early 1920s as we bought Ford Model T's and began to explore our own country, for work and for pleasure, without depending on railroad schedules and stops.

Over time, each big oil company has focused on different parts of the system. At any given time, some oil companies had more crude oil than they could refine and sell, while other companies did not have enough to meet the needs of their refineries and gas stations. Yet the industry giants always battled for the attention and patronage of American motorists at their branded gas stations. This is the story of those wars.

The Standard Oil Trust

Clevelander John D. Rockefeller saw great opportunity when petroleum was discovered in Pennsylvania in 1859. Kerosene derived from oil was used to fuel lamps, replacing whale oil. The railroads, America's first giant industry, also used lubricants to keep their trains rolling. In 1863, Rockefeller and his partners invested in their first refinery, in Cleveland. Over the next forty-eight years, this small group of men created company after company to exploit the opportunities in oil. Savvy, ambitious, and sometimes ruthless, Rockefeller made every effort to control the refining and transportation of petroleum. By 1870, the partners incorporated the Standard Oil Company of Ohio.

Incorporation laws at the time varied greatly from state to state. Many states required that the company be incorporated in that state in order to operate there. In New York, a corporation was not allowed to own another corporation. But New Jersey allowed it. This led to the creation of separate companies with names like Standard Oil (Ohio), Standard Oil (New York), and Standard Oil (New Jersey).

In 1882, he and his partners secretly pooled all their shares in their multitude of companies into the Standard Oil Trust, to some degree evading the state limitations. Outsiders may have thought that the companies were competitors, when in fact they were all part of the giant trust, which refined as much as 85% of the nation's petroleum. In the 1890s, many other industries copied Rockefeller's ideas, creating trusts to attempt to monopolize industries (many of those efforts failed in their efforts to monopolize).

Standard Oil used its market position in refining and pipelines to control the flow and pricing of oil. At the same time, Standard lowered it prices by operating more efficiently and making continuous improvements in the system.

But people still did not trust the Trust, especially as they discovered the secret linkages between the many component companies. Ida Tarbell's expose of the Standard Oil Trust, despite its many flaws, became a bestselling book. The Standard Oil Trust was an easy target: the railroads blamed it for low prices to carry the oil and hated the competition from Rockefeller's pipelines. Those who produced oil at the well, selling to Standard, and those who sold kerosene in the cities, buying from Standard, thought the Trust had too much control over their lives and businesses. Everyone thought the kerosene produced by the Trust should be even cheaper.

Americans had always been wary of monopoly. By the start of the twentieth century, populist politicians and leaders like Teddy Roosevelt were ready to "bust the trusts." And the most famous, largest, and most hated trust of all was Rockefeller's Standard Oil. After plentiful investigations by Congress, in 1911 the U.S. Supreme Court found Standard guilty of monopoly and ordered the trust to be broken up into thirty-four separate companies. Those companies set the stage for the emergence of the oil industry in the twentieth century.

Rockefeller's Children

The thirty-four companies created out of the Trust varied in size and focused on different aspects of the industry. There were pipeline companies, a few crude oil producers, and even Chesebrough, the makers of Vaseline. But the biggest parts of the empire were the refining entities. And the largest of them, representing over forty percent of the Trust's assets, was the Standard Oil Company of New Jersey, commonly called "Jersey Standard." This company was the nation's largest refiner of oil.

Another large child of the Trust was Standard Oil of Indiana, called "Stanolind," which owned the largest single refinery in the nation, in Whiting, Indiana, across the state line from Chicago. A third refiner was Standard Oil of California, or "SoCal," but this was a smaller company: California had not yet risen to the prominence it would gain later in the twentieth century.

The Standard Oil Company of New York, or "Socony," was primarily an exporter of kerosene, sending the Trust's products all over the world. There were also Standard Oil Companies of Ohio, Kentucky, Nebraska, and Louisiana. The Ohio Oil Company was one of the more rare producing companies in the Trust, controlling wells in Western Ohio. The Atlantic Oil Company served Pennsylvania and Delaware. The Continental Oil Company served the great plains east of the Rocky Mountains. The Magnolia Oil Company primarily served Texas.

Despite the tarnished reputation of the Trust, the Standard Oil name was still known across America, and had great brand value. So when the Trust was broken up in 1911, each of these companies was assigned a geographical region in which they had the rights to market petroleum products under the Standard Oil name, sometimes just using the letters "SO." This map shows how the nation was divided up:

Gas Station Wars: Rockefeller to Dinosaurs to Tigers in Tanks

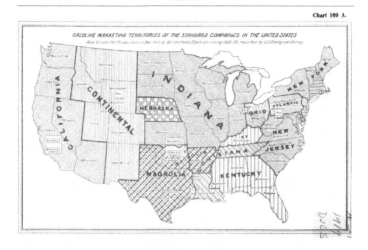

Chart 109 A.

Note that the map is titled, "Gasoline Marketing Territories." The map was printed in 1919, eight years after the breakup. In the early years of the oil business, gasoline was considered a useless by-product of kerosene production, and often thrown away. With the rise of the automobile, especially after the breakup, the refiners had to invest in new technologies in order to get more gasoline out of the crude oil. By 1919, gasoline had become an important product to all of the Standard companies. Standard of Indiana not only owned the big Whiting refinery, but also had the largest marketing territory of any of Rockefeller's offspring.

Over the next one hundred years, these children of Rockefeller would battle each other, enter each other's trade areas under different brand names, buy and sell oil companies, venture more heavily into crude oil production, focus and defocus on gas stations, and sometimes even partner with each other. Yet, as time passed, they were not the only major players in the oil industry.

Three Big Thorns in the Side of the Standard Companies

The largest and certainly longest-lasting of Standard's competitors was (and is) the Royal Dutch Shell Company. Shell was created in 1907 through the merger of two older companies, the British Shell Transport and Trading Company and the Royal Dutch Petroleum Company. The Dutch had oil in what would become Indonesia and found more oil elsewhere. British Shell had the facilities to trade and move that oil around the globe. Shell's first foray into the United States came when they supplied their Asian oil to California Standard. When "SoCal" found its own oil in California, Shell lost that contract, and began producing, refining, and marketing oil in the golden state.

(British giant British Petroleum – "BP" – did not become a factor in the United States until late in the twentieth century.)

Rockefeller and his partners were slow to recognize the potential of Texas oil after the big gusher was hit at Spindletop in East Texas in 1901. Others were not so slow. Two future big competitors arose from the Texas oil strikes.

Gulf Oil was the successor to companies created in 1901 at Spindletop. In the next few years, the wealthy Mellon banking family of Pittsburgh, who also backed Alcoa Aluminum and other companies, got control of this competitor.

In 1902, wildcatter Joe Cullinan founded the Texas Company to exploit new finds in Texas. This company, too, was soon controlled by eastern capitalists. The company branded its gasoline and stations "Texaco."

Gulf, like other companies in this story, went on to find oil around the globe, including in the Middle East. The Texas Company, "Texaco," had a greater emphasis on marketing and retailing oil.

The foreign invader Shell and the two Texas upstarts Gulf and Texaco soon provided serious competition to the various Standard Oil companies.

More and More Competitors

These future giants were not the only foes for the Standards. Harry Sinclair built a major oil company from his start in the middle of the continent. The company went on to make Dino the dinosaur famous across America. Cities Service company and the Ohio Cities Gas company both provided natural gas to city utilities. In their search for more natural gas, they discovered oil and soon were selling gasoline, under the Cities Service and Pure Oil names, respectively.

Richfield and Union Oil were California upstarts. The Pew family of Philadelphia founded Sun Oil. Their fortune led to the creation of the Pew Research Center, known today for its polls and surveys. Highly successful wildcatter Frank Phillips and his brothers created Phillips Petroleum, later using the Phillips 66 brand. Tide Water Oil used the Tydol brand in the east and later merged with Associated Oil's west coast operations, known for their "Flying A" logo.

In the automobile age, all of these names became familiar to the motoring public, though each focused on particular regions of the nation. At first, there were no truly national oil marketing companies; no company had gas stations covering the whole country.

The Gas Station: 1920s and 1930s

The first products of the industry, lubricating oils and kerosene, were initially sold in cans by grocery stores, country general stores, and other retailers. Before the automobile, there were no gas stations. As Henry Ford's Model T, introduced in 1908, began to take off (and drop in price), those same stores provided gasoline in cans.

Auto sales and usage boomed, and soon those retailers began to put curbside pumps along city streets. These were tall and thin, and often sat right on the curb, where we might find a parking meter today. This system only added to the traffic congestion of the big cities, where horses and carriages still competed with the new automobiles.

Independent gasoline dealers and local and regional oil distributors, called "jobbers" in the industry, began to open dedicated filling stations in the 1910s. Many of these stations were "unbranded" as the big oil companies had not yet focused on the power of branding. Customers did not know the quality or purity of the gasoline they bought.

One of the most innovative local gasoline retailers was the American Oil Company and Lord Baltimore filling stations of Baltimore, both owned by the Blaustein family. They and other retailers developed stations with their own driveways, moving their customers off the streets and out of the way of traffic. Over time, service bays were added and the stations began to sell tires, batteries, motor oil, and other auto accessories. Gasoline pump makers also kept innovating, eventually leading to the self-service pumps we know today (which were initially banned by fire marshals for being too dangerous).

The big oil producers and refiners began to understand that the public would trust branded products. To keep their refineries busy, they needed to promote their brands and sign up more independent gasoline dealers, both jobbers and gas station owners. With its big refinery and large marketing region, Indiana Standard led the way, later acquiring the Blaustein's American Oil, branded as "Amoco." Each company tried to architecturally differentiate its stations, a practice that continued after World War II.

New York Standard, "Socony," formerly a petroleum exporter, began to exploit its assigned trade area, New York State and New England. Socony also bought marketer Vacuum Oil Company, General Petroleum to enter the California market, and Magnolia in Texas. In the process of its acquisitions, Socony acquired the Mobil brand and Pegasus, the flying red horse.

Giant Jersey Standard, with its large refining capacity but lack of crude oil supplies, bought the very big Texas producing and marketing company Humble Oil. That acquisition also led Jersey Standard to enter the gas station market in Texas. Prevented from using the Standard name outside its limited geographical area, the company experimented with many different names, including Humble, Esso, and Enco, before settling on Exxon in the 1970s.

In 1926, these were the largest American sellers of gasoline to consumers via service stations:

Company	1926 Share of U.S. Gas Station Sales
Standard (Indiana)	10.9%
Standard (New York)	9.4%
Gulf	6.9%
Sinclair	6.7%
Texas Co.	6.4%
Standard (New Jersey)	6.4%
Shell	5.3%
Atlantic	4.1%
Standard (California)	3.4%
Tide Water	2.6%
Standard (Kentucky)	2.5%
Standard (Ohio)	2.4%
Pure	2.3%
Union of California	1.4%
Continental	1.4%
Richfield	0.8%

In the 1930s, auto use continued to rise, and more companies developed more "branded gasoline" stations. These gas stations were organized in many different ways. Rarely were they owned and operated by the big oil companies. Some were operated by jobbers who resold the branded gas. Others were owned by independent businesspeople, who either owned the station or leased it from the big oil companies. Sometimes the station operator owned his own building and simply bought the gasoline from the big oil companies and used their signs and marketing.

The oil companies provided subsidies, cheap rents, signs and marketing materials, and sometimes even the pumps and other equipment. By the late 1920s, Texaco was sponsoring national radio programs, further enhancing their brand and its appeal to the station owners. Eventually, each oil company also offered its own credit card, in order to induce customer loyalty.

Gas Station Wars: Rockefeller to Dinosaurs to Tigers in Tanks

Since the old Standard Oil companies could not use the Standard name outside the areas shown in the map, they all adopted new names for at least those stations outside their assigned territories. This table shows the evolving brand names and the number of stations operated under the major brands during this era:

Company	Number of Gas Stations		
	1929	1932	1938
Standard (Indiana)/Amoco	9,187	13,556	11,241
Socony-Vacuum/Mobil	6,702	18,406	9,045
Texas Co./Texaco	5,571	23,459	9,607
Shell	3,082	8,623	6,572
Gulf	1,793	10,174	7,438
Standard (Ohio)/Sohio	1,418	2,696	2,314
Continental/Conoco	1,332	5,814	1,666
Cities Service/CITGO	1,031	2,869	2,515
Tide Water-Associated	880	1,233	2,166
Union of California/Union 76/Unocal	550	915	4,053
Pure	464	952	36
Atlantic	394	580	131
Phillips/Phillips 66	380	1,490	1,572
Sun/Sunoco	345	474	682
Skelly	285	388	630
Standard (New Jersey)/Esso/Exxon	156	17,012	417
Ohio Oil/Marathon	134	324	15
Sinclair		14,244	9,611

(data on Standard of California is not Available)

Note that most of the companies had fewer stations in 1938 than they had in 1932. Some of this was because of the Great Depression, but much of the drop came from replacing low-volume, low-profit stations with bigger, more efficient ones. Shell in particular has a long history of building bigger stations, and even today has a far greater share of the U.S. gasoline market than you might think based on how many stations the company has.

The Gas Station in the Second Half of the Twentieth Century

America's post-World-War-II economic boom was accompanied by increased travel, further boosted by the Eisenhower Interstate Highway System begun in the 1950s. The oil companies intensified their battles for market share at the pump. Television ads for Texaco promoted "The Man Who Wears the Star." Shell proclaimed premium fuels and gave drivers advice on driving safety and auto maintenance. Gulf tried selling lower-grade fuel at a lower price, Gulftane. Sun Oil (Sunoco) offered a higher grade of fuel, and eventually had pumps on which the customer could select from multiple grades of gasoline. Individual oil companies handed out as many as thirty million free road maps a year. Customers were wooed with trading stamps, free glassware, contests, and premiums of every sort.

In the course of this boom, the oil companies continued their history of mergers and acquisitions. SoCal bought Standard Oil (Kentucky) with its valuable southeastern territory in 1961. Union of California bought Pure in 1965. Atlantic and Richfield merged to form Atlantic-Richfield (ARCO) in 1966. ARCO in turn bought Sinclair in 1969. In 1968, British Petroleum entered the US by buying Ohio Standard (and later buying ARCO and Indiana Standard, which had been renamed Amoco after its primary brand). With each merger, after selling off some stations and territories as required by the monopoly-wary Federal Trade Commission, new names appeared in new geographical areas.

Many companies tried to enter the lucrative California market, but were often rebuffed by the strength of SoCal, now branded Chevron, and the two smaller west coast companies, Union 76 (Unocal) and Richfield.

Gas Station Wars: Rockefeller to Dinosaurs to Tigers in Tanks

Texaco, Shell, Gulf, and even Phillips 66 made efforts to serve all forty-eight states, but sometimes had to back off from their efforts. Discoveries of new oil, depletion of old wells, and construction of new refineries all played a role in each company's strategy. And all along, fewer, bigger stations replaced smaller, older ones. Rockefeller's small Ohio Oil company evolved into Marathon, which bought and developed the Speedway brand with its very large stations with many pumps. Others followed its lead. Self-service pumps came on the scene in a big way. Convenience store chains led by 7-11 entered the business. The convenience stores could add gasoline without adding employees, drawing more frequent traffic to buy their other merchandise.

Here are the top sellers of gasoline in America during this period:

Company	Share of U.S. Gas Station Sales		
	1954	1966	1970
Texas Co./Texaco	7.9%	8.5%	8.1%
Standard (New Jersey)/Esso/Exxon	7.8%	7.8%	7.4%
Socony-Vacuum/Mobil	7.8%	6.4%	6.6%
Standard (Indiana)/Amoco	7.7%	7.6%	7.3%
Gulf	6.8%	7.2%	7.1%
Shell	6.6%	8.0%	7.9%
Sinclair	5.0%	3.8%	
Standard (California)/Chevron	4.4%	4.9%	5.0%
Sun/Sunoco	3.6%	3.0%	4.2%
Phillips/Phillips 66	3.3%	3.4%	4.0%
Cities Service/CITGO	3.1%	2.3%	2.0%
Tide Water-Associated	2.4%	1.9%	
Atlantic	2.2%		
Pure	2.1%		
Union of California/Union 76/Unocal	1.8%	3.2%	3.3%
Standard (Ohio)/Sohio	1.7%	1.6%	1.5%
Continental/Conoco	1.6%	2.1%	2.4%
Standard (Kentucky)	1.6%		
Richfield	1.5%		
Ohio Oil/Marathon			1.7%
Atlantic-Richfield/ARCO		3.3%	5.6%

The oil crisis and Arab Oil Embargo of the 1970s, accompanied by much higher gasoline prices, brought much of this post-war expansion to an end. The fates of individual companies varied, as some were better managed (Exxon, Chevron, Shell) than others (Mobil, Gulf, Texaco).

The Last Forty Years

Since 1980, the industry has witnessed continuous change. Many stations changed hands. In 1985, Socal, now renamed Chevron, bought Gulf and converted their stations to the Chevron brand. (Some stations lived on as Gulf in the northeastern U.S.) Shell and Texaco merged their U.S. refining and marketing operations. Texaco the producer and refiner was bought by Chevron in 2000 but many of their stations were taken over by Shell, retaining their Texaco signs for a few years. In 1998, Exxon took control of Mobil, creating an even larger behemoth. (The Federal Trade Commission had many times stopped the mergers of much smaller companies, but perhaps now it was becoming apparent that the big companies had challenges of their own, and threats of monopoly power were no longer a concern.)

Full-service gasoline stations disappeared except in Oregon and New Jersey, where self-service is still illegal. Service bays also went away as Jiffy Lube and similar companies rose up. The "Man who wears a star" and takes care of your car – and washes your windshield and checks your oil – is long gone. AutoZone, O'Reilly, NAPA, and Advance took over the auto parts and accessories business while new tire store chains stole that lucrative part of the business.

The biggest change in recent decades has been the rise of the big chains operating combined gas stations and convenience stores. Convenience store giants 7-11 and Circle K were joined by regional operators like Maverik in the middle of the country and Pennsylvania's Wawa and Sheetz. Speedway's big, multi-pump locations were followed by upstarts including QuickTrip (QT) and Racetrac. Truckstop operators Flying J, Pilot, and Love's built large new facilities. In 2020, the parent company of 7-11 paid $21 billion to buy the Speedway outlets from Marathon Oil. Now approaching 70,000 locations worldwide (not all sell gas), 7-11 is the world's largest retail chain by store count.

Yet, through all these turbulent changes, one brand name reigns supreme at America's gas pumps, and it is not even an American brand. As of 2019, Shell held an estimated 12.5% share of "motor fuel" sales in the United States, double the 6-6.2% shares of ExxonMobil and Chevron. Shell may not have the most stations, but their sales per station is high. Globally, Shell is sold through 46,000 branded locations, more places than either McDonald's or Starbucks, or any other oil company (BP is second with 30,000+ locations).

Possible Marketing Lessons

A side story has relevance here.

In about 1970, your writer was browsing the stacks in the big University of Chicago library, a block from his dormitory. He stumbled across a dissertation or paper on oil company marketing. While the details are lost in his memory, he recalls that the main conclusion of the study was that the strongest brand in America, the most trusted and respected at the time, was the one reflected in this powerful logo:

Standard (Indiana) Logo

As indicated in the preceding paragraphs, Indiana Standard did not stick with this logo, eventually changing to Amoco and now BP. Socony changed to Mobil, Jersey Standard to Exxon. Once prominent brands Texaco, Gulf, and Sinclair declined and sometimes disappeared in mergers. It is hard to believe that all these changes did not affect customers and their loyalty. (An even greater case can be made for the branding destruction done by all the mergers in the banking industry.)

So who "won" these battles at the pump? Shell won. Shell is the one company that has had the same logo, the same brand identity, from the outset. The company's success in the United States has been through internal growth rather than a lot of big acquisitions. Though Shell has been as ambitious as the other companies in finding new oil and controlling tankers and refineries, the company seems to have kept its eye on marketing more than any competitor. In recent years, it passed up ExxonMobil to become the world's biggest oil company in revenue. (In 2020, BP took the lead, followed by Shell and then ExxonMobil.) Perhaps John D. Rockefeller has finally met his match, in these two "foreign intruders" that have had such a big impact on American business history.

Originally published on AmericanBusinessHistory.org on September 5, 2021.

Some Most Interesting Characters

Chapter 25
Superwealth: A Historical Perspective

Few business subjects fascinate people as much as the very wealthy. Our obsession with celebrity goes back centuries but seems to have accelerated in recent decades.
Forbes produced its first list of the richest Americans in 1982 and later started publishing it annually, though such lists have been made off and on for over a century.

The latest list was published last month, showing the top Americans as Jeff Bezos at $177 billion, Elon Musk at $151 billion, and Bill Gates at $124 billion. Only one non-American was in this mix at the top of the list, French luxury goods baron Bernard Arnault (CEO, LVMH Moet Hennessy Louis Vuitton) at $150 billion. Of course these numbers are only estimates, given the difficulty of valuing real estate, art, and other assets, though *Forbes* works hard at it and has a lot of experience by now. And the numbers change daily, especially for people with large holdings of public company stocks like Bezos and Musk.

(Mark Zuckerberg, Warren Buffett, Larry Ellison, and Google founders Page and Brin are just below the $100 billion mark in the latest list.)

Our job here at the American Business History Center is always to add some historical context – how rich are these people compared to the superwealthy of the past? That exercise requires adjusting historical dollar figures to today's values and today's economy. There are several ways to make these adjustments.

In our articles, we generally use an inflation index, which gives a rough idea of what those old dollars might buy today. Some who have compared wealth over time have looked at people's wealth relative to the US Gross Domestic Product when they were alive (or at the time of their death). Authors Michael Klepper and Robert Gunther used this method in their popular book, *The Wealthy 100: From Benjamin Franklin to Bill Gates – A Ranking of the Richest Americans, Past and Present*, published in 1996. At that time, their method listed Bill Gates as the richest living American but just thirty-first in the overall historical list of 100 individuals.

With all the controversy surrounding the superrich – and their taxes and divorces – it seems a good time to take another look. And to try yet another method of adjusting the historical data.

For our list, we looked at the wealth of the superwealthy compared with the total national wealth of all the people in the United States. That total currently stands at about

$130 trillion at yearend 2020, according to the latest government data. (The total includes non-profit organizations, but they represent a small fraction of the total.) Mr. Bezos holds about one-seventh of one percent of that total American wealth.

We used that same method to look back in time, using the estimated "wealth at time of death" numbers from *The Wealthy 100* book. We arrived at these "2020 equivalent" numbers (in billions of dollars) for the top historical (and present) people:

	Name	Industry	Year	Percent of National Wealth	In 2020 Dollars
1	John D. Rockefeller	Oil	1937	0.374%	$ 448.8
2	John Jacob Astor	Furs, Real Estate	1848	0.282%	$ 338.4
3	Cornelius Vanderbilt	Shipping, Railroads	1877	0.278%	$ 333.6
4	Andrew Carnegie	Steel	1919	0.168%	$ 201.6
5	Jeff Bezos	ECommerce	2020	0.148%	$ 177.0
6	AT Stewart	Retailing	1876	0.136%	$ 163.2
7	Elon Musk	Automobiles, Space	2020	0.126%	$ 151.0
8	Henry Ford	Automobiles	1947	0.122%	$ 146.4
9	Marshall Field	Retailing	1906	0.115%	$ 138.0
10	Jay Gould	Railroads	1892	0.111%	$ 133.2
11	Richard Mellon	Banking, Investments	1933	0.106%	$ 127.2
12	Andrew Mellon	Banking, Investments	1933	0.106%	$ 127.2
13	Bill Gates	Software	2020	0.103%	$ 124.0
14	Fred. Weyerhaeuser	Timber	1914	0.101%	$ 121.2
	John D. Rockefeller @ peak wealth		1913	0.495%	$ 594.5

When viewed in this way, the "concentration" of wealth, at least at the very top, is less now than it was one hundred years ago. At the same time, the top current people are "far richer" than were the top billionaires (and eccentrics) in the mid-twentieth century, such as Howard Hughes, J. Paul Getty, HL Hunt, and Daniel Ludwig.

As in *The Wealthy 100* book, today's rich are not at the top of the historical list. (If the inflation index is used to adjust the wealthy of the past, much lower numbers show up for the rich of bygone days, leaving today's rich at the top.)

Taken together, it strikes us that no one today approaches the relative wealth achieved by John D. Rockefeller, and probably the other names in our list. At his 1913 peak, when his Standard Oil Trust was broken up by a Supreme Court Decision, Rockefeller was perhaps three times as wealthy as Bezos is today, using the method we have used. He also had many partners whose wealth would show up not far below those listed above, including his brother William Rockefeller, Henry Rogers, Edward Harkness, Henry Flagler, and Oliver Payne.

Others high on the list would include railroad barons Edward Harriman, Russell Sage, Leland Stanford, Mark Hopkins, Charles Crocker, and CP Huntington. Other industrial titans would also rank highly, such as financier JP Morgan, Carnegie partner Henry Frick, magazine publisher Cyrus Curtis, sewing machine magnate Edward Clark, and meatpacker Philip Armour.

All those individuals would be worth at least $40 billion in today's economy based on their share of the national wealth at the time of their deaths, ranking them up with the twenty richest Americans in the newest *Forbes* list.

Among more recent billionaires, Sam Walton at the time of his 1992 death was worth an estimated $22 billion, which would convert to about $112 billion in 2020, just missing the list in the table above.

While we always enjoy "playing with numbers," more interesting to us are the achievements and contributions to society made by these businesspeople, or lack thereof. Rockefeller, Carnegie, Ford, Weyerhaeuser, and the Mellons created large enterprises that still exist today. Most were also great philanthropists.

Please check back on our website in 50 or 100 years to see how Bezos, Musk, and Gates appear in retrospect!

Originally published on AmericanBusinessHistory.org on May 6, 2021.

Chapter 26
Two Entrepreneurs Who Helped Create Florida

Every state has a fascinating history, including the role of business and entrepreneurship. The swamp that was much of Florida did not develop until the late 19th and early 20th centuries. Two men, both named Henry, were perhaps the most important in that development. They brought railroads to the state to make it accessible and built beautiful hotels to make it worth the trip. Henry Flagler made the east coast of the state "happen." Henry Plant did the same with the west coast. Their efforts led to the growth of the state which continues to make headlines today. Here is a brief look at these two very different men and their accomplishments. We start with the first born of the two, Henry Plant.

Henry Plant

Henry Bradley Plant was born in Connecticut in 1819. Eager to go to work, he passed on the chance to attend Yale and instead became a "captain's boy" and deck hand on a steamboat that ran from New Haven to New York. As part of his duties, he handled express packages, improving their organization and handling. By the 1840s, he had gone to work for one of the large express companies that worked with the railroads and steamship companies to expedite packages. (The largest express company was American Express, whose founders later created another one, Wells, Fargo, when American Express decided not to expand to California.)

In 1853, he moved to Jacksonville, Florida, recommended for his sickly wife's health. The trip took eight days. Upon getting to know the then-tiny village, Plant became excited about the future of Florida. They returned north, whereupon Plant was given responsibility for all the activities of the big Adams Express Company south of the Potomac and Ohio Rivers. This was a major challenge, as the transportation network of the south was years behind that of the north. When the Civil War approached, Adams Express worried about the future of its southern operations and sold them to Henry Plant. He organized the Southern Express Company in 1861.

Southern Express was named the Confederacy's agent for collecting tariffs and moving money. Understandably in a difficult position given his Yankee heritage, Plant feigned illness and sailed to Bermuda, then Canada, and then France and Canada again before returning to New York.

After the Civil War, he returned to the south to reclaim leadership of Southern Express. But the railroad system was worse than ever, much of it destroyed in the war. So

Plant began buying up small southern railroads at foreclosure sales in the late 1870s. Over the next twenty years, he developed and expanded a large transportation system, "the Plant System," including fourteen railroads, 2,100 miles of track, steamship lines, and hotels. His system opened up central Florida, allowing orange growers to ship their products north. He proceeded to build down the southwest coast of the state.

Between 1887 and 1898, he built hotels from Sanford to Tampa to Fort Myers. Two of the most beautiful were the Tampa Bay Hotel and the Belleview Biltmore near Clearwater, one of America's largest wooden buildings.

Henry Plant worked his entire life and became one of the richest men in the south. He died in 1899 at the age of seventy-nine. Three years later, his system was absorbed by the Atlantic Coast Line Railroad, which ran from Richmond, Virginia to Jacksonville.

Henry Flagler

Henry Morrison Flagler, eleven years younger than Henry Plant, was born in Hopewell, New York in 1830. At the age of fourteen, Flagler moved to Ohio where his stepbrother Stephen Harkness lived. After working in a retail store and a grain business owned by a Harkness relative, in 1862 Flagler co-founded a salt mining company in Michigan, but that business failed.

Returning to the grain business in Bellevue, Ohio, he got to know Clevelander John D. Rockefeller, who was an agent for another salt company owned by the Harkness family. By the mid-1860s, Rockefeller had left the grain business to enter Cleveland's emerging oil refining industry, which used the newly discovered petroleum found in nearby parts of Pennsylvania. In 1867, Rockefeller asked Flagler's stepbrother Stephen Harkness to invest $100,000 in Rockefeller's new oil business. Harkness agreed, on the condition that Rockefeller hire Henry Flagler to watch over Harkness's investment.

It will come as no surprise that Rockefeller and his partners made a success of the business, Standard Oil, which continues today in numerous offspring including ExxonMobil and Chevron. Henry Flagler was perhaps the most important person in the company after Rockefeller himself. When John D. Rockefeller was asked if the Standard Oil company was the result of his thinking, he answered, "No, sir. I wish I had the brains to think of it. It was Henry M. Flagler." The story of Standard Oil, John Rockefeller, and his many partners is well-told in dozens of books and other sources.

In 1877, Henry Flagler moved to New York City, eight years before Standard Oil relocated from Cleveland to the Big Apple. While he continued to serve on the Standard Oil board of directors, a very, very wealthy Flagler retired from active management in 1882.

Meanwhile, he, like Henry Plant, became enthusiastic about the future of Florida. Also like Plant, his first trip was to Jacksonville to improve his wife's health. When she died, Flagler married her caregiver. After the wedding, they traveled to nearby historic St. Augustine, but Flagler found the transportation and hotel infrastructure lacking. Between 1885 and 1887, he built the 540-room Ponce de Leon hotel there.

Looking south down the east coast of Florida, Flagler began to envision an "American Riviera." He gradually acquired and built a railroad south from Jacksonville to Palm Beach, spending a fortune cutting through the swamp. As he expanded his Florida East Coast Railway, he kept building hotels, including the 1,100-room Royal Poinciana and the

Palm Beach Inn (later renamed The Breakers) in Palm Beach.

In 1912, Flagler extended the Florida East Coast Railway to Key West by building an elaborate causeway system across the Florida Keys. That part of the railroad was severely damaged in the hurricane of 1935 and was never rebuilt, instead replaced by a highway.

Henry Flagler died in 1913 at eighty-three, worth about $60 million ($1.6 billion in 2020 money).

Epilogue

Others followed the trail to Florida along the paths pioneered by Plant and Flagler, using their transportation systems to get there. Until the creation of Amtrak, their two railroads hauled thousands of passengers from the northeast to Florida on beautiful passenger trains.

The Atlantic Coast Line, the 1902 successor to the Plant system, later merged with the parallel, competing Seaboard Air Line Railroad, which went through more evolutions before becoming part of the CSX system, one of the four giant American railroads today. Trains headed down the east coast of Florida to Miami had to transfer to Flagler's Florida East Coast, which also changed hands and since 2017 has been owned by copper mining and railroad company Grupo Mexico. Both continue to be critical parts of Florida's transportation infrastructure, hauling freight in and out of the state.

Originally published on AmericanBusinessHistory.org on December 18, 2020.

Chapter 27

Forgotten Business Giant: Charles M. Schwab

We are all familiar with the visionary entrepreneur Charles R. Schwab who pioneered the discount stock brokerage industry in the 1970s. But almost no one remembers the unrelated Charles M. Schwab, one of the most important business leaders in American history.

Born in modest circumstances in Pennsylvania, at the age of thirty-five this Charles Schwab was running one of the most important companies in America. At thirty-nine, he became President of the world's first billion-dollar corporation. He then went on to build yet another company which at its peak was the third largest industrial company in the nation, the size of Ford and General Electric combined. Charles Schwab built a mansion in New York City, the largest single-family home ever constructed in Manhattan. He played a key role in the Allies' victory in World War I. At times he was celebrated as America's greatest business leaders; at others he was vilified in the press. Here is his intriguing story.

Beginnings

In 1861, John Schwab and Pauline Farabaugh, both children of Catholic immigrants from Germany, were married in the small mountain town of Loretto, Pennsylvania. A center of Catholicism, Loretto was known for the presence of the renowned Father Gallitzin, one of the few priests in "the west," in whose church the two were married. They moved to nearby Williamsburg, where their first-born child, Charles Michael Schwab, came along in 1862. When young Charlie was twelve, they moved back to Loretto, where he grew up in the remote little town.

From the earliest age, Charlie seemed destined to be an entertainer. He loved to perform for his family, do tricks, and play the piano and organ – he even went so far as to teach those keyboard instruments to others. His father worked as a weaver in his grandfather's woolen mills, which got a contract to make blankets for the Union armies in the Civil War. While not wealthy, the family was comfortable.

Charlie's father also owned a livery stable and got a contract to deliver mail in the area. Outgoing, curious Charlie would pick up the mail in the larger town of Cresson, which also had a railroad stop. In order to make some extra change, he would meet the incoming trains and grab people's luggage before they realized what had happened, then take them to their destination. He loved meeting people. In school, he learned bookkeeping, surveying, and engineering and was a voracious reader, especially of history and biography. The boy began to have big dreams, unlike his father who was easy-going and satisfied with life as it was.

In 1879, at seventeen, without a high school degree, Charlie Schwab set out for the big world – moving about seventy miles to Braddock, near Pittsburgh, where he got a job at $10 a month as a store clerk. He was soon working twelve-hour days and doing the bookkeeping for the store. A regular customer for the store's cigars was "Captain Bill" Jones, the most important person in town. Jones ran Braddock's massive (for the time) Edgar Thomson steel works, owned by Andrew Carnegie and his partners.

Impressed by the boy's energy and enthusiasm for work, Jones offered him a starter job at the steel mills at $25 a month. Charlie's first task was to carry the rods used by surveying teams in the engineering department. (The Thomson works were named after the President of the Pennsylvania Railroad, where Carnegie worked early in his career. Not only did that railroad carry steel and ore for Carnegie, but it was the mills' biggest customer for steel rails, an important product.)

Steel Man

With his energy and commitment to "proving himself indispensable," Charlie Schwab continued to catch the attention of his supervisors. One time, when Jones had a major new engineering project in mind, the head of engineering asked him which young engineer to assign it to. Jones said, "Just ask all of them to work late tonight, overtime (without extra pay), and I will observe them." The only one who never looked at the clock was Charlie, and he got the job.

At twenty-one, Charlie married Emma Eurania "Rana" Dinkey, a few years older than he was. They remained married until her death, eight months before Charlie died.

Rana did not share Charlie's love of the spotlight and lively lifestyle, and over time became extremely obese. But she did enjoy the gifts and attention that Charlie showered on her.

Jones had to make weekly reports to Carnegie in Pittsburgh and grew tired of the time and travel, so Charlie took over the task for him. Carnegie, a believer in promoting from within and paying his top men well, took a liking to the youngster and saw in him the management potential he was always seeking. Charlie quickly proved his total knowledge of the steel business. What he didn't know, he read up on at night or asked the veterans in the mills. (Throughout his life, everyone was amazed at Schwab's photographic memory. He could memorize whole speeches in a minute and never forgot a statistic he had seen in a report.)

At the same time, the energetic and extroverted Schwab developed the ability to talk to anyone and was respected by the men in the mills, no matter their position or age (most were much older than he was). If he found a worker smoking in the mills, against the safety rules, he took the worker aside and gave him a fine cigar "to smoke after work, outside the mill" (Schwab always carried the cigars with him but did not smoke and was not a heavy drinker).

At twenty-three, Schwab earned the thanks of Jones and Carnegie when he designed and built a bridge to carry molten steel over some railroad tracks, accomplishing it ahead of schedule and under budget. Jones gave Charlie a diamond pin and Carnegie gave him ten $20 gold pieces.

Carnegie was always among the first to adopt new technologies, at first the Bessemer steelmaking process, then the open hearth process. At each stage, Charlie became his "go-to" expert, designing, building, and running the works. The two men were made for each other: both ambitious, both aggressive, and both visionaries compared with their competitors. They also believed in developing their subordinates, paying them bonuses for work well done, and continuously lowering costs and selling steel at lower prices than their competitors. In recessions, Carnegie took the opportunity to expand, build new facilities, and buy out weak competitors. All these attitudes and behaviors stayed with Charlie Schwab long after he left Carnegie's employment.

One promotion led to the next, until, in 1886, the twenty-four-year-old Charlie Schwab was appointed as the general superintendent of another steel works that Carnegie had acquired and was improving. The works were in Homestead, Pennsylvania, a few miles closer to Pittsburgh than the big Edgar Thomson works in Braddock. Schwab's salary zoomed to $10,000 a year (about $300,000 in 2021 dollars).

When big rail customer Pennsylvania Railroad was disappointed in the quality of some of Carnegie's rails, the railroad began to explore the internal chemistry of the steel. Few in the steel industry had studied such chemistry. Charlie Schwab set up a lab in his home kitchen and quickly became an expert.

In 1887, a British steel maker offered Charlie $50,000 a year to run the big works in Birmingham, England, even agreeing to a five-year contract with annual increases. In 2021 money, that would have been $1.5 million for the twenty-five-year-old, but Schwab turned the offer down when the Brit would not agree to also paying big salaries to Charlie's lieutenants.

Rising to the Top

Captain Bill Jones took charge when one of his Thomson

works' furnaces jammed in the fall of 1889. The Furnace exploded and Jones died shortly thereafter. 10,000 men and their families lined the streets for his funeral.

Carnegie needed to replace Jones, but did not want Schwab to leave Homestead, where he was doing an exceptional job. Charlie persisted until Carnegie gave his approval. At twenty-seven, Charles M. Schwab became the general superintendent of the biggest steel works in America. He had been working for Andrew Carnegie for ten years.

Like Carnegie, Schwab rewarded his employees for high productivity but also drove them hard. He believed in carrots much more than sticks. One day he asked the men coming off a shift, "How many heats has your shift made today?" When they said "Six," he wrote a big 6 in chalk on the floor. The next morning, the overnight shift had erased it and written 7 in its place. The next day, the day shift had again erased it and written 10.

In 1892, workers called a strike in the Homestead works, which became violent and made national headlines when armed Pinkerton's men unsuccessfully tried to oust the strikers. Schwab was called back to Homestead to help settle the situation, which was ultimately resolved. While throughout his career Schwab fought unionization like almost every other industrialist of the era, he also had a rapport with workers that most did not. He did not fear meeting directly with the union organizers and leaders of the workers in his efforts to settle labor issues. He talked to virtually every worker on the day and night shifts, knowing them by first name. During this crisis, Schwab lived at the plant and worked seventy-two hour stretches, with only a few short naps. The man was tireless.

(While the steel industry paid better than most American factories, and far better than European steelmakers, pay rates were 12 to 30 cents an hour for ten-and-a-half hours

Sunday through Friday and five-and-a-half hours on Saturday. These hourly rates did not increase if the workers had to work overtime beyond those hours, which they often did.)

Upon his return to Homestead, Charlie Schwab was given his first equity in Carnegie's operations – a one-third of one percent ownership.

Carnegie Steel was a major supplier of armor for ships and big guns for the US military. In 1893, some disgruntled employees filed a suit claiming that the company had misled government inspectors on the quality of the armor, violating a big contract with the Navy. Carnegie and his men, including Schwab, thought the inspectors did not understand steel and were interfering with their work. The steel involved had superficial flaws, but the steelmen knew that it was sound. So they fudged their reports. In testing, all the armor exceeded the contract standards. Nevertheless, the issue became a widely publicized scandal and the first major public black mark on Schwab's record, one which was raised any time someone had a beef with him in the future.

Carnegie continued to reward those who served him well. He told Schwab he would give him 1% of the company, and if he did well in the next six months, raise that to 2%. But in just five months, Carnegie gave him 3% instead.

Charlie Schwab always lived life to the fullest, and by his own standards. While Carnegie was a puritan who fired any executive who drank too much, gambled, or chased women, Schwab was of a different stripe, despite his Catholic education and upbringing. While Charlie and Carnegie became best of friends and frequent golfing partners, Charlie had to keep his other side secret from his boss. He loved a good poker game and sired a daughter with a nurse who was caring for his niece. While he made sure the child was financially secure and even visited her, their relationship never became public knowledge in Charlie's lifetime.

Throughout these tribulations, Carnegie Steel continued to innovate, to lower costs, and to lead the industry, producing far more steel than any competitor. In 1890, profits reached $5 million. In 1893, the nation was struck with a major recession which lasted a few years. Many companies did not survive and most steelmakers lost money. Yet even in the depths of the recession, Carnegie Steel made a profit of $3 million, and by 1897 made $7 million.

In April of that year, Charles M. Schwab, thirty-five years old, was named President of the Carnegie Steel Corporation. Profits reached $11 million in 1898, $21 million the next year, and $40 million in 1900, a remarkable record. Few corporations of any type were as profitable. Andrew Carnegie and Charlie Schwab were on top of the world.

The Sale

While Charlie Schwab was renowned in the world of steel and a leader of industry groups, he was less known to the broader business world, in large part because he was overshadowed by Carnegie. In December of 1900, he was invited to present at a dinner of New York's top businesspeople and bankers. (Over time, Schwab developed the reputation of one of the nation's best orators and after-dinner speakers.) JP Morgan and the other top leaders of the New York business community attended. Charlie gave a speech in which he outlined a vision of a large, integrated steel organization which could make the best steel at the lowest prices while giving its workers job security. After dinner, he had a chat with Morgan, who had formed the General Electric company a few years earlier and was a leading advocate of industrial consolidations. Morgan asked Schwab to list the companies that he thought would best fit into a giant steel company. The ultimate list understandably included Carnegie Steel.

Though Schwab was only thirty-eight, Andrew Carnegie was sixty-five and more interested in giving away his wealth than making more money. Yet Charlie hesitated to bring the idea to Carnegie, instead approaching Mrs. Carnegie. In the final event, the Morgan syndicate paid Carnegie and his partners $400 million in (very safe) bonds of the new corporation, the United States Steel Corporation. Charlie Schwab, as 6% owner of Carnegie Steel, received $24 million worth of the new bonds (about $800 million in 2021 dollars).

In April of 1901, the thirty-nine-year-old Schwab was named the first President of US Steel. The corporation, commonly called "Big Steel," was the first corporation whose assets exceeded one billion dollars, far larger than any other enterprise in the world. The holding company controlled 213 steel mills and transportation companies, 78 blast furnaces, 41 iron ore mines, 112 ore barges, 57,000 acres of coal and coke properties, and nearly 1,000 miles of railroad tracks. The company dwarfed all other steel companies in revenues and profits.

Charles Schwab was now a national figure. While anti-business forces decried the giant steel "trust," business leaders came to see Schwab as one of the greatest industrial managers of the era, if not the greatest. He joined the circle of the top business leaders of the era, gambling with John "Bet-A-Million Gates" and socializing with Kings and Presidents.

Charlie and Rana (they never had children) moved to New York City, where in 1901 they began construction of the largest mansion in the city, named "Riverside." Located at

72nd Street and Riverside Drive, overlooking the Hudson, the home had over ninety bedrooms served by six elevators. It had a sixty-foot indoor swimming pool, its own power plant, one of the biggest pipe organs in the city, a gymnasium, a bowling alley, and its own telephone system and switchboard. Capped by a 116-foot tall lookout tower which gave a view of the city, the mansion took four years to build and cost $3 million, plus millions more on furnishings. Manhattan had never before and has never since seen such a huge single-family freestanding dwelling.

At the same time, Schwab developed a fabulous estate back in Loretto, covering 1,000 acres and employing hundreds of workers and servants. The giant parallel stairways that led up to the main mansion were separated by a continuous, electrically operated waterfall.

At the same time that Charlie seemed to reach the top of the business world, he also found himself with much less authority. Andrew Carnegie found good men, paid them well, and left them alone, a philosophy shared by Schwab. But the Chairman of US Steel, Elbert Gary, was a lawyer and judge without a deep background in making steel. Gary and the other board members tended to be more conservative than Schwab with his desire to always expand, to always invest in new technologies and plants. Charlie especially ached under the board's desire to sell steel at high, stable prices, whereas he wanted to keep prices low, competing for big jobs, as had Carnegie Steel. The two sides increasingly clashed over policy. (Gary later did authorize the building of one of the largest steel mills ever built, on the south shore of Lake Michigan, to serve the "western market." The company built a model town there, named after Judge Gary: Gary, Indiana.)

At the same time, Charlie was also free of Andrew Carnegie's puritanical beliefs, and could be more relaxed about "being himself."

Charlie and Rana then took off on a long vacation to Europe, something they (or more often he alone or with a mistress) continued in future years. They crossed the Atlantic in eight suites on a French luxury liner. In January of 1902, they arrived in Monte Carlo, where Schwab's longstanding love of gambling led him to the tables. Crowds and reporters gathered around as the famous American placed huge bets and often won. Charlie did not anticipate the reaction in the States. Not only did the newspapers consider his behavior scandalous, but his old friend Carnegie sent him letter after letter telling him how disappointed he was, berating Schwab in the harshest language. He told Schwab that he must resign from the Presidency of US Steel, and many American newspapers said the same thing. Carnegie's letters so distressed Charlie that he became sick and lost weight. His doctors ordered him to rest, and he returned to Europe, though he continued to stay in regular touch with the affairs of US Steel as its President. It would take years before Schwab and Carnegie would heal the wound and again become friends.

Upon returning to New York, the conflicts with the board, intensified by the bad press over his gambling, led many to demand Schwab's resignation from US Steel. This did not happen immediately, as JP Morgan stood behind Schwab, believing in his managerial talent. Morgan also felt that a businessman's personal behavior was his private business. (For this and other reasons, Morgan and Carnegie were never close. And while most titans of the era like Morgan and Rockefeller shunned the press and publicity, Charlie was always eager for attention, ready for an interview or a speech.)

In 1903, forty-one-year-old Charles Schwab resigned the Presidency of US Steel and left the Board of Directors the following year.

Round Two: Bethlehem Steel

With his enormous wealth, Charlie had three major uses for the money. First, he took care of himself, with his mansions, the finest automobiles money could buy, and valuable books and works of art. Second, he loaned money to anyone who would ask for it, financed their business ideas, and sent regular checks to all his relatives. But thirdly, he still had plenty of money to invest. He helped create the International Nickel Company and other successes.

While many might have retired at that point, that was out of the question for Charles Schwab. He knew only hard work and loved the steel industry, for which he had become the leading public spokesman.

His largest investment was in a small steel company in eastern Pennsylvania, the Bethlehem Steel Company. While still at US Steel, he bought the whole company as a personal investment. Tiny compared to US Steel, Bethlehem made a profit of $1.4 million a year. (US Steel was making profits of $70-100 million a year at the time.) Like Carnegie Steel, Bethlehem supplied the Navy with armor plate. The company was also a major maker of gun forgings for the same ships. When a group of investors decided to create a shipbuilding trust by merging several major shipbuilders, they wanted to include Bethlehem. Charlie offered to sell them Bethlehem for $9 million cash, but the promoters had no cash and instead offered him $30 million in stocks and bonds in the new company, US Shipbuilding, which offer he accepted.

The Shipbuilding company turned out to be a financial disaster. Most of the shipyards were badly run and in disrepair. Above all else, they were losing money. In less than a year, US Shipbuilding was bankrupt. Following lawsuits and more bad press for Schwab, he ended up again in control of the company, which was again named Bethlehem Steel.

From that difficult start, Charlie assembled a team of talented managers and built up Bethlehem. He continued the kinds of policies he and Carnegie had used to make Carnegie Steel a great success. He found a young man, Eugene Grace, who worked as hard as Charlie did. Grace, like Charlie, rose rapidly even before he was forty, and ultimately became the President of Bethlehem. A scandal hit the papers when it was revealed that Grace was being paid a bonus of over a million dollars a year on top of his $12,000 annual salary. Grace and Schwab developed a working relationship very much like the earlier one between Schwab and Carnegie.

In 1910, Bethlehem was making a profit of $2 million a year. From 1915 through 1929, the company usually earned about $15 million but, in some years, as much as $40 million. By the late teens, lists of the largest industrial companies of America ranked Bethlehem third, behind US Steel and Standard Oil of New Jersey (later named Exxon). (Prior to the Securities and Exchange Commission requiring that companies report their sales numbers to shareholders, many companies did not reveal that "confidential" information. Thus size lists at the time were based on assets rather than sales, as has been the standard practice since at least 1950.)

Over this period, Bethlehem rose from being an insignificant steel maker to become the clear second largest company in the industry, passing up much older firms like Jones & Laughlin. This growth was propelled by three factors. First, the company was the world's largest shipbuilder, which led to huge contracts with the Allies in both World Wars. Second, Schwab took a big risk on a new concept in structural steel used in buildings. He obtained the patents on the Grey beam, an H-shaped beam that was stronger, lighter, and less expensive than that used previously. No other big steel company believed in the beam, but Schwab did. As a result, Bethlehem beams were used in an estimated 80% of the skyscrapers built in the 1920s boom in New York City, including Rockefeller Center and Madison Square Garden. Third, Bethlehem aggressively acquired other mid-sized steel companies, including Midvale and Lackawanna.

Via those acquisitions, Bethlehem Steel operated giant steel mills near Buffalo at Lackawanna, New York (employing 20,000 at its peak) and at Sparrows Point near Baltimore. Maryland. Both works were far larger than the original Bethlehem operations in Bethlehem, Pennsylvania.

Wartime Wizard

Whatever damage that had been done to Schwab's image by his prior scandals was undone during World War I. By the end of the war, he was an international hero.

Before the United States entered the war, the British Admiralty under Winston Churchill asked Schwab to come to England. When the Germans announced their submarines would torpedo any British passenger ships, few dared risk the crossing. Schwab's ship proceeded under guard and rescued 900 people when the ship ahead of it was hit. Schwab made it across the Atlantic and proceeded to the war offices, where the top people in the British Navy told him they needed twenty submarines as fast as possible. Wiring home in coded messages, Schwab said he could get it done. While submarines normally took over a year to build, he said he could start delivery within six months. He sailed home with a large contract and a multimillion-dollar deposit on the order.

Upon arrival in America, Charlie was immediately called on the carpet in Washington, where President Wilson and others made it clear he was in violation of the law and could not build the submarines: America had declared itself neutral and would not provide any weapons to either side in the European conflict.

Charlie returned to England, where Churchill was outraged and called Charlie a lying cheat. Then Schwab told him he had worked out a solution. The parts of the submarines would be made in the US, but then shipped to a British-owned shipyard in Montreal, where they would be assembled. This process was cleared with US authorities, Bethlehem's people took over the Canadian shipyard, and all the subs were delivered on time or earlier, and on budget. Charles Schwab earned Churchill's enduring admiration.

Once America entered the war, the US government created an agency called the Emergency Fleet Corporation (EFC). Its task was to ramp up the building of cargo and troop ships. But it failed. When the US wanted to send 100,000 troops a month to the European front, American shipbuilders under the command of the EFC could not meet the demand. After months of poor results, they turned to Schwab and begged him to come run the EFC. He turned them down, as he felt it would be a conflict of interest as the owner of big shipbuilder Bethlehem Steel. In order to put pressure on him, the government people arranged for him to meet with President Wilson, who had been a frequent adversary of Charlie's. When Wilson came out of another meeting, he walked up to Charlie and thanked him heartily for agreeing to take the job. Schwab was unable to resist, but made a series of demands, including that he be given total freedom and authority, that he only be paid a dollar a year, and that he not be involved in any dealings with Bethlehem. To no one's surprise, the EFC was soon pumping out ships and beating deadlines, its troop ships carrying 350,000 soldiers a month to Europe.

These events again put Charles Schwab in the spotlight, a miracle worker and wartime hero.

Years later, in an all-too-common political circus, members of Congress and the government tried to claw back the profits Bethlehem had made during the war. They wrongly accused Schwab of having a conflict of interest, which he had carefully avoided. While nothing came of the uproar, it dragged on for years and again placed Schwab's name in vilifying newspaper articles.

The Descent

Bethlehem Steel continued to prosper in the 1920s, but like virtually every American business, was hit hard by the 1929 stock market crash and Great Depression. In 1932, Bethlehem lost over $19 million. Ever an optimist, the aging Charles Schwab continually preached that recovery was just around the corner, but it was not to be. As his fortune shrunk, he was forced to part with Riverside, offering it to the City of New York as a home for the Mayor at half of what it cost to build. But Mayor Fiorello LaGuardia thought it a bad time to live lavishly and turned it down. Ultimately Charlie's creditors took over the mansion, and years after he died it was demolished and replaced by apartment buildings.

In January of 1939, Rana died. While their marriage had rarely been intimate and Rana was aware of his philandering, there was a mutual support between them that never died. A depressed Charlie moved into a small apartment on Park Avenue. Much to his despair, he had to cut back on the generous checks he had been sending to friends and family. Eight months after Rana's death, in September 1939, Charles Michael Schwab, age seventy-seven, died of a heart attack.

Schwab's estate showed assets of $1.4 million and debts of $1.7 million, making him technically bankrupt when he died. The executors were his younger brother and another man. Against the brother's wishes, the other man, more conservative, required that Schwab's Bethlehem stock be sold before it might drop even lower in price. Had the estate held on to the stock, it would have soon become solvent as Bethlehem again became a major wartime supplier.

Bethlehem After Schwab

In 1938, Bethlehem made a profit of $5 million. In the 1950s and 1960s, it consistently made profits of over $100 million a year, maintaining its position as the nation's number two steel maker by a good margin. Schwab's protégé Eugene Grace continued to be the dominant force in the company until the late 1950s.

Yet, by the 1970s and 1980s, the steel industry came under tremendous competitive pressure from both foreign steel makers with newer plants and from domestic "minimills" using newer technologies like electric and oxygen furnaces. Many companies merged and were bought and sold by various parties. As the industry shrunk, they could not honor their pension plans. Bethlehem had five retired workers for every active worker, the reverse of the ratio in its glory days.

Despite the best efforts of its management, in 2001 Bethlehem Steel declared bankruptcy. Its facilities were ultimately bought by the Indian Mittal Steel company, and then became part of the world's largest steel maker, ArcelorMittal. In 2020, that giant sold its US operations to Cleveland-based Cleveland-Cliffs. The only operating remnant of Bethlehem today is the large plant at Burns Harbor, Indiana, which Bethlehem built in the 1960s. The former Lackawanna and Sparrows Point grounds near Buffalo and Baltimore, which employed tens of thousands of men, are now under "brownfield" redevelopment. The Bethlehem works in the company's hometown include a casino and entertainment and arts complex, with some of the furnaces still standing but inoperative.

The company's headquarters in Bethlehem, the Martin Tower opened in 1972, was the tallest building in the city. It was demolished in 2019. In yet another twist, before its closure it was the operations center for business information company Dun & Bradstreet, owners of the Hoovers website, a company co-founded by your writer.

Summary

Like all men (and women), Charlie Schwab was a flawed person. None of us is perfect. Yet a close study of his management methods can teach much to managers today. His success in developing and running two top companies in one industry is perhaps unique in business history. His speeches and enthusiasm inspired tens of thousands of employees. His steel holds up some of the world's most famous buildings and his armor and ships helped win two world wars. Yet, like all of us, his dust returned to dust, and with it, even the world's awareness of his existence.

(For a much more detailed examination of Schwab's life and achievements, read *Steel Titan: The Life of Charles M. Schwab*, by Robert Hessen, and *Industrial Genius: The Working Life of Charles Michael Schwab*, by Kenneth Warren. Warren also wrote *Bethlehem Steel: Builder and Arsenal of America*, which covers the company before and after Schwab. All three of these books are excellent.)

Originally published on AmericanBusinessHistory.org on February 26, 2021.

Chapter 28
Father of Modern Sales: The Remarkable Mr. Patterson

In our opening chapter on the three greatest companies in American history, we listed both General Motors and IBM. Neither of those companies would have been the great successes they were without the contributions of proteges of John Henry Patterson, though he did not work for either company himself. Sales methods used around the world today might not exist without John Patterson. One of the great technology companies, still going today, would not exist without him. Yet few know of him or his story. Patterson was one of the great business builders in American history. A complex man, he was a ruthless tyrant but also led the way in better treatment of (some of) his employees. Here is a brief look at this most interesting gentleman.

Beginnings

John H. Patterson was born in 1844 near Dayton, Ohio, the seventh of eleven children. He served briefly in the infantry in the Civil War and developed an admiration for military discipline. He would later write, "I believe that a business ought to be like a battleship...in cleanliness, in order, in the perfect discipline of the men, in the readiness for use of every part of the plant." After graduating from Dartmouth College in 1867, he returned to Ohio and went into business. He started as a toll-collector on a canal, then went into coal and wood selling. In 1879 he and one of his brothers began a partnership which operated retail coal yards and coal mines.

One of their operations was a grocery and general store in Coalton, Ohio, which sold supplies to the miners. Patterson would later recall, "At the end of three years, although we had sold annually $50,000 worth of goods, on which there was a large margin, we found ourselves worse off than nothing. We were in debt, and could not account for it." He found out his employees were failing to collect from credit customers and were giving merchandise away to their friends.

In 1878, Dayton saloon owner James Ritty had developed the first primitive wooden cash register, named the "Incorruptible Cashier," to reduce theft from his cash drawer. Patterson bought four of the machines and his losses were eliminated. Gradually investing in the cash register business, Patterson by 1884 had control of that business and its patents, renaming the company the National Cash Register Company. John Patterson was forty years old. From that point forward, the short, wiry, intense

Patterson devoted his life to dominating the cash register business and to getting registers into every saloon and retail store in the world.

Taking Over the World

Under Patterson, who lived until 1922, the National Cash Register Company (often called "the Cash") went on to sell thousands, then tens of thousands, of their machines and succeed in dominating the industry, which had many competitors. In order to do so, he faced stiff opposition from the retail and saloon clerks, who resented the lack of trust implied if their employer bought a cash register. Patterson and his brother owned the whole company, which did not go public until after he died. Rather than recount the growth of the company here, we focus on Mr. Patterson, his style, and his impact on the world of business.

To say that Patterson was ruthless may be an understatement. As part of his sales strategy outlined in the paragraphs that follow, he used every trick in the book to drive competition out of business. Failing to do so, he bought them out, buying up most of the industry. His methods included dropping prices below cost to meet cheap competitors ("predatory pricing"), running ads targeting specific competitors claiming their products did not work, making clones of competitors and selling them under different brand names (not National), and taking competing machines and rigging them to fail, then using them to demonstrate their weaknesses to potential customers. He also sued any and all comers for infringing on National's patents, and usually won, as the National machines were in fact the most advanced. When a competitor did bring about a good innovation, he bought them out and incorporated the improvements in National's machines.

These practices eventually caught up with Patterson and his associates when the government tried and convicted them for their many misdeeds. He was headed for jail when the verdict was overturned upon appeal. But it is also possible that the government backed off when Patterson "saved" the people of Dayton in the great flood of 1913. He used all his resources and plant facilities to rescue, feed, and house the people of the devastated city.

The Selling System

In his usual, methodical, disciplined system, John Patterson also used every trick in the book to develop a selling system and motivate his salespeople, who were relentless. He "carpet-bombed" potential customers with direct mail flyers, to the extent that one retailer wrote the company, "Let up. We done you no harm." National Cash Register was among the earliest and heaviest advertisers as it promoted its products and ridiculed the competition.

Patterson, always with a blackboard at hand so he could draw his many diagrams, spurred on the sales force with motivational slogans, pep talks, cheering sessions, and company songs. Patterson pioneered the idea of a sales manual, which ran to hundreds of pages of specific instructions as to how to dress and how to deal with reluctant customers. The salespeople had to memorize and use exact scripts. He was the first, insofar as we know, to develop sales quotas for each salesman, who were assigned exclusive territories so as to avoid competition between salesmen and to encourage them to share ideas and best practices with each other. Each salesman and their supervisor had to write up daily reports sent to headquarters in Dayton. These practices spread to other industries, often by hiring ex-National salesmen, and continue in use today.

The Employer

There were two sides to Mr. Patterson when it came to his employees. On the one hand, in his huge Dayton plant, he was a leader in what was at the time called "Welfare work," which meant treating the employees to extra benefits. He added daycare for employees' children, cafeterias, lunchtime entertainment programs, a beautiful landscaped factory environment, and classes of all types in his schoolhouse. Other companies followed his lead.

On the other hand, Patterson's ruthless, tyrannical nature also came through. Anyone who violated his many edicts, from how they ate to how they presented themselves, was fired on the spot. One person began a talk with, "I am not very good at public speaking," at which point Patterson replied, "Then, why are you speaking? Sit down!" The man was then out of a job.

In another classic Patterson story, he asked a factory manager if he was satisfied with his plant. The man said, "Yes, we have great workers and make great products, I am totally satisfied." Patterson then fired him, because he thought dissatisfaction was key to success.

Any executive who was too good, who assumed too much authority or challenged Patterson, was dismissed immediately. Even one top executive who worked for him for decades and ran the company after Patterson's death admitted that he never really could "relax" while Patterson ruled. Yet John Patterson's drive, his passion for selling, and his underlying belief that it was only right that he sold all the cash registers in the world, led to continued success and growth. He was a hero and model to some, the devil himself to others.

The "Offspring"

National's early cash registers required hand-cranking. When electricity became more readily available, eliminating this tiring effort became a priority, but no electric motor was small and light enough to fit inside a cash register. So two of Patterson's engineer-inventors, Charles Kettering and Edward Deeds, developed a small electric motor that met the need.

Auto industry pioneer Henry Leland, head of the Cadillac division of General Motors, had a friend whose arm was broken when an auto crank kicked back. The friend died from the resulting infection. So Leland looked around for a better way to start cars and heard about Kettering and Deeds' work for The Cash. After overcoming many difficulties, Kettering developed the electric starter, which Cadillac put in all their cars. General Motors wanted more electric starters, so Kettering and Deeds started a new company, Dayton Engineering Laboratories Company, known as DELCO. GM bought DELCO, Kettering became the chief scientist-inventor at GM and thus a very wealthy man. Charles Kettering went on to lead the development of the diesel locomotive and leaded gasoline, earning many patents and propelling General Motors to great success.

Edward Deeds became a leading Dayton industrialist, partnering with the local Wright Brothers in aviation and helping merge Pratt & Whitney with Boeing, creating United Aircraft and United Airlines. After Patterson died, Deeds returned to National Cash Register to run the company in the dark days of the Great Depression.

A good friend of Kettering's at The Cash was top salesman, and later sales manager, Richard H. Grant. In the mid-1920s, he, too, was lured away to General Motors to join his friend Kettering. While Grant gets too little credit in most history books, his application of what he learned from Patterson was key to GM passing Ford in sales in the late 1920s. Many innovations in projecting sales levels and supporting dealers (unlike Henry Ford) became key to GM's success. Grant continued as GM's top sales executive and a member of the company's board of directors (alongside Kettering) into the 1940s.

Yet the most important, or at least most famous, of Patterson's proteges was top National salesman and later sales manager Thomas J. Watson, Sr. In 1914, Watson was hired away from National to run a small maker of office equipment, the Computing-Tabulating-Recording Company. Watson renamed the company after its Canadian subsidiary, the International Business Machines Company. He and his son Thomas Watson, Jr., built IBM into the greatest information technology company in the world.

National Cash Register Since Patterson

Over the years, rebranded as "NCR," the company continued to dominate the retail cash register business. The company entered the banking equipment business, which is today the largest generator of company revenues and profits. NCR claims to be the largest maker of ATM's but derives most of its revenue from selling software and services. NCR, now relocated to Atlanta, is also a powerhouse in retailing and restaurants. Annual revenues are about $7 billion.

Every day, millions of people around the world interact with NCR equipment, quite a legacy for a very determined, obstinate, difficult man. Yet John Patterson's greatest legacies are the sales systems he developed and the many great companies that applied and adapted his best ideas.

Originally published on AmericanBusinessHistory.org on July 9, 2021.

Chapter 29

Forgotten Empire Builders: Cleveland's Van Sweringen Brothers

Here we present, in bullet point form, a classic story of shattered dreams.

At the American Business History Center, we focus our energies on those companies (and their founders and leaders) which became household names or large businesses. Yet history is littered with smaller "bit players" on the economic stage. Some of them, like the unique, tragic Van Sweringen brothers of Cleveland, left lasting marks on their cities. While we hesitate to give such interesting people short shrift, we figure it is better than no shrift at all.

- 1879 – Oris Paxton Van Sweringen, always known as OP, is born near Wooster, Ohio.

- 1881 – Younger brother Mantis James Van Sweringen, MJ, is born near Wooster, Ohio.

- 1900 – The family moves to Cleveland, the 7th largest US city.

- The two brothers are known as "the Vans." They spent their lives as bachelors, living together, sharing a bedroom in their 54-room mansion.

- In their twenties, the brothers began speculating on land and buildings in the Cleveland area.

- 1909 – The Vans begin acquiring land east of Cleveland which had formerly been owned by the Shaker religious community. The Shakers believed in celibacy, and thus did not grow and prosper. This land is developed by the Vans into the Shaker Heights community, noted for curved streets, an early shopping center, and high design standards. But the lots sell slowly, so the Vans decide they needed better transportation to downtown Cleveland. They plan a high-speed (50 mph) electric rapid transit line from Shaker Heights to the center of Cleveland, where they acquired land.

- 1915 – The Vans acquire the Nickel Plate Railroad, which runs from Buffalo to St. Louis via Cleveland, in order to have trackage rights connecting their suburb to the city, yet away from city streets. They use debt and holding company structures to control their expanding empire. For example, one company would own 51% of another, then that company would own 51% of the next, with the Vans in control of all the companies.

- 1923 – The Vans announce they are building Terminal Tower in the center of Cleveland as a terminus for their Rapid electric line, but also to serve the New York Central passenger lines. The most famous American train, the Twentieth Century Limited, will stop there enroute between Chicago and New York. The complex will be topped by a tall office tower.

- During the booming 1920s, the Vans continue to build their financial empire, buying up more railroads to connect to the Nickel Plate and coal mines to provide coal for their trains. By 1929, they control the Chesapeake & Ohio, the Erie, the Missouri Pacific, and the Texas & Pacific, giving them a system which reaches from New York and Washington, DC to El Paso, Texas, one of the most extensive rail systems ever created in America.

- 1929 – Their empire is valued at $3 billion.

- 1930 – The Terminal Tower complex opens, built at a cost of $179 million. The tower, at 771 feet, is the second tallest building in the world when it opens and remains the tallest American building outside New York City until 1964. To avoid vibrations from the trains running underneath, the building's foundations drive 200-250 feet below street level. The office building and rail terminal are joined by the 1918 Hotel Cleveland, owned by the Vans, on one side and Higbee's, Cleveland's leading department store, on the other side.

- The stock market crashes and the Great Depression sets in. The Vans' complex stock and debt structure collapses.

- 1935 – Seeking a savior, they find George Ball of Muncie, Indiana. He and his brothers' Ball jar company is a major customer of the Nickel Plate. He, like the Vans, dislikes and distrusts the eastern bankers to whom the Vans are indebted. Ball and another investor buy the entire empire at auction for $3.1 million, with the agreement that the Vans can buy it back for that amount when they have that much money again.

- December 1935 – MJ dies of a broken heart (literally) at the age of fifty-four.

- November 1936 – On a train enroute to New York to negotiate with the bankers, OP dies of a heart attack, following his brother by less than a year, at age fifty-seven.

- The seventy-four-year-old George Ball never expected to outlive the two men who he was trying to help. He has no real interest in empire building, and the Vans vast business interests are purchased by Wall Street speculator Robert R. Young and Woolworth fortune heir Allan P. Kirby. Young is the brother-in-law of artist Georgia O'Keefe.

- 1950s – With the support of Texas oilmen Clint Murchison and Sid Richardson, Young gains control of the big New York Central Railroad. But, suffering from depression, he commits suicide in 1958 at the age of sixty.

- Despite this tale of repeated tragedy and broken dreams, the Terminal Tower complex continues to shine brightly over Cleveland and Shaker Heights remains one of the most beautiful American suburban developments.

Originally published on AmericanBusinessHistory.org on May 29, 2020.

Chapter 30
The Tragic Story of the Fox in Fox Network and Fox News

Fox News and the Fox Network have become part of the daily lives of millions. Yet few know where the name "Fox" came from, other than the historic Twentieth Century-Fox Studios. That movie-making part of the Fox empire was recently sold by Rupert Murdoch to Disney, which is dropping the Twentieth Century-Fox brand. There was a real man behind all this, and his life was fascinating.

William Fox was born in Tolcsva, Hungary on January 1, 1879, his parents' first child. They soon moved to New York where they lived in poverty. When young William broke his arm, they could not afford treatment, and he lost the use of his arm for life. William was followed by twelve brothers and sisters, only six of whom lived to adulthood.

Like fellow future movie barons Adolph Zukor (Paramount), Marcus Loew (M-G-M), and Samuel Goldfish (later changed to Goldwyn), he began his career at the bottom rung of the apparel business. By 1912, like Zukor and Loew, he had invested in the booming nickelodeon business in New York City and soon had a small chain of theaters and a fortune of $500,000 ($13 million in today's money).

Desiring a good flow of films to show, Fox started making and distributing movies. He expanded his theater chain by buying and building theaters. In the mid-twenties, he bet big on sound for film, buying key patents. The Fox studio became a leader in sound movie production, alongside Warner Brothers. Fox spent $10 million on a big new studio in Los Angeles. He became obsessed with keeping up with fellow New Yorkers and industry giants Zukor's Paramount (which owned over 1,000 theaters) and Loew's M-G-M.

Fox Movietone newsreels were the first newsreels with sound. The company produced four new newsreels a week, created by seventy crews around the world. Fox had the only sound-and-film recordings of Lindbergh's takeoff for Europe and interviews with world leaders like Mussolini. These newsreels were shown in Fox's theaters and those owned by other movie companies.

William Fox was a great showman and had some of the largest and finest "picture palaces" built, eventually owning over 500 theaters. He built almost-twin theaters in St. Louis and Detroit with about 5,000 seats each, two of the nation's largest. Large Fox theaters were also operated in Brooklyn, Philadelphia, Atlanta, and San Francisco. He purchased the 5,920-seat Roxy in New York, which generated $100,000 per week in revenue ($1.5 million today).

By the beginning of 1929, William Fox was on top of the world. Despite only having the use of one arm, he was an expert golfer, hitting three holes-in-one playing one-handed. He owned a mansion on Long Island and a huge yacht. He owned 53% of Fox Studios and 93% of Fox Theaters, but had borrowed heavily at high interest rates to build his empire, which was valued at $300 million ($4.5 billion today).

In March 1929, William Fox announced that he had an agreement to acquire control of M-G-M from Marcus Loew's widow and other stockholders, creating the largest entertainment company on earth. But in July 1929, before the deal closed, Fox's speeding Rolls Royce collided with a housewife in her Chrysler. Fox's chauffeur died and William Fox almost expired, requiring transfusions of rare blood and spending three months in the hospital. By the time he got out of the hospital, the stock market had crashed and the deal fell through.

The bankers seized control of William Fox's empire. He was convinced that they stole it from him. He battled on in the courts for years. William Fox ended up in bankruptcy. In 1936, he committed perjury and paid off a judge in the bankruptcy case. This resulted in William Fox spending five months in prison in 1943. The disgraced and embarrassed William Fox then completely left the film business, dying nine years later at the age of seventy-three.

Despite this fall from grace, the Fox name lives on in our lives. His Los Angeles studio property became Century City, an important local landmark. Many of his theaters have been demolished, but the giants in Detroit and St. Louis have been restored, as has the smaller theater in

Atlanta. His life is a classic illustration of the rewards – and risks – of being an entrepreneur. Big dreams can become big nightmares, yet still leave a legacy.

Originally published on AmericanBusinessHistory.org on July 31, 2020.

Chapter 31
Baseball, Broadcasting, & Compact Cars: Forgotten Mr. Crosley

This chapter presents another one of our short "bullet point" biographies.

When I recently told a friend the story of Powel Crosley, Jr, she said, 'Why haven't I heard of this guy?" To which the answer is, "There are tens of thousands of entrepreneurial men and women we've never heard of, who shaped our

lives." Check out the life of my "old friend," the incredibly innovative Powel Crosley:

- Born in 1886 to a successful Cincinnati lawyer and his wife

- Is followed by three siblings, including younger brother Lewis who helps carry out Powel's dreams for their entire working lives

- Tinkers with automobiles at an early age, dreams of being a race car driver and an automaker

- Drops out of college after dabbling in law and engineering

- Sells cars and works for automakers in Indiana to learn the business

- "Almost" drives a race car in the Indianapolis 500

- Prospers in the auto accessory business, selling "add-ons" that did not come with the car

- Age 34, 1921: wants to buy a toy radio for his son, but finds they cost $100 ($1500 today); buys a twenty-five-cent book about radio instead

- He and son build their own radio, then he hires university-trained engineers to design a cheap radio

- By the end of 1921, the Crosley "Harko" radio is offered to the public for $7

- By 1925, radio takes off and Crosley is one of the world's largest radio makers, possibly #1

- Powel and his brother become wealthy; Powel owns

fishing islands, hunting preserves, and mansions in Ohio and Florida

- Realizing that having a radio station would help sell radios, the Crosleys launch WLW radio station in Cincinnati, at first 500 watts of broadcast power, then 1000, 5,000, 10,000; Crosley also does early television experiments

- WLW reaches 50,000 watts, one of the relatively few "clear channel" stations in the nation

- WLW reaches much of the Eastern United States, develops unique programming like Ma Perkins and overnight music show Moon River; nicknamed "the Nation's Station"

- In 1934, WLW technicians boost power to 500,000 watts, the most powerful station in the world; can be heard in South America and Europe

- Also in 1934, seeking more content for WLW, Powel buys the Cincinnati Reds baseball team, which was broke and about to leave Cincinnati, leads the way in live sports broadcasts

- In 1935, Reds have the first night-time baseball game, under the lights and on the radio from Crosley Field; game attendance then booms and other teams adopt night games and radio broadcasts

- After five years, in 1939, pressure from smaller stations leads FDR and federal government to make WLW come back down to 50,000 watts

- Throughout the 1930s, Crosley's company adds

other appliances; invents and patents the "Shelvador" – the first refrigerator with shelves inside the door

- Crosley dabbles in making airplanes, without success

- At the 1939 Indianapolis 500, his company launches the Crosley car, the first real compact car (top speed 50 mph, 50 miles per gallon fuel efficiency, 80-inch wheelbase, and 39-cubic-inch engine); 5,700 are sold by the onset of WW II

- In World War II, Crosley becomes a major defense supplier, making 150,000 radio sets, bomb fuzes, military vehicles, and many other key items

- During the war, the government uses Crosley technology to broadcast our messages to Europe from Cincinnati; just before the atom bomb is dropped on Hiroshima, government prepares to ship WLW's 500,000-watt transmitter to Asia, but it is not needed

- In 1945, fifty-eight year old Crosley is bored with radio and sells his station and appliance businesses to Avco Corporation, former owner of American Airlines

- But he believes in his economical little car; his new 1946 "CC" model sells for $850 ($11,300 today)

- Crosley Motors is the first American car company to use disc brakes on all models

- In 1948, Crosley sells almost 25,000 cars

- As General Motors, Ford, and Chrysler clinch their

domination of the US auto industry, Crosley gives up in 1952 after selling about 84,000 cars (now collectors' items). Owners now or then include Humphrey Bogart, Gloria Swanson, Frank Lloyd Wright, Nelson Rockefeller, and Boy George.

- Powel Crosley, Jr., dies in 1961 at the age of seventy-four

There is a lot more flesh and detail available on this fascinating story, most easily found in the biography *Crosley: Two Brothers and a Business Empire that Transformed the Nation*, by Rusty McClure, David Stern, and Michael Banks.

Originally published on AmericanBusinessHistory.org on April 24, 2020.

Chapter 32
Malcolm McLean: Unsung Innovator Who Changed the World

In 1937, 24-year old Malcolm McLean (later changed to Malcom) delivered a load from the south to the New Jersey docks for export. He had been in the trucking business for two years. The rural North Carolina native was running a gas station when he learned he could make $5 a load to truck the gas to his station. He bought a truck, paid for on time, and began to build a trucking company with his brother Jim and sister Clara. On this day in 1937, legend has it that, as he watched the stevedores gradually unload his truck bale by bale, and load the ship equally slowly, he dreamed of a day when the whole truck trailer could just be lifted onto the deck in one motion. His dream would have to wait almost 20 years.

Young McLean proved himself an innovator in the trucking industry. By 1945, he had 162 trucks, hauling primarily textiles and cigarettes from North Carolina to the northeast. When soldiers returned from World War II, they were eligible for GI loans to finance vehicles, including trucks. He offered them haulage contracts as independent operators, allowing him to indirectly benefit from the financing offers. In this way, he added 600 more trucks to his fleet between 1947 and 1949.

In those days, before the Interstate Commerce Commission was eradicated, the ICC had full control over where truckers went, how much they charged, and what they carried, all in the name of "fair competition." Competitors could protest any move you made – in a committee room that took forever to make decisions rather than in the fast-moving marketplace dictated by customers. His trucks carried RJ Reynolds tobacco to the northeast by roundabout routes, and usually came home empty since he did not have the ICC authority to bring other goods home. McLean bought or leased other truck lines to gain better routes and freight rights. Above all else, he was always seeking efficiencies: ways to lower his costs and thereby lower his rates, although the ICC sometimes rejected his applications to charge less (the other truckers and the railroads fought him all the way). By 1954, McLean Trucking was the 8th largest US trucker in revenue, but 3rd in after-tax profits.

But McLean never stopped thinking about how to make ocean shipping more efficient, how to skip all that loading and unloading that took at least 8 days on each end of each ship's journey. This idea was not his invention – in 1929 ships took railcars to Cuba, and the military had experimented with small containers during World War II. To all that studied the issue, the problems seemed intractable: tight government regulations that stifled creativity, powerful longshoremen's unions who would fight to protect their jobs, ships that were not built for containers, docks that could not handle container ships and had no cranes to lift such heavy loads, no money to do any of this, and on and on. Not only would changing the system take lots of money, it would take lots of persuasion. Others could not see through the fog. But to McLean, "It just made too much sense." His colleagues report that he could not see problems like others saw them – he took big issues and broke them down into components, which he attacked one at a time.

Realizing that oil tankers travelled with empty top decks, in 1955 McLean bought an oil tanker and added a steel deck. On April 26, 1956, the ship Ideal X sailed from Newark toward Houston with a whopping 58 containers on board. As he watched the ship sail, one top longshoremen's official reportedly said, "I think they ought to sink the sonofabitch." Despite all the prior experiments, this was the birth of successful containerization. It was driven by a man who thought in terms of systems, of how to integrate things and make them happen, rather than only in terms of the individual components.

In time, he acquired the Waterman Steamship Company of Mobile as a base of operations. The ICC said he could not be in the trucking business and the shipping business at the same time, so he got out of trucking. His friends thought him nuts. A young banker at First National City Bank of New York (now Citibank/Citicorp) named Walter Wriston agreed to finance the purchase of Waterman with a $22 million loan, but his bosses rejected the deal as too risky. McLean went to the bosses, made his case, and in reference to Wriston said, "He may just be a trainee, but he's going to be the boss of both of you pretty soon." He got the loan. Wriston, considered by many to be the most important commercial banker of the late 20th century, went on to preside over the giant bank from 1967 to 1984. (My first job out of college was at First National City from 1973 to 1975, so I was fortunate to hear speeches by the visionary Wriston who gave us the Certificate of Deposit and early on promoted the ATM and credit card as well as global corporate banking.)

One of McLean's key moves was to not patent the container. Instead, he backed the people at the Fruehauf trailer company to develop the containers, and insisted that the technology be made available to the entire industry, including all his competitors. But they all thought he would fail, that containers would never make it. Over time, McLean made peace with the longshoremen and with the all important ports. His later ships could carry over 200 containers. By the mid-1960's, The Port Authority of New York committed to spend $332 million to build a container port at Elizabeth, New Jersey. In April, 1966, in his first transoceanic sailing, his Sea-Land Service sent a ship from Port Elizabeth to Rotterdam, arriving four weeks faster than any prior ship when loading time was included. The Dutch shipping executives booed McLean and his team when they celebrated, but shippers loved him; the clock could not be turned back.

By the late 1960s, Sea-Land was highly profitable. It played a key role in delivering supplies for the Vietnam War. In 1969, McLean sold the company to his old friends at RJ Reynolds for $500 million, of which he received $160 million. He joined their board but was soon uncomfortable and resigned the position, saying "I am a builder and they are runners." His empire later ended up in the hands of the CSX railroad and the Maersk shipping lines.

Never idle or lacking for ideas, in 1978 he got back into container shipping, raising $1.2 billion for 12 super-large "Econoships" which could hold over 2,000 TEU's each (TEU = Twenty-foot Equivalent Units; containers are either 20-foot or 40-foot). His idea was to have giant ships circling the globe at the equator, with smaller ships loading and unloading the giants. But this time the tide temporarily turned against him. Falling oil prices hurt his competitive advantage, and shipping price wars broke out. In 1986, when he was 73, McLean's new idea resulted one of the biggest bankruptcies in history up to that time. This man was in many ways an entrepreneur's entrepreneur – dreamer, doer, calculated risk taker. He died in 2001.

But what did McLean give us? Did he really change the world?

Based on numerous sources, it looks like containerization, once widely accepted, reduced shipping and loading costs by at least 80%, and perhaps 90%. In the old days, freighters spent up to 2/3 of their time in ports, loading and unloading. Port turnaround times, which were as high as 3 weeks, dropped to 24 hours. While still a problem, the rates of merchandise theft dropped dramatically once the goods were sealed away out of sight, untouched by human hands from origin to destination. Containers also took the place of many warehouses – they are their own warehouse, and retired containers are now being used to build houses for humans as well.

By 1996, the largest container ships could hold 5,000 TEUs, far more than even McLean's "Econoships." His ideas of loading and unloading around the globe became real. Today the largest new ones can carry 19,000 TEU's (though no ports in the western hemisphere can handle ships that large). There are over 30 million TEU's in use worldwide, with 5-6 million in transit at any given time. (An estimated 27 containers a day, 10,000 a year, fall off ships, usually due to high seas – but still a tiny loss relative to the traffic!)

The bottom line is that world commerce could not take place the way it does without McLean's innovation. Cold beer comes from Germany in refrigerated containers, just in time auto parts move around the world, and fresh fruit from the tropics arrives on our table – all for far less money that it would have cost under the old system. The final cost of products from around the world is 5-10% less due to containerization, saving the world hundreds of billions of dollars.

Especially impressive was McLean's integrated systems thinking. He saw himself in the transportation business, not in trucking or shipping. He understood that business was not just processes and numbers, but it was dealing with people, with unions, government regulators, competitors, and customers. Malcom McLean put it all together, like King C. Gillette and his razors and blades, Steve Jobs and iTunes, and George Eastman and his film development service with reloaded Kodak cameras shipped back to the customer in ten days ("You press the button and we do the rest"). He built a platform. Not many entrepreneurs and inventors think this extra mile. And he had the confidence and persistence to pursue his impossible vision until it became real. Of McLean, Wriston later said, "Malcom McLean is one of the few men who changed the world."

As to the present and future, here is a quote from the great book *The Box* by Marc Levinson:

"No one in the early days of container shipping foresaw that this American-born industry would come to be dominated by European and Asian firms, as the US-flag ship lines, burdened by a legacy of protected markets and heavy regulation, proved unable to compete in a fast-changing world."

Those giant 18,000-TEU ships are built by Daewoo in Korea (for $190 million each), the engines are from Germany (MAN, controlled by Volkswagen), and operated by Chinese firms and the biggest shipping company of them all, Maersk from tiny Denmark. But no one profits more from containerization than the American consumer.

For further reading:

The best book that tells this story is: *The Box: How the Shipping Container Made the World Smaller and the World Economy Bigger.*

Another excellent book: *Box Boats: How Container Ships Changed the World*

If you want to study McLean and many other great business leaders, you cannot beat this book, exciting and well-written. Get the hardcover because the paperback does not include the same compelling images and illustrations: *They Made America: From the Steam Engine to the Search Engine: Two Centuries of Innovators*

For a take on the importance of thinking in systems to business strategy, here is an outstanding book: *Good Strategy Bad Strategy: The Difference and Why It Matters*

This book contains the best short description of the great George Eastman story: *Technology in America – 2nd Edition: A History of Individuals and Ideas*

Originally published on Hooversworld.com on May 30, 2015.

Chapter 33
The Business History of Woodstock

Too often, when we see great entertainment or a great event, we forget that someone had to dream it up, organize it, and finance it. Fifty years ago this month, from August 15 through 18, 1969, the most famous music festival of all time took place in Bethel, New York. "Woodstock – an Aquarian Exposition: 3 Days of Peace and Music" drew more than 400,000 people to hear music ranging from Joan Baez to Jimi Hendrix, from the Who to Sly and the Family Stone. Blockbuster records and an Oscar-winning documentary film followed, as well as a library full of books and stories about the festival. Despite all the hoopla, few know the business story behind Woodstock.

Step back to the 1930s, when Alexander Block of the Block Drug Company introduced Polident, a denture cleaning product. His daughter married a man named Roberts, and in 1945 they had a son, John Roberts. By 1966, when John turned twenty-one, his grandfather and mother had died, and he inherited about $250,000 from the family denture fortune. However, he could only spend the interest on this money (which he did), not receiving the principal until he was older – one-third when he turned twenty-five, one-third at thirty, and one-third at thirty-five. Freshly graduated from the University of Pennsylvania, John Roberts did not know what he wanted to do in life, but he had money – the equivalent of $2 million today.

John Roberts soon hooked up with Joel Rosenman, a recent graduate of the Yale Law School and the brother of one of John's friends at Penn. Like John, Joel was also seeking his life's path. Both men thought the entertainment industry would be interesting. By the spring of 1967, John and Joel, twenty-two and twenty-five years old, were rooming together in New York City. They decided to create a television series. The idea was about rich kids (like themselves) looking for investment opportunities. Each episode would tell the story of a business adventure – or misadventure. The problem was that they did not have enough business ideas to create the episodes. So, on March 22, 1967, they put a tiny ad in the *New York Times* that read:

"Young men with unlimited capital looking for interesting, legitimate business opportunities and business propositions."

John and Joel received over five thousand replies to the little ad. They proceeded to meet with dozens of people with crazy schemes. They also built a recording studio in New York called Media Sound.

In this process, their lawyer called and suggested they meet with Michael Lang and Artie Kornfeld. The lawyer warned the businesslike John and Joel not to be put off by the appearance of Michael and Artie. John and Joel did not know what to think when the heavily-fringed Michael Lang and the equally spacey Artie Kornfeld showed up at their apartment-office. Twenty-three-year-old Lang had owned a headshop in Miami and promoted concerts. He was well-connected in the music industry. Twenty-five-year-old Artie Kornfeld had already written and produced dozens of hit records, most recently for a band called the Cowsills, and was the youngest vice president at Capitol Records.

Michael and Artie wanted to build a recording studio in the Catskill Mountains north of New York City, near the homes of several prominent musicians including Bob Dylan. Busy with their own studio in New York, John and Joel were not interested in doing that. But along the way, they asked Michael and Artie how they were going to launch and publicize the rural studio. The answer was that they planned to have a big music festival with all the local musicians, drawing attention to the relatively remote location.

From these conversations evolved the idea of a giant music festival in the Catskills. But there was one problem. Not only did John and Joel not have "unlimited capital," but John was not old enough to access his inheritance yet. After being turned down by banker after banker, John found one who was willing to loan John up to $800,000, using his future inheritance as collateral.

Thus was born a business, Woodstock Ventures, with the four men as partners, and the festival in Bethel, near Woodstock.

There is no need to recount here the story of the festival and the great music performed there, as that history is readily available in many books and on the Internet. (The best way to grasp Woodstock is to watch the movie, one of the greatest documentaries of all time.) Suffice it to say that it was a huge success. But not without problems: traffic jams, heavy rain, farmers' fields overrun by hippies, and multiple lawsuits brought by local property owners.

The Woodstock festival sold $1,800,000 worth of tickets.
But expenses including $250,000 for the musicians totaled
$2,800,000. There was plenty of cleanup to be done and
about eighty lawsuits to be settled. The four partners knew
that the long-term rights to the recordings and film would
be valuable, but they were essentially broke. Their
immediate problems scared them (and scared their banker
even more).

For many reasons, the four partners began to squabble,
businessmen John and Joel on one side and hippies Michael
and Artie on the other. They agreed to split up, with one
group or the other buying out the others' share of
Woodstock Ventures. John and Joel gave Michael and Artie
$31,750 each for their shares (equal to $220,000 today).

About the same time, Warner Brothers, which had secured
the recording and movie rights, paid Woodstock Ventures
$1,000,000. $600,000 went to clean up the grounds, pay
attorneys, and settle lawsuits. When all the dust settled,
the net loss was $100,000. Gradually, royalties on records
and the movie came in, and John and Joel had broken even
on their investment by the late 1980s.

Despite their differences, John, Joel, and Michael reunited
to put together Woodstock '94. Michael also produced
Woodstock '99.

John Roberts died at the age of fifty-six in 2001. His estate
still collects royalties. Joel, Michael, and Artie each went on
to illustrious careers. All four men wrote books about their
Woodstock experience. Artie Kornfeld has done over 5,000
radio interviews.

In 2001, British pharmaceutical giant GlaxoSmithKline
spent $1.2 billion to purchase the Block Drug Company, by

then including Nytol sleep aids, Tegrin medicated shampoo, Super Poli-Grip, and many other over-the-counter products.

Without Polident, we might never have heard of Woodstock, New York.

Sources: *Woodstock: The Oral History*, by Joel Makower (1989) and *Young Men with Unlimited Capital: the inside story of the legendary Woodstock festival told by the two who paid for it*, by John Roberts, Joel Rosenman, and Robert Pilpel (1974). There are many other excellent books on Woodstock, with several published for the 40th and 50th anniversaries in 2009 and 2019.

Originally published on AmericanBusinessHistory.org on August 23, 2019.

Lessons

Chapter 34
Six Simple Steps to Building A Great Lasting Company

One of our key goals at the American Business History Center is to learn lessons from the successes and failures of the past. In most of our weekly articles, we leave it to our readers to draw their own lessons, although we occasionally touch on what can be learned from these histories and biographies. In this week's article, which is adapted from a post we published at Hooversworld.com six years ago, we try to draw some general conclusions based on our fifty-eight years of studying thousands of companies in hundreds of industries.

In 1837, a blacksmith in Grand Detour, Illinois, struggled making plows for local farmers. The traditional cast iron plows that were used back East did not cut through the moist Midwestern loam like they did sandy Eastern soils.

The blacksmith used a steel sawmill blade, resulting in a plow better suited to the prairie. He only sold a few plows the next few years, while the big manufacturers were selling tens of thousands. But he persisted, and made a success of the business. The man was John Deere. Deere's company emerged as the largest farm equipment maker in the world by 1963, surpassing industry giant International Harvester that was created by J.P. Morgan in 1902. Today, after 184 years in business, John Deere is led by its 10th Chief Executive Officer (CEO), a remarkable record of steadiness at the helm.

Today's headlines leap off the page with new business models, disruptive innovators, and unicorns – companies which are valued at over $1 billion soon after founding. It is easy to believe that building a company is complex, that it takes the "right" connections, or that the "rules" are changing all the time. Or, worse yet, that it is easy to create and build a solid company.

I started studying business in 1963, when I was 12 years old, in order to better understand General Motors which dominated my hometown, Anderson, Indiana. I cannot count the number of companies (and non-profits), big and small, in every industry and every part of the world, that I have investigated since then. This curiosity led me to start the company that became Hoovers.com, one of the world's leading providers of company profiles and other information.

My conversations, observations, and above all else reading and study have led me to the following conclusions.

If you read the business best sellers or the blogs, you may think it is "all" about corporate culture, cutting the right deal, great branding, financial management, technology, efficiency, or many other factors.

Each of these does play a role, sometimes a very important one, but will only work if the organization is built on the durable foundation of the six steps described below.

Most great lasting companies are built in a very similar way, which is neither complex nor hard to understand. But it can be difficult to carry out, hard to live by. Here I break it down into six steps. Of course every industry, every era, and every leader must customize these ideas to fit their situation, and the execution of an idea can indeed become complex: consider what it takes to "execute" UPS or FedEx each day: millions of decisions made in thousands of locations.

1. **See or find a real need of society.** This need can be enormous, or it can be in a niche. It can be fundamental or fluff. From energy-efficient cars to better chocolates, there are opportunities everywhere around us. There must be people who need and will love what you design.

Often founders have the need themselves, or a loved one has it. The founders of TripAdvisor got tired of bad advice from their travel agents. The founders of Home Depot and of Walmart would have created their empires working for other, existing retailers, but were "forced" to do it on their own when the old-timers wouldn't listen. The inventor of the supermarket, one of America's most important innovations, could not convince the bigwigs at the chains he worked for to try his new idea. So he went out on his own and did it and changed the world. As did Malcolm McLean, inventor of containerized shipping.

2. **Build a better mousetrap**, something that truly adds value for your customers, that is clearly differentiated, that improves their lives, and that they are willing to pay for. The entrepreneur knows that there is almost always a better way to do things.

3. Then improve your product or service every day, for as long as the enterprise continues. One of the founders of Ancestry.com told me the company added a new feature, usually historic records, every working day. The Japanese are famous for their dedication to "continuous improvement." Some of the big ecommerce and other websites which rose up in the last 10 years seem to no longer invest in improvements. Others, like TripAdvisor, get better and better. Old leaders like Sears and Kmart go to sleep while more agile upstarts like Walmart change their world.

There are a million things to distract leaders from their core products and services: financial engineering, big "transformative" deals, acquisitions, dealing with Wall Street's analysts and Washington's regulators, and on and on. Those things may earn headlines. A shoe company making its shoes last a year longer does not. But that's what makes companies last longer.

Over time, great, "learning" organizations build their "knowledge base." They get better and better at what they do. This the ultimate form of growth – internal, organic. The great business historian Alfred Chandler repeatedly pointed out how companies have risen and fallen due to expanding or shrinking their knowledge base.

Continuous improvement drives how one thinks about competitors. Over and over I have heard, "If you do that, the big companies will stomp you out." Or, "Others with deeper pockets will copy you and crush you." If these statements become true, you have chosen an awful business, or you do not have an idea that is truly better.

Great companies usually start small, with a single product or line that is superior. As they evolve and learn, their competitors are left in their dust. As long as you keep moving, you should not have to worry about anyone else.

They didn't have the idea and they don't have their heart in it. Only naïve financial minds believe that "deep pockets" can win any battle. Did the US military win in Vietnam? Did Kmart stomp out Walmart? Did Howard Johnson's stop McDonald's, and McDonald's in turn kill off Starbucks? Did Hilton nip Holiday Inns in the bud? Did Blockbuster abolish Netflix?

People and organizations must above all else stay hungry. The greatest causes of failure in large organizations are hubris, satisfaction, and complacency. If you think the battle is over and you have won, you have probably lost.

4. Continuously listen to, talk to, question and observe your present and potential customers. Too few executives really know what it is like to be a customer of their own products and services. Too few bankers have waited in line in the drive through or used a failed app – or studied the apps of their competitors. Great enterprises obsess on customers.

5. Be ambitious and believe in growth at an appropriate rate. If you have something that makes the world better, don't you owe it to your customers, your employees, your owners, and your suppliers to do it on a larger scale? Whether that means expanding your business where it is, or opening stores or branches around the globe, great enterprises know there is no such thing as sitting still: you either grow or die. (Though if you get too big or too diverse, losing focus, you may need to split into smaller enterprises to grow effectively, as United Technologies has recently done.)

Your growth must reflect the industry you are in and its growth rate, local or national dynamics, and most important of all, your own capabilities. A common failure of startups and venture-backed companies is over-acceleration, driving the company so fast it goes off the road on a curve. On the other hand, in public companies sometimes the expectations are set low to make life easy for the highly paid executives.

6. Believe in yourself. I sat on the board of Hoover's when the majority desired to sell the company. "We need to be part of a bigger company in order to prosper," said the "sophisticated" investors. But Morningstar, another upstart in the business information industry, never bought the idea that "we have to be part of a big outfit to survive" and continues as a strong, independent company, with a market valuation of almost $12 billion. I am confident Walmart turned down many offers back when it was not in the top 50 retail chains. Great companies which endure over the decades have a commitment to their independence. They believe in themselves.

While those pursuing other models of organizational success, such as "built to flip," may get the headlines and occasionally big "scores," I believe any review of the great companies of the world will usually find these steps at the core of the organization. This applies equally to non-profit organizations. I believe that the criteria of the most successful long-term equity investors, such as Warren Buffett, are very similar to what I have enumerated here.

Published on AmericanBusinessHistory.org on September 23, 2021.

Index

Made in the USA
Coppell, TX
28 March 2022

75648410R00198